SACRED
STORY

An Ignatian Examen For The Third Millennium

William Watson S.J.

Other Books by William Watson, SJ

Inviting God Into Your Life:
A Practical Guide for Prayer

Reflections and Homilies:
The Gonzaga Collection

Forty Weeks:
An Ignatian Path to Christ with Sacred Story Prayer

Sacred Story Rosary:
An Ignatian Way to Pray the Mysteries

Sacred Story Affirmations

The Whole-Life Confession

My Sacred Story Missal

Understanding the Spiritual World

Advance Praise for Sacred Story

William Watson's *Sacred Story* is a huge undertaking. It is a new, enlarged and redeveloped book of Ignatius' *Examen*. *Sacred Story* probes profoundly into the dynamics of Ignatius's personal journey—into his sacred story—and the discernment of spirits that embellish and enlighten it. William Watson's treatment of the Discernment Rules, so essential to the practice of *Examen*, is very well done. Watson finds the integral development of Ignatius's own life as essential elements for the *Examen*.

He uncovers a paradigm of the *Examen* in the Autobiography with the two conversions of Ignatius, which is very insightful. Despite my familiarity with the *Autobiography*, I had never thought of this before. Also, I can see now after reading *Sacred Story* that the key insight of Ignatius' surrendering his scruples over confessing past sins was the most important decision of his life—a tipping point for him personally and a defining element of Ignatian Spirituality.

George Aschenbrenner, S.J.
Washington, D.C.

William Watson's *Sacred Story* is an exceptional work. It masters the difficult task of integrating spirituality and psychology and creates an original, rigorous, brilliant and scholarly book. It is an excellent contribution to Ignatian Spirituality and spirituality in general. The author has the ability to take the classic Ignatian Examination of Conscience and recreate it with great originality and scholarship.

It illuminates with brilliant insights and accuracy the fields of both psychology and spirituality. Books like this rarely come along once a decade.

Javier Melloni, S.J., Th.D.
Author, *The Spiritual Exercises in the Western Tradition*
Professor, *Faculty of Theology of Catalonia*

William Watson's *Sacred Story* is a seminal, brilliant tour de force—erudite, well researched and deeply pondered. It is a passionate book, full of the urgency of one who is speaking of what he knows and of what he lives. It is a book born not merely from well-grounded scholarship but from deeply personal experience and struggle. Read it and be amazed, as I was.

Watson does for the Examen what Jerome Nadal did for the Jesuit Constitutions (when Nadal explained the Constitutions to the Jesuit communities he visited in the very early days of the Society of Jesus). Watson links any proper and full appropriation of the *Examen* to the experiences of St. Ignatius' life, particularly to his conversion, and to the program of the *Spiritual Exercises*. This is a novel approach, and one, in my opinion, which is holistic, rich, fertile and fruitful.

David Keith Townsend, S.J. Director, *The Seven Fountains Spirituality Centre, Chiang Mai, Thailand*

Fr. Watson deftly and elegantly translates Ignatius Loyola from the sixteenth to the twenty-first century and reveals him to be an accessible and astute guide for all—no matter faith, path or denomination—who seek spiritual discernment, moral wisdom, psychological growth and universal truth.

Gabor Maté, M.D.
Author, *In The Realm of Hungry Ghosts: Close Encounters With Addiction*

Making St. Ignatius' practice of the Examen meaningful in the 21st century, useful for self-knowledge and self-transformation, and respectful of the complexities of each individual psyche immersed in modern culture seems at best to be daunting and at worst, impossible. Yet that is precisely what Fr. William Watson, S.J. has accomplished in his fresh, clear, interdisciplinary and contemporarily relevant approach to the Ignatian Examen – *Sacred Story – An Ignatian Examen for the Third Millennium*. This book would have achieved great purpose if it had accomplished but one of its objectives: presenting an insightful and valuable cultural critique; unearthing new scholarly insights into the texts of St. Ignatius Loyola; or probing the depths of interaction between spirituality and psychology.

But he does so much more. His real quest is to find a practical, usable approach to a profound relationship with the Lord, which avoids superficiality in its practicality and needless complexity in its profundity. By taking the time he needs to develop his insights into the human psyche, the stories he needs to illustrate his points, and the scholarship that underlies a deep understanding of the spirit of St. Ignatius Loyola, Watson weaves a rich unified tapestry of practical, sage instruction on how to find the Lord in the depths of self-examination and the sacred story that emerges from it.

Sacred Story is a "must read" for those seeking knowledge of the spiritual and psychological obstacles that may present themselves in our individual spiritual quest – along with the tools for discernment and authentic reflection needed to overcome them.

Robert J. Spitzer, S.J., Ph.D.
President, *Magis Institute* Author, *Five Pillars of the Spiritual Life*

In *Sacred Story*, Bill Watson retrieves the heart and soul of Ignatian Spirituality. In this timely work on the prayer of the *Examen* Watson demonstrates that the ancient practice of this essential prayer can enrich and sanctify contemporary lives. Aptly identifying the millennial sin of narcissism, Watson's book offers an attractive paradigm that makes the *Spiritual Exercises* accessible and mobile. This book pushes the boundaries of our understanding of the *Examen* and challenges all who embrace an Ignatian way of life to deeper transformation. Bill Watson has done a profound service in giving us *Sacred Story!*

Damian Dzynda, Th.D.
Author, *Archbishop Romero: A Disciple Who Revealed the Glory of God*
Director of Formation, *Church of the Transfiguration, Pittsford, NY*

Fr. Watson has written a thorough and reflective guide for the *Examen*. He has surveyed many recent authors on one or other aspect of the *Examen*, how to present it and how to understand it. Ignatius' spiritual genius is on display in his discernment principles linked to the *Examen* practice. He teaches us to discriminate between feelings that come from God, expressing our true human nature, from those whose origin reflect inspirations from the one Ignatius identifies as the "enemy of human nature." Fr. Watson has shown how the *Examen* can help priest and laity alike navigate the confusing currents of human sentiment to find the authentic expression of one's human nature.

This study clearly illuminates how Ignatius' discernment rules always lead one to the authentic expression of that human nature, discoverable through one's affect and feelings. And as Ignatius' teaches, the authentic expression of human nature always aligns with Scripture, tradition and the teaching Church. The need of a thorough re-consideration of Ignatius of Loyola and his teaching about our direct relation to God has been obvious for some time. The insight and thoroughness of this book is to be commended. Father Watson has given us a chance for an in-depth second and third look at the great *Examen* tradition of Ignatius and his "thinking with the Church."

James V. Schall, S. J. *Georgetown University*
Author, *A Philosopher in Society: The Political Philosophy of Maritain*

In his *Sacred Story*, Fr. William Watson invites followers of Ignatian Spirituality to enter more deeply into this mystery by the understanding and practice St. Ignatius of Loyola's general and particular *Examen*. His new exposition of Ignatius' conversion story in the *Autobiography* reveals the genesis and practice of the *Examen* in Ignatius' life. In his new hermeneutic of its origins, Watson demonstrates how this essential Ignatian prayer discipline, so vital in the early history of the Society of Jesus, gains a powerful new relevance for our contemporary spiritual, theological and psychological moment in these early years of Christianity's Third Millennium.

Sacred Story is invaluable for anyone sincerely interested in understanding the *Examen* as Ignatius used it: to follow Christ in the most concrete details of day-to-day life. What we have through Fr. Watson's *Sacred Story* is a new roadmap to achieve St. Ignatius' *Magis* in our own day.

Thomas Sherman, S.J.

Professor of Philosophy, *Arrupe College of Philosophy, Harare Zimbabwe*

Fr. Bill Watson, S.J., has created a landmark study on the Ignatian *Examen*. The *Sacred Story* offers profound new insights into the *Spiritual Exercises*, *Examen* and the Rules for Discernment. Fr. Watson accomplishes this critical achievement through a detailed analysis of Ignatius' progressive conversion in the *Autobiography*.

As a Jesuit for 50 years, I now appreciate the Autobiography in a completely new light and understand for the first time St. Ignatius' unique version of the Examination of Conscience. In a creative, fresh, and very accessible fashion for contemporary Catholics and Christians, Watson unlocks the personal, daily life spiritual tool of the *Examen*.

I highly recommend *Sacred Story* for anyone who desires a greater intimacy with God and a better self-understanding through this practical, holistic, and experiential spiritual growth method."
John Mossi, S.J.,
***Santa Clara* Spiritual Director and Retreat Guide**

"The *Examen* Prayer as taught by Fr. Watson grounds the new evangelization in the gift of discernment of spirits. When practiced faithfully the New Jerusalem is seen, and the Church enjoys living in an on-going culture of Pentecost."
Fr. John Horn, S.J.
Rector, *Kenrick Seminary; Co-Founder Institute for Priestly Formation*

The "Narrow Gate" of the Ignatian *Examen* offers a path to spiritual growth that is missing in today's dominant culture. This is an age when the search for God and hunger for spiritual life is longed for, but often lost in spiritual, psychological and moral confusion. Fr. Watson's work offers a new, more accessible approach to the *Examen* that is a valuable and needed resource for people today."
Mary Cross, Ph.D.
Director of Adult Spiritual Formation, *Archdiocese of Seattle*

Fr. Watson's *Sacred Story* is a seminal and insightful new version of St. Ignatius' classic *Examen* Prayer. *Sacred Story* provides a guided step-by-step process with practical tools that allows God's grace and consolation to restore "psychological imbalances" caused by sin and dysfunction.

Sacred Story reminds us that cultural, psychological and spiritual forces are constantly filling the human consciousness with noise. How can we filter the noise of the world and invite into our lives the authentic voice of God's word? *Sacred Story* can help any practitioner accomplish this. It will be a tremendous blessing for laity, priest and religious who are seeking a more integrated spiritual and psychological life in Christ.

Dr. Christina Lynch:

Director, Psychological Services, *St. John Vianney Theological Seminary, Denver*

Dedicated to Our Lady of the Way

IMPRIMI POTEST
Patrick Lee, S.J.

IMPRIMATUR
J. Peter Sartain
Archbishop of Seattle

Unless otherwise indicated, Scripture quotations are from the Holy Bible, *New American Bible, revised edition* © 2010, 1991, 1986, 1970 Confraternity of Christian Doctrine, Washington, D.C.

Cover Art: *Heart as a House*, Jerry A. Fenter
Jacket Design: William Watson, SJ

ISBN: 0615667368
ISBN 13: 9780615667362

SACRED STORY

An Ignatian Examen For The Third Millennium

WILLIAM WATSON S.J.

Foreword by

J. Peter Sartain

George Aschenbrenner, SJ

David Keith Townsend, SJ

About the Author

Fr. William Watson, S.J., D. Min., has spent over thirty years developing Ignatian programs and retreats used by Georgetown University, Seattle University, Santa Clara University, Gonzaga University and Loyola College in Baltimore. He has collaborated extensively with Fr. Robert Spitzer in the last fifteen years on Ignatian retreats for corporate CEOs. In the spring of 2011 he launched a non-profit institute to bring Ignatian Spirituality to Catholics and Christians of all ages and walks of life. The Sacred Story Institute is promoting third millennium evangelization for the Society of Jesus and the Church by using the time-tested *Examination of Conscience* of St. Ignatius.

Fr. Watson has served as: Director of Retreat Programs at Georgetown University; Vice President for Mission at Gonzaga University; and Provincial Assistant for International Ministries for the Oregon Province of the Society of Jesus. He received his Doctor of Ministry degree in 2009 from The Catholic University of America (Washington D.C.). He also holds Masters degrees in Divinity and Pastoral Studies, respectively (1986; Weston Jesuit School of Theology, Cambridge Massachusetts). He is a specialist in Ignatian Spirituality and the Ignatian Examination of Conscience.

We Request Your Feedback

The Sacred Story Institute welcomes feedback on this book. We are developing versions of the *Sacred Story Examen* method for many different groups. Please visit our website to leave us your comments, ideas, suggestions and inspirations for how to make this a better resource for Catholics and Christians of all ages and walks of life. Let us know groups you believe special versions of *Sacred Story Examen* might be researched and developed.

Contact us at: *admin-team@sacredstory.net*

Sacred Story Institute
1401 E. Jefferson Suite 405
Seattle, Washington, 98122

Acknowledgements

Many mentors, friends and guides deserve recognition. Gordon Moreland first instructed me in the Ignatian *Examen* as a Jesuit Novice. Joe Tetlow, through his writings, reintroduced me to its practice at the end of my Tertianship. Michael Buckley taught me to ask the right question and John Mossi how to answer it clearly. George Aschenbrenner, David Townsend and Joe Tetlow read sections of this book and offered sound advice and guidance. John O'Malley and Michael Maher clarified some important historical details. Javier Melloni opened me to Ignatius' early spiritual reading.

Michael Brown and Gabor Maté awakened me to see Ignatius' life, spirituality and *Examen* with fresh eyes.

The communities at Jesuit High School in Portland, Oregon, and Arrupe Jesuit at Seattle University, supported me while I wrote. The Trappist's of Our Lady of Guadalupe in Lafayette, Oregon, continue to provide welcome and silence while I journey through my own sacred story.

Thanks are not enough.

Contents

Author's Preface

Spiritual guides are tempted by two opposed extremes. The first is a legalistic spirituality akin to that of the Scribes and Pharisees. It places heavy burdens on people without helping to carry the load. The second temptation is a popular but decadent Christianity without boundaries. Its law is a vaguely defined love that Bonheoffer rightly dismisses as cheap grace.

The true guide is a servant who lays down his life to protect those in his care. Few servants are willing to descend into the mystery, mess and murkiness of the human heart to help those seeking integrated spiritual growth. For a guide—a true servant—can only take people as far along the narrow road as he or she has been willing to travel.

Fortunately for us there came a point in Ignatius' early journey where he gave up seeking "spiritual persons." No one could give him the help he needed. What he needed required a new science of the heart, with new spiritual disciplines. The costly grace of Ignatius' journey began in sinful addiction, descended into scrupulous religious torment, and finally opened to graced illumination.

His *Spiritual Exercises* reveal the template of his own progressive conversion and forge a new paradigm for the Christian's journey back to God. They include *Rules* of spiritual guidance as well as a two-level *Examen* method. Both are highly evolved consciousness disciplines that teach us how to recognize our authentic identity. These disciplines invite an emotional awakening to life events and patterns of sin and dysfunction and help people discern Divine spontaneities from those Ignatius identifies as coming from the enemy of human nature.

The spontaneities from a Divine source or those of the enemy of human nature have a unique spiritual signature. By learning the signatures and choosing thoughts, words, and deeds appropriately, one can achieve integrated spiritual growth and wholeness. Nothing typifies contemporary culture more than the demand for spiritual authenticity that can be validated by one's own emotional and affective experience. Ignatius' spirituality provides such validation if applied faithfully. Grace abounds.

Ignatius is a perfect archetype for contemporary culture. He had most of the emotional, intellectual, and psychological complexes that make people today fear any limit to the free expression of their instinctual drives: dysfunctional family, compulsive appetites, addictive personality, narcissism, greed for celebrity and wealth, sexual self-indulgence and a love of violence. He did what he wanted because it suited him. This did not make him any less attractive and compelling a personality. In fact he had considerable charm and allure. But his true identity was masked by his sinful addictions, sexual indulgence and narcissism. When the brilliance of his authentic human nature is finally unmasked he becomes the most practical spiritual guide of modern times.

At the dawn of the Age of Discovery God used the complexity of Ignatius' spiritual and psychological wounds to fashion a set of spiritual methods at once sublime, strategic, lean and eminently practical. Ignatius' spirituality and his *Examen* is as dynamic, relevant, transformative and vital as ever. His disciplines are a key to the heart's deepest desires. His methods can respond to the deepest social, religious and spiritual crises of any age.

Ignatius' discernment *Rules* and *Examen* predate and inform healing tools now used by twelve-step recovery programs and the mindfulness and presence-oriented disciplines of today's best-selling authors. In addition, his teachings and techniques align with ancient masters of many religious traditions. In Ignatius' discernment principles we have rules to confront sin's roots in the spiritual and psychological dysfunction resulting from early-life traumas. We also have rules to interpret the stress, anger and anxiety that fracture our consciences with constant black noise. New psychological methods proven effective to reprogram and balance the biochemical systems of the brain, even after years of depression and addiction, are congruent with Ignatius' insights and discernment *Rules*.

The extraordinary Russian Theosophist and Catholic convert Valentin Tomberg recognized Ignatius' universal spiritual genius. Ignatian spirituality he affirms embodies "the calm warmth of complete certainty due to the cooperation of human effort and revelation from above."[1] Tomberg believes Ignatius has discovered the grail path to the resurrected Christ, residing at the center of the cosmos, and every human heart. Ignatian spirituality, for him, represents the transformative wisdom of the Buddha-Avatar to come, whose mission is to light the path to He who is the Way, Truth and Light.

Some claim that Ignatius' spirituality and methods are outdated. They are in fact rigorous, strategic, practical and effective. The last Jesuit General Congregation affirmed that mediocrity has no place in Ignatius' worldview.[2] Nor does mediocrity in any way characterize his spiritual disciplines. Ignatius himself affirmed that spiritual growth while arduous was effective when generous hearts engage it courageously. The daily *Examen* embodies a radical, daily commitment to Gospel discipleship that seeks salvation through the narrow door [Mt 7:13].

Even if modern spiritual guides forget or are simply too anxious to invite conversion through the narrow door, Ignatius' *Examen* will show you the way. It will shorten your journey on what is at times a fearsomely confusing passage but one that leads to astonishing luminosity, interior freedom, wholeness and peace. And the Ignatian *Examen*, holistically practiced, is perhaps the preeminent spiritual discipline for what is the most vital, difficult and distant of all missionary efforts—the journey to your heart.

The *Examen* embodies Ignatius' courage to wake from sleep and to face the mortal wounds of body, mind and spirit that block the path to interior, spiritual freedom. If, like Ignatius, we are willing to take this journey and travel deep into our hearts, we will "find God in us, around us in everything" and have the ability "to know his will and put it into practice."[3] The human effort required is the graced surrender of self-will, as Ignatius finally accepted at Manresa. Ignatius invites all who engage his spirituality and *Examen* to know God's will, and in grace, surrender to it. St. Ignatius, pray for us.

Foreword Comments

Serving the Church as an Archbishop in the early decades of the Third Millennium is at once a privilege and a challenge. It is a privilege because of the opportunity to proclaim to the youth, women and men of our day the Truth who is Jesus Christ, and to offer them a living relationship with him in the Church. Our Lord desires to make us friends and apostles, and when we accept his invitation, he satisfies the deepest hungers of our hearts. Still, we face the supreme challenge of finding the most effective means of communicating his Truth. The restlessness of our age seeks him, often unwittingly. But how will we help people find him?

Pope Benedict XVI reminded the Jesuits at their 35th General Congregation in 2008 of their proud history of proclamation and encounter between Gospel and culture. He invited them to be courageous and intelligent in ministering on the frontiers of faith and culture; to remain faithful to the Magisterium so that the truth and unity of Catholic doctrine is preserved in its totality; and to reserve special attention to the ministry of the Spiritual Exercises. Of the Exercises, he said: "It is for you to make it a precious and efficacious instrument for the spiritual growth of souls, for their initiation to prayer, to meditation, in this secularized world in which God seems to be absent."

Jesuit Father William Watson's *Sacred Story—An Ignatian Examen for the Third Millennium* responds to all three of the Holy Father's missions. Father Watson combines a missionary's determination and creativity to reach the far frontiers of the human heart in contemporary cultures, a scholar's search for the truth faithful to the genius of the *Spiritual Exercises,* and (as a son of Ignatius) zeal to preserve and illuminate the unity of the Church's doctrine. I am already seeing the fruits of *Sacred Story* in the work of the Sacred Story Institute in the Archdiocese of Seattle. May this book and the Institute serve both the Society of Jesus and the Church's great work of the New Evangelization in the Third Millennium.

J. Peter Sartain
Archbishop of Seattle

Many years ago, in the summer of 1971 an insight of Ignatian discernment had evolved slowly for me. This gradual development also sparked a new view for me about the examen. A daily practice of discernment: that is what the examen was for St. Ignatius. Then I came to understand why the *Examen* prayer was so centrally important for him beyond any other spiritual practice.

The *Examen* demanded for today's challenging life must cut to the core of our heart to find a heat and fire beyond our own invention and control. Though the contemplative insight of a faithful heart burns deep and firm, it always flashes forwarded to challenging service.

The most dangerous issue confronting our culture is to learn to deal with violent sudden and explosive impulses. Though we can unhealthily try to squelch these strong feelings, such violent explosives simmer in all our hearts and flail out often beyond our control. Without realizing such explosive power resides within us or without an ability to control such eruptions, we all face disaster. Learning to control these violent impulses is the greatest challenge facing our families, our culture and our world. We read of this disaster in our newspapers, police reports and various electronic images. From international wars to individual suicide, these human explosives kill and destroy people more and more. In many ways these sudden violent eruptions are the worst issue facing our families and cultures.

Facing, learning and helping to control these activities can be the most important issue for the *Examen*. In years gone by, children often learned from parents and family how to deal with these attacks. But so much of our family structure has now fallen apart – and all of us are now available to deadly disaster. Prisons will not stop this problem. An external punishment of penalty is never enough by itself to destroy these incendiary crashes.

Facing and dealing with these impulses must cut deep inside our human hearts. No external force can solve this issue. Discernment of spirits with its ordered dynamics, always central to the Ignatian *Examen*, can provide a faithful human education for simmering emotions, unreflective thoughts and explosive impulses. This is the deep-seated heart of the Ignatian *Examen*. Never automatic, it requires gutsy work and tough decisions if we are to avoid the deadly disaster that faces us all.

Ignatius had to learn and burn through these disordered and dangerous inner impulses for him to recognize and accept the firm and tender love of his sanctity. The *Examen* will always cut deeply into our harsh felt spirits of love to reveal our true identity. The *Examen* will always play an important role in the basic human education we all need if God's Glory is to glow more and more in our universe.

George Aschenbrenner, S.J.
Washington, D.C.

I am not the only person to have wrestled with the interpretation and the regular practice of the Ignatian *Examen*, both in one's own life of prayer, as well as in assisting others seeking help. In the decades following Vatican II's call of all to holiness, a few books, and several articles have been written, offering interpretations and patterns of practice regarding the *Examen*. William Watson's *Sacred Story*, does this too, in a manner that rings true to the authentic Ignatian tradition and which, at the same time, bursts the categories of traditional phrases that can restrict understanding. Like the wise scribe applauded by Jesus, Watson addresses us contemporary women and men in the psycho- social language in which we are immersed and by which we try to understand our world and ourselves in our various roles and societies. This is one heck of a blockbuster of a book.

Watson is in earnest about the centrality of the Ignatian *Examen*. He attempts something that I am not aware having been tried before – seeing and understanding the *Examen* as arising totally out of the story of St. Ignatius' life and reflected experience. Watson does for the *Examen* what Jerome Nadal did for the Jesuit Constitutions (when Nadal explained the Constitutions to the Jesuit communities he visited in the very early days of the Society of Jesus). Watson links any proper and full appropriation of the *Examen* to the experiences of St. Ignatius' life, particularly to his conversion, and to the programme of the *Spiritual Exercises*. This is a novel approach, and one, in my opinion, which is holistic, rich, fertile and fruitful.

This perspective for appreciating the *Examen* is not solely historical. Watson with great attentiveness and clarity of thought makes use of contemporary psychosocial understandings of our human nature to enter more deeply into the person of Ignatius Loyola. Our attention is drawn to the influences, both personal and societal, on St. Ignatius, onwards from his conception into a proud and ancient Basque family. These are the influences (spirits) that give shape and form to a person, any person. Looking at St. Ignatius in this manner, allows Ignatius to raise the level of our own awareness of the influences that have and continue to shape us. Ignatius' person, and his coping with the issues raised in his own life, touch and resonated with my own different person, with my own, not-too-dissimilar issues, in my own different time and different place.

St. Ignatius Loyola emerges as a rich, complex and multi-layered personality. Engaging with Ignatius reveals how rich, complex and multi-layered I am as well. But I am also brought face-to-face with the demands of the effort to deal more adequately with the rootedness of the various influences that have formed me, and the pervasiveness of the habits that have colonised my perceptions, and of the judgements that arise from those perceptions. Watson issues challenging warnings to anyone wanting to enter into the *Examen* programme of St. Ignatius. Watson enumerates five challenges that might hinder and trip up a person from persevering in the prayer of *Examen*.

In order to both encourage and assist a person in developing his or her own prayer of *Examen*, Watson gives us a well-thought-through, highly organised, systematic programme of exercises that gradually and progressively introduce us into the practice and heart-felt understanding of the presuppositions and building blocks on which the full *Examen* grows. He gives guidelines for healing and growth. Watson does not underestimate the personal courage and the spiritual stamina to be prayed for in this task. Through a re-contextualising of the Ignatian rules for discernment of spirits, the *Examen's* vitality and relevance is recovered, and the *Examen's* supernatural powers are rediscovered.

Watson's very valuable and practical contribution to Ignatian studies, and particularly to a deeper appreciation of the centrality of the *Examen*, moves both its practice and its understanding to a new level as we continue to ask "Where do you live?" of the God who "is not far from any of us, since it is in him that we live, and move, and exist, as indeed some of your own writers have said: *We are all his children.*"

Watson gives much to ponder and to digest. Food for a lifetime: feeding my own *Sacred Story*.

David Keith Townsend, S.J.
Chiang Mai, Thailand

Introduction

The Examen Problem

Mid-last century two Christian scholars separated by distance and discipline identified the same threat as humanity's gravest. C.S. Lewis and Josef Pieper wrote that loss of the examined life, contemplative rest, and God consciousness is eroding culture and destroying humankind.[4]

Lewis' *Screwtape Letters* sketch a plan for humanity's destruction through the blinding of people's awareness of the present and the eternal. The goal is a world devoid of reflective contemplation.[5] Pieper's *Leisure, the Basis of Culture,* affirms that the very survival of Western society hinges on the re-establishment of contemplative rest (leisure) as the preeminent, foundational value of an enlightened and creative culture.

Each writer identifies the fundamental challenge confronting the person seeking a measure of self-reflection. For Pieper, the world of total work is annihilating all unstructured time thus rendering impossible the capacity for self-awareness to open human consciousness to "the-world-as-a-whole."[6] Lewis sees a strategist's hand in this global, evolutionary trend toward darkened conscience. The world of noise and chaos will in the end silence every heavenly voice as well as human sensitivity to the inner stirrings of conscience.[7] Pieper sees the erosion of a contemplative, reflective space slipping away with such "monstrous momentum" that he wonders whether its loss and the hyperactivity filling the void has demonic origins. His solution is to reclaim a space for leisure that provides "contact with those superhuman life-giving forces that can send us renewed and alive again into the busy world of work." [8]

A divine counter-strategy for nullifying the demonic forces that Lewis and Pieper unmask is found in the Psalmist's words: "Be still, and know that I am God." Jesus too affirms that "the Kingdom is among you."[9] These Scriptural prescriptions speak to us, but shouting much louder are the cultural, psychological and spiritual forces arrayed against the awakening of human consciousness to the world as a whole. These overpowering forces gain strength each day. We are losing touch with the intimate presence of God in and among us. In fact, we are in the full bloom of what Thomas Merton described as violent hyper-activism.[10] The threat, while still gaining force, is primeval. Strategies to confront it are as ancient as the threat itself. God, working through both the Chosen People, and the Church's saints has provided us countless spiritual resources to meet it head-on.

Ignatius of Loyola, born over four hundred years before Pieper and Lewis, created a method of attentive prayer called the *Examination of Conscience.* The discipline was Ignatius' way to be conscious—to stay awake—so as to reject temptations from the enemy of human nature and respond positively to God's graces. Ignatius incorporated the discipline into his *Spiritual Exercises* and encouraged its use beyond retreats. It became one of the principal pastoral tools of the early Jesuits in their European and missionary apostolates. It is a discipline Ignatius performed hourly and continued to practice up to his death.

Yet the *Examen,* Ignatius' synergistic partner to the *Spiritual Exercises,* is a practice that for most is difficult and inconstant. Writing thirty years after Pieper and Lewis, George Aschenbrenner called attention to the trouble *Examen* practitioners encounter staying awake and seeing God in the present moment. One of the most repeated lines from his landmark article is the opening sentence: "*Examen* is usually the first practice to disappear from the daily life of the religious…all the reasons amount to the admission (rarely explicit) that it is not of immediate practical value in a busy day."[11]

Aschenbrenner reframed the *Examen* as discernment of *consciousness* thinking that a narrow moralism was blocking its use and efficacy. He and many other commentators from the same era changed the understanding of this spiritual discipline but not its popularity. In three articles on the *Examen* written between 1972 and 1988 Aschenbrenner sees the use of the *Examen* among the ranks of religious women and men holding steady, i.e., practically nonexistent. In 2006 he writes: "Entry into the practice of examen that is regular and perduring is not easy for many people. They start to practice it because it seems important, but it just does not last."[12]

About This Book

How and why did Ignatius develop the *Examen*? What is it supposed to accomplish for those who practice it? Why do people choose to forgo this discipline that has proved over the centuries to be invaluable and essential to spiritual growth and the discernment of spirits? What are the contemporary cultural crises confronting today's would-be *Examen* practitioners provoking distrust, fear, or dismissive attitudes towards it? How can an *Examen* faithful to Ignatius' original method be modernized to address the mindset of today's Christians?

This book offers a new analysis of Ignatius' progressive conversion (which he details in his *Autobiography*) to answer these questions. In *Beginnings and Challenges*, we examine Ignatius the man and the events in his life, especially his confrontation with addiction, sinful habits, and narcissism. Analyzing his *Autobiography's* terse text, four paradigmatic elements come to light that encapsulate significant Ignatian insights. In addition, analysis of Ignatius' early conversion as an organic process reveals connections between his two conversion experiences at Loyola and Montserrat/Manresa, the *General* and *Particular Examens,* and the two sets of discernment *Rules*.

Ignatius' fundamental conversion at Loyola tracks a process of *General Examen*. Here Ignatius identifies his most manifest sins and addictions. The temptations at this purgative stage of development force the insights leading to the discernment *Rules* of the First Week. These foundational discernment *Rules* are essential for all who seek to identify and withdraw from sensual temptations. These purgative sufferings typify the Catholic mystical tradition's "dark night of the senses."

Ignatius' integrated conversion at Manresa is the critical tipping point in his life. It provides the insights necessary to shape the *Particular Examen* process. Through the scrupulous anguish and harrowing of Montserrat and Manresa Ignatius identifies his core sin. The temptations at this illuminative stage of development force the insights leading to Ignatius' discernment *Rules* of the Second Week. These *Rules* help one to discern the temptations directed at the spiritual sin of pride which lurks beneath one's manifest sins. The mystical tradition identifies the sufferings associated with dismantling narcissism's superstructures as the "dark night of the spirit." It is this deep surrender to God that is the signature—the *Magis* or Holy Grail—of Ignatius' spirituality including the *Examen*.

This investigation of Ignatius' two-tiered conversion is accompanied by a study of the spiritual disciplines of his *General and Particular Examination of Conscience* (*GE* and *PE*) and the difficulties they pose for practitioners. The structure of the *Examen* is analyzed, as is its use in early Jesuit history. Critiques of the Ignatian method from modern commentators name five challenges these methods present to believers today. This calls for a deep analysis of the *Ignatian Paradigm*, which forms the core structure of the *Examen*. In the end, the Ignatian *Examen* is revealed as a revolutionary, dynamic, holistic, efficient, and thoroughly contemporary spiritual discipline. Solutions to these five supposed challenges are inherent in Ignatius' methods and spirituality.

The second part of this book, *Recovering the Examen's Vitality and Relevance*, explores the four key components that comprise Ignatius' *Examen* in a new method titled *Sacred Story*. These are: Ignatius' *Rules* for Discernment and an analysis of their development during Ignatius' progressive conversion; an explanation of how the *Rules* have been revised for the *Sacred Story* method and an investigation of updates to the *Particular Examen*. There is finally an exposition of the five-point *Examen* structure called "chapters" in the *Sacred Story* method. These both encompass and intensify the *Examen's* core purpose revealed in the *Ignatian Paradigm*.

Part three, *Writing Your Sacred Story* details the components of *Sacred Story* practice and how to integrate it into one's life. Key components are the rules of engagement, the foundational spiritual diagnostic exercises, and Ignatian Confession, modeling Ignatius' own. There are instructions for practicing *Sacred Story* shaped by scores who have engaged its disciplines and revised Ignatian discernment *Rules* in a narrative format created especially for *Sacred Story*.[13]

The more you understand about Ignatius' conversion and the *Examen* and trust what you understand, the more likely you will be to open your heart to its practice. In reading the history, challenges, and the reasons for updating this powerful spiritual discipline you have already begun its practice.

It is my prayer that you will consciously and courageously follow in Ignatius' footsteps by living his life-changing *Examen* in the form of a *Sacred*

Story. Invite the Divine Physician to open your mind and heart to reveal your *Sacred Story* and, like Ignatius, help shape this final epoch of human history, becoming a co-laborer in the Divine work of reconciliation.

William Watson, SJ
Feast of Our Lady of the Way

Part One

Beginnings and Challenges

Anyone who is not totally dead to self will soon find that he is tempted and overcome by piddling and frivolous things. Whoever is weak in spirit, given to the flesh, and inclined to sensual things can, but only with great difficulty, drag himself away from his earthly desires. Therefore, he is often gloomy and sad when he is trying to pull himself away from them, and easily gives into anger should someone attempt to oppose him.

—Thomas à Kempis, *The Imitation of Christ*

1

Fundamental Conversion and the General Examen

A Unique Discipline by a Unique Disciple

Ignatius was not the first to examine his conscience, nor the last. Every philosophy student reading Plato's dialogues learns that a life unexamined is not worth living. The Delphic saying, "know thyself," is ubiquitous. Disciples of Zen have been seeking self-consciousness for over fifteen hundred years. Buddhists practice mindfulness. Disciples of contemporary masters like Eckhart Tolle seek self-consciousness and are buying millions of his books seeking peace and enlightenment. Followers of Christ have devised numerous ascetical practices and prayer disciplines over the millennia to sensitize their consciences to grow spiritually. But there is something new and unprecedented in the method of conscience examination developed by St. Ignatius. His method is closely linked to his life story, and the conversion journey he details in his *Autobiography*.

Shortly after the decisive events that transform Ignatius' life from soldier to pilgrim, he travels from his home at Loyola to Montserrat and Manresa. His sojourn lasts from late February to late March of 1522. We know from Ignatius' biographers and recent scholarship that two important spiritual works were available to him during this time. One, the *Book of Spiritual Exercises* by Garcias Cisneros, the abbot of Montserrat, contains a full compendium of spiritual wisdom and practices from the Western Tradition. Cisneros included lengthy, detailed methods for examining one's conscience.[1] The other book was Thomas à Kempis' *The Imitation of Christ.* It held pride of place with the New Testament in Ignatius' cell while he was General.[2]

The *Imitation* contains two short entries on methods for examining one's conscience. The most lengthy and detailed is reserved for a priest prior to celebrating Mass. Included also are longer passages for staying recollected over the course of the day.[3] The *Imitation* was a book so close to Ignatius' heart that it gained wide popularity among the early Jesuits.[4] *The Practice of Perfection* contains the most detailed accounts in the early Society of the use and practice of Ignatius' two *Examen* methods.[5] Its author, Alphonsus Rodríguez, identifies many sources that support the techniques of the *GE* and *PE*. However, he states that their value for Christian growth is based upon Ignatius' "reason and experience."[6] Both the *Imitation of Christ* and Cisneros' compendium of Christian wisdom inspired Ignatius. But Ignatius' distinctive *Examen* methods are shaped by other forces.[7] In order to discern the true origin of Ignatius' unique examination method we need to explore his conversion process as detailed in his *Autobiography*.

Ignatius told his story to Gonçalves da Câmera, minister of the house. As scribe, da Câmera relates that Ignatius had good recall of events and communicated things with such clarity that da Câmera did not need to press him for further information.[8] A full third of Ignatius' *Autobiography* is dedicated to the first two years of his conversion. An analysis of this period in Ignatius' life reveals new insights about his spirituality and his distinctive spiritual methods. Specifically, four paradigmatic events—significant with respect to Ignatius' life and also to the spirituality that marks his legacy, including the *Examen*—come to light. Before beginning to analyze Ignatius' remarkable conversion story, however, it is best to step back and take a measure of the man and his family of origin. This will provide both preface and foundation for the critical transformations he recorded for posterity in the *Autobiography*.

Ignatius the Man and the Loyola Family

Records indicate Iñigo (Ignatius) Lopez de Oñaz y Loyola's family enjoyed status, wealth, and a history of aggression. Several decades before Ignatius was born, Enrique IV of Castile ordered the armament strongholds of the Oñez de Loyola family demolished in an effort to staunch the family's violent behavior. Rebellions, assassinations, and robberies are some of the profane fruit on the Loyola tree. Numerous entries in family records indicate pious works and the pay out of "conscience money" to shrines as attempts to atone for their transgressions. Probably more telling is the fact that nothing in the Loyola family records indicates grief or regret for their "ferocious hatreds and terrible vendettas."[9] The culture of the times was violent, but as a family, the Loyola name gained special renown. Their nobility traced back to an unbroken line of service since the 12th century to the kings of Castile. Yet their sense of entitlement encouraged them to rebel against that same authority.[10]

If aggression was a way of life for the men of Loyola, sexual exploits equaled the episodic violence. Known for high piety and low morals, "fathering bastards" was a family legacy.[11] Records show Don Beltrán, Ignatius' father, had at least three illegitimate children. Ignatius' elder brother, a priest, had a concubine with whom he fathered four children. While biographers admit the Loyola's possessed a strong, reflexive Catholic piety, it is portrayed as "that peculiar brand of faith that could willingly shed blood in defense of religion and celebrate the victory with a night of unbridled lechery."[12]

Ignatius by upbringing was properly initiated into the culture of aggression and desire. At the age of twenty-four, he and his brother were convicted of nighttime misdemeanors that records reveal were both premeditated and "most outrageous."[13] They attacked a cleric from a family against whom the Loyolas had a vendetta. The Loyola family name is the likely reason Ignatius escaped prosecution. Polanco, Ignatius' secretary, wrote: "Though he was attached to the faith, he lived nowise in conformity with it and did not avoid sin. Rather he was much addicted to gambling and dissolute in his dealings with women, contentious and keen about using his sword."[14]

For years writers circulated stories that Ignatius himself had a bastard child. Nothing can either be affirmed or denied in this case. His lifestyle and family history make it likely, and if not a fact, then possibly only by circumstance of biology or grace. Joseph de Guibert sums up the man: "very careful about his personal appearance, anxious to please the fair sex, daring in affairs of gallantry, punctilious about his honor, fearing nothing. Holding cheap his own life and that of others, he was ready for all exploits, even for those that are but an abuse of strength."[15] A Freudian analysis of Ignatius and all the Loyola men as phallic narcissists gives a secular psychological tag to this mid-tier noble clan.[16]

Ignatius Discovers his Conscience

In May of 1521, Ignatius was thirty years old. A soldier of four years, he commanded a troop of two hundred men on the walls of the Spanish town of Pamplona. They fought against twelve thousand superiorly armed French soldiers. His courage in commanding against such odds has the hallmark of bravery. In his *Autobiography*, however, Ignatius reveals his conduct during this battle to be that of sheer arrogance. He persuaded the commander, against the wishes of every other single soldier, to engage the battle. The Battle of Pamplona was a twenty minute skirmish that ended when a cannon ball shattered Ignatius' leg. Ignatius' pride endangered his own life, as well as the lives of his comrades. Many of his soldiers were injured and one died.[17] French soldiers brought Ignatius home to Loyola. A period of convalescence punctuated by boredom-induced daydreams leads to a series of insights that awaken his conscience.[18]

The French soldiers, who ferried Ignatius home, bound his fractured leg. The bone set poorly, was dislocated on the trip, and required a second surgery. The operation nearly killed Ignatius. The leg healed but with an unsightly knob. Some months after the second surgery, and close to recovery, Ignatius insisted doctors perform an excruciating operation to cut away the knob. This was a dangerous cosmetic procedure endured for image and vanity that "quite alarmed" his brother.[19] Painful leg-stretching to improve his gait followed the surgery. In his own words Ignatius initiated and endured these procedures because he "had made up his mind to seek his fortune in the world" and "to gratify his own inclinations."[20]

The cannon ball, the near-death experience from surgery, and the reckless cosmetic procedures: none of these created a saint. Contrary to pious clichés, the Jesuits did not "gain a father" at Pamplona. Ignatius' awakening came in a less glamorous moment. Bored and confined to his room while his leg was stretched he requested books of knightly exploits and chivalrous romances popular with men of his social class.[21] No books of this type existed in the Loyola castle. Instead, his sister-in-law Magdalena offered her four-volume copy of Ludolph of Saxony's, *The Life of Jesus Christ*, along with the *Flos Sanctorum*, a collection of short stories of the most popular saints.[22]

The books introduced a new narrative theme into Ignatius' vain daydreams:

> By the frequent reading of these books he conceived some affection for what he found there narrated. Pausing in his reading, he gave himself up to thinking over what he had read. At other times he dwelt on the things of the world which formerly had occupied his thoughts. Of the many vain things that presented themselves to him, one took such possession of his heart that without realizing it he could spend two, three, or even four hours on end thinking of it, fancying what he would have to do in the service of a certain lady, of the means he would take to reach the country where she was living, of the verses, the promises he would make to her, the deeds of gallantry he would do in her service. He was so enamored with all this that he did not see how impossible it would all be, because the lady was of no ordinary rank; neither countess, nor duchess, but of a nobility much higher than any of these.[23]

Reading Magdalena's books also introduced holy thoughts of making a pilgrimage to Jerusalem into Ignatius' vain fantasies. A totally new narrative now fought for pride of place with Ignatius' vain daydreams. Entertaining the dueling daydreams brought contentment and delight for hours on end. But Ignatius saw something in his post-daydream ruminations that is attributable only to grace:

> [O]ne day his eyes were opened a little and he began to wonder at the difference and to reflect on it, learning from experience that one kind of thought left him sad and the other cheerful. Thus, step by step, he came to recognize the difference between the two spirits that moved him, the one being from the evil spirit, the other from God.[24]

These two sets of fantasies are radically opposed in both character and content. Later in his *Spiritual Exercises* he would come to identify these polarities as the *Two Standards* of Christ and Satan.[25] Ignatius' "eyes being opened a little" in this, his reflecting on reflection, commences his attunement to the discernment of the spirits. It will translate into a constant and life-long examination of his conscience.

The Ignatian Paradigm and the General Examen

Ignatius' emerging consciousness of two polarities was quite superficial at first. His holy books produced "some affection" for the daydreams they engendered.

The notable difference between polarities was contentment versus dissatisfaction. But his conscience was sensitized and his conscious awareness of differences gained depth. Reading his autobiographical account, three unfolding events reveal these changes:

- The discovery of different spirits at play in his inner self, and affirmation of those causing sustained contentment over those that leave him dissatisfied, leads him to:

↓

- "think seriously of his past life and the great need he has of doing penance for it," and from this follows:[26]

↓

- the aspiration to go to Jerusalem, "which a generous soul on fire with the love of God is wont to desire."[27]

In Ignatius' account, these three awakenings are immediately followed by a "vision" revealing the same general pattern. The vision "confirmed" for him the authenticity of his holy desires:[28]

- A vision of Mary and the Christ child that produces intense consolation, leading to:

↓

- a felt revulsion of his past life, in particular sins of the flesh, with "great disgust" of sufficient intensity that he feels it:

↓

- "wiped out" the "images" from his thoughts,[29] leaving him:

$$\downarrow$$

- "without a care in the world," to read and reflect on the saints and the life of Christ, and freeing him during this time of his greatest consolation to:

$$\downarrow$$

- "gaze upon the heavens and the stars...because when doing so he felt within himself a powerful urge to be serving our Lord."[30]

These two consecutive clustered sequences are similar and paradigmatic: graced seeing preceding knowledge of sin and atonement, followed by a desire to serve and act on the Lord's behalf. The pattern in these initial awakenings can be traced in the structure of the yet-to-be-written *Spiritual Exercises*. The *Exercises* begin the First Week with meditations on the corruption of creation by sin and a personal call to repentance. The Second Week comprises meditations on the life of Christ and exercises to help one discern how to follow Christ in one's own life. Week Three deepens the commitment to follow Christ by reflecting on his passion and death. The Fourth Week consolidates one's commitment to serve Christ and to find him "in all things" with the Contemplation to attain God's love.

These linked events describing Ignatius' awakening also summarize the flow of the *Examen* structures in the *Exercises*:

A graced experience of God's love opened Ignatius to: ⇨ ⇩	**GIVE THANKS FOR FAVORS RECEIVED** ⇩
A dissatisfaction with vain fantasies which led to surrendering to holy day-dreams, characterized by consolation, which in turn ⇨ ⇩	**PRAY FOR GRACE TO SEE CLEARLY** ⇩
Caused him to review his life and actions leading to: ⇨ ⇩	**GIVE A DETAILED ACCOUNT OF CONSCIENCE: GENERAL AND PARTICULAR** ⇩
Grief with yearning for penance and repentance for his past sins, culminating in: ⇨ ⇩	**ASK PARDON FOR ONE'S FAULTS** ⇩
Ignatius' passion to amend his life and a desire to love God wholeheartedly. ⇨	**RESOLVE AND AMEND TO SERVE GOD**

This is the first of four paradigms in the early conversion narrative. It is an archetypal structure of conversion and vocation. This sequence is titled the *Ignatian Paradigm* because it distills the spiritual arc of both the *Exercises* and the *Examen*. It is Ignatius' "first conversion" and fundamental "election."[31]

The graces of this first conversion event, reinforced by Ignatius' spiritual reading, mirror the structure of both the *Exercises* and his five-point *Examination of Conscience*. Ignatius first learns how to listen to and reflect on his inner experiences. The new data his reflection uncovers helps this decisive event to unfold. The elements of that unfolding will eventually constitute a finely tuned method of spiritual conversion and discernment.[32]

Ignatius' mastery of his most visible sins is only the beginning of his conversion journey. He has acquired a general understanding of the patent disorder in his life, but deeper insights are still to come. The process of Ignatius' conversion from this point forward leads him to a more particular, keenly focused awareness of the fundamental disorder at his heart's center.

2

Integrated Conversion and the Particular Examen

Signs of Growth

The period from August of 1522 until February of 1523 is distinguished by discoveries linked to Ignatius' awakening conscience. He is enlightened by graced attentiveness to understand the difference between good and evil as they manifest in his thoughts, words and deeds. He learns to embrace those spontaneities from God and reject those from the enemy of human nature. From this point forward, Ignatius plunges into a deep confrontation with the roots of his disordered life, which over time fully awakens him to the Divine light within.

Indications exemplifying both spiritual growth and a stripping of self abound in the *Autobiography*. After his vision in August of 1522, Ignatius becomes scrupulous about truthful speech.[1] He settles accounts with those to whom he owes money and spends the remainder of his money on repairing and adorning a shrine of Mary.[2] In addition, he admits to knowing little about humility, patience, charity, or discretion but wants nonetheless to perform penances and do great deeds for God.[3]

When a Moor offends Mary's perpetual virginity, he surrenders the Loyola blood lust to the whims of the mule he is riding.[4] Purchasing pilgrim's clothes, writing a confession over three days, yielding his dagger, and giving his rich clothing to a beggar, he resists the esteem of others.[5] And regarding his personal appearance, Ignatius, who "had a good head of hair" and was "delicate" about caring for both hair and nails, confronts pride of appearance by letting both grow wild.[6]

All these events are recounted simply. One can feel the piety and intensity of his burgeoning faith after he secretly gives his clothes to the beggar and kneels all night at the Virgin's altar.[7] The altercation with the Moor is more symbolic of Ignatius trying to master the violent Loyola temper. It will take more time to develop the intense, heartfelt Marian devotion that will soon characterize his spirituality and mystical experiences. Indeed, he prefaces the account by stating he is simply mimicking the "outward" actions of the saints.[8]

There is genuine emotion, however, for the beggar who became a victim of his charity. This event might well mark the first time Ignatius awakens to the sufferings his actions cause another, and someone well beneath his social class.[9] The charity he offers to this beggar can be considered the first recorded example of what will become for Ignatius a life-long priority to work on behalf of society's least.

The Truth Paradigm: Naming Sin and Addiction

On his journey from Loyola to Montserrat, Ignatius recounts an experience that marks the second paradigmatic event of his progressive conversion. What is titled the *Truth Paradigm* enfolds a temptation that carries with it the potential of annihilating his newly chosen ascetical path. Many can control vices, sin, and addictions for some weeks or months. Mastering those for the remainder of one's life is another matter entirely.

Ignatius lived for thirty years with the wealth, prestige and protection of the Loyola name. Along with an addiction to gambling, he was sexually promiscuous, possessed an explosive temper, and was conceited and touchy about his honor. According to some psychological profiles, Ignatius was quite insecure. In his personal appearance and dress he was vain and careful. Ignatius like we have already stated, was not a likely candidate for sainthood.

Anyone contemplating a lifetime of abstinence and asceticism could rightfully be paralyzed by fright at the prospect of overcoming this intense spiritual and psychological matrix of pride, passion, addiction and sin.. It is in light of this problematic history, and his fragile yet maturing faith, that Ignatius is tempted by "a rather disturbing thought which troubled him, representing the difficultly of the life he was leading."[10]

Ignatius sensed the "voice of the enemy" taunting him with fear and dread at the thought of suffering for "seventy years." He decisively confronted the threat: "You poor creature! Can you promise me even one hour of life?"[11] Successfully overcoming the temptation, he remained "at peace." Here on after he experienced successive alterations between intense desolations and consolations that caused him awe: "What kind of new life is this that we are now beginning?"[12]

In defiant rejection of this fearsome threat, Ignatius resolutely commits himself to surrendering his former life of sin. At this point, he consciously embraces a life-long journey of self-mastery and ascetical practices. More significantly, he proclaims the "truth" that the temptations are mirages. The black noise of the addictions, sinful habits, and pleasures of his past that promise "life," cannot satisfy his authentic human nature. Awakened by grace, he speaks that truth out loud.

This second conversion paradigm is titled the *Truth Paradigm*, for Ignatius confronts the ancient lie that sin and addiction's promise of life— however it assaults us—is false. In his *Rules*, Ignatius calls Satan the "enemy of human nature."[13] This title expands our understanding of sin and temptation's multi-pronged attack on the human person. The effects are manifest physiologically, psychologically and spiritually; i.e., through one's entire human nature. And the "life" the tempter holds forth to the one tempted is a lie, no matter whether promised benefits are physical, psychological or spiritual.

The structure of the *Truth Paradigm* looks this way:

An enemy voice evokes Ignatius' fear of a lifelong struggle with his sinful habits. ⇨ ⇩	**CONSCIOUS FEAR AND ANXIETY OVER SURRENDERING SINFUL AND ADDICTIVE HABITS** ⇩
Ignatius rejects the "enemy of human nature" and confronts his false promises. ⇨ ⇩	**CONFRONTING THE THREATENING "VOICE" OF SIN AND ADDICTION WITH THE "TRUTH" THAT THEY BRING DEATH, NOT LIFE** ⇩
Peace is restored after truthfully naming sin and addiction as death dealing. ⇨	**PEACE RETURNS AND ANXIETY DISSOLVES**

In naming and confronting his temptations Ignatius is rewarded with both peace and profound insight into the discernment of spirits that fill him with "awe." The *Truth Paradigm* entails a confrontation with the counterfeit but fearsome dread that a life-long commitment to self-mastery inspires. These early lessons in standing down the enemy's fear tactics define the very structure of the *Exercises'* First Week *Rules for the Discernment of Spirits (Rules)*.[14]

As such, the *Truth Paradigm* highlights the reflection and discernment necessary in the ongoing general examination of conscience required for persons firmly committed to the Gospel's narrow path. Gabor Maté's research, discussed later, provides important physiological evidence to the spiritual dimension of this *Truth Paradigm*. Challenging "false narratives," so often unconscious in the black noise of our lives, and unhooking from the pseudo-comfort of the addictions and habits they encourage, enables psychological healing by re-wiring the brain and balancing its biochemistry.

Contextualizing Ignatius' Sins and Narcissism

Ignatius' commitment to the asceticisms of his newfound faith brought him ultimately to the greatest crisis of his conversion journey. The event forming the *Truth Paradigm* happened before Ignatius entered a church for prayer.[15]

As proclaimed in the first sentence of his *Autobiography*, his confrontation with narcissism follows immediately and defines his pre-conversion years.[16] Exploring Ignatius' past indicates how his harrowing by scrupulosity is both spiritual and psychological.

Doña Marina Sáchez de Licona, Ignatius' mother, died shortly after giving birth to him. Upon her death, Ignatius was removed from the Loyola manor house and nursed by María de Garín, the wife of a blacksmith living about half a mile from the family home. Meissner states: "research in this area tends to confirm the association of early maternal deprivation through death, divorce, or separation with relatively severe forms of life-long psychopathology".[17] Idígoras, a modern biographer of Ignatius, complements this analysis:

> This primordial bonding between Íñigo and his mother, or rather the nonexistence of such a bonding, suggests the absence of the protective, liberating, fostering maternal presence that would have given him early direction, basic confidence, and would have opened up new objectives for him. This absence of affective nurturing during his early years could have even resulted in retarded physical growth. Íñigo was a runt, hardly a representative of the Basques, who are considered the tallest of the Spanish people. The lack of nurturing by a mother engenders habits of depression later in life; it affects that way one reacts to and relates with others; it incites vague feelings of guilt. Again we cite Rof Carballo, who has written extensively on the relationship between psychoanalysis and religion, on this particular point: "Deep within the recesses of his affectivity, every wandering adventurer is responding to the hidden and irresolvable need to compensate for the lack of that maternal nurturing, whose function is to provide the child with affective perimeters."[18]

Both Idígoras' and Meissner's insights dovetail with the research of Karen Horney. Psychological disturbances are the source of neurotic patterns or "trends" that, having unconscious roots, indicate efforts to cope with early traumatic childhood experiences.[19] About these trends, Horney writes:

> They represent a way of life enforced by unfavorable conditions. The child must develop them in order to survive his insecurity, his fears, his loneliness. But they give him an unconscious feeling that he must stick to the established path at all odds, lest he succumb to the dangers threatening him…When this initial development has once occurred is it necessarily lasting? The answer is that although he will not inevitably retain his defensive techniques there is grave danger that he will… in the absence of strong counteracting factors there is considerable danger that the trends acquired not only will persist but in time will obtain a stronger hold on the personality.[20]

Rudolf Allers and Gabor Maté provide more evidence of the personality challenges caused by early-life trauma. Their theories expand upon and complement those of Meissner, Idígoras, and Horney. Allers, considered Freud's last brilliant pupil, views early childhood trauma and deprivation as key to character development problems later in life.[21] Gabor Maté also points to maternal deprivation and early life stress as a root cause of serious maladaptive behaviors and psychological problems.[22] Maté's study on stressors in childhood development discloses the source of a narcissistic personality and his or her addictive tendencies:

> Addiction is primarily about the self, about the unconscious, insecure self that at every moment considers only its own immediate desires— and believes that it must behave that way. In all cases the process arises from the unmet needs of the helpless young child for whom this constant self-obsession appears, to begin with, as a matter of survival. That he cannot rely on the nurturing environment becomes his core myth. No such environment even exists—or so he has come to believe in his bones and in his heart, which were parched by early loss…[T]he addict hasn't grown out of the stage of infancy

that has been called the narcissistic phase, the period when the fledgling human being believes that everything happens because of her, to her, and for her.[23]

Evidence of the type and intensity of stress and/or trauma that Ignatius encountered in childhood can be deduced from his behaviors. According to Horney's theories, (and with added insights from Meissner, Idígoras, Allers and Maté), stresses from Ignatius' early development are probable contributing factors to his addictions and sinful narcissism. Indeed half of Horney's trends fit Ignatius' personality to a tee.[24]

If precursors for Ignatius' sinful narcissism and addictive habits can be inferred from lack of maternal influences, what about paternal influences? The Loyolas had a sense of their own nobility and a willful entitlement that emboldened them to fight against their own king. Ignatius, the last born child of the Loyolas, was insignificant in size and family rank but displayed traits of this willful entitlement.

By right the oldest brother would inherit the entire Loyola estate. Ignatius would have to fend for himself to make his mark in the world. Subject to the "patriarchal and arbitrary manner" of his father, Ignatius was given the tonsure and enlisted in a clerical militia. This is a career that he would rebel against in "stubborn opposition to this plan of his father."[25] He saw his future career as something greater than living his years out as a country pastor on the family estate now owned by his brother. The example of his father Beltrán Loyola, a feudal lord of Guipúzcoa, and the Loyola tradition of entitlement, would be "far-reaching."[26]

Pride, wealth, family status, military prowess, valor in battle, and a reflexive faith are part of Ignatius' noble breeding. He identifies these characteristics of his upbringing later as "riches, honor, and pride:" *Spiritual Exercises*: *SpEx* [142].[27] When Ignatius is sixteen years old, his father Beltrán dies. Upon the death of his father, all of the family wealth, prestige and property pass to Ignatius' oldest brother. Ignatius, now alone in the world, must fight for a place of honor befitting the Loyola name and temperament. He has no intention of serving the Church. Instead he will seek to make his mark serving the king and achieving military glories.[28]

The commanding sixteen year-old that leaves home upon his father's death carries into the world his sufferings, emotional deprivations, addictive traits, sinful habits, and narcissistic pride. The world he enters is the princely court of one of his relatives, Don Juan Velasquez de Cuellar at Aravalo. It will be another fifteen years before Ignatius begins to name, source, and confront the sins and addictions at the root of his disordered dreams and extreme passions. When enlightenment strikes it is scrupulosity that initiates his harrowing passage toward integrated spiritual growth and mystical wisdom.

The Harrowing Struggle with Scruples: Ignatius Confronts His Core Sin

Ignatius spent three days writing out his confession after arriving at Montserrat. The year was 1522. It was his desire to make the confession on the feast of the Annunciation. With the detailed guide provided by Abbot Cisneros' book, it seems that every category and shade of sin Ignatius committed in his thirty years could be catalogued, written down, confessed and dispatched. It is noteworthy that Ignatius' account of this significant spiritual rite of passage is recounted as a simple fact: "He made a general confession in writing which lasted three days."[29] There are no indications of the shame, disgust, and remorse mentioned earlier during his initial awakening at Loyola. Nor are there statements of spiritual elation or mention of graces accompanying the event. But a harrowing experience looms.[30]

After his confession, Ignatius began to worry whether he had honestly detailed all his sins and was terribly distressed:

> But at this time he had much to suffer from scruples. Although the general confession he had made at Montserrat had been entirely written out and made carefully enough, there still remained some things which from time to time he thought he had not confessed. This caused him a good deal of worry, for even though he had confessed it, his mind was never at rest.[31]

The Montserrat confession was made with full diligence.[32] Nonetheless, Ignatius began a habit of confessing and re-confessing the same sins. Neither this practice nor the spiritual persons he sought for advice to manage his troubling habit brought release. Finally, confiding his troubles to a spiritually astute doctor from La Seo Cathedral in Zaragoza, he was advised to re-write his general confession to solve the problem. However it was to no avail. The scruples returned.

His scruples not only returned, but as he examined his sinful memories, he saw details he believed had escaped his notice. For this, he felt even more guilt and agony. This worrisome obsession of focusing on finer and finer details caused him intense suffering and damage.[33] He was afraid to tell his confessor to "order him in the name of Jesus Christ" never to confess past sins again. Providentially, the confessor did make this recommendation, and without prompting, but with this caution: unless the matter "was something absolutely clear."[34] Unfortunately, this did no good for Ignatius because for him "everything was quite clear"[35]. "Thus he remained with his hard labor."[36]

Back in his room at Manresa, Ignatius became increasingly desperate and frightened. By this time, this crisis of his scruples had lasted at least two months, if not longer.[37] It was damaging psychologically and spiritually. Crying out to God to cure his scruples, Ignatius pleaded: "Rescue me, O Lord";[38] "no trial would be too great for me to bear."[39] As a man used to physical torture, such as enduring the butchery and reconstruction of his leg, we can only imagine the intensity of the spiritual and psychological agony he suffered. To bargain with God for even worse physical pain in exchange for release from this excruciating mental distress is notable.

Ignatius is not forthcoming on the specific nature of his scrupulous agonies. But scrupulous pathologies can stem from a temporary developmental problem linked to a conversion experience. They can also lead to an emotionally based obsessive-compulsive disorder (OCD). Scrupulous obsessions "include, but are not limited to, blasphemy, violence, psychological harm and sexual obsessions."[40]

Ignatius' scrupulosity defies easy categorization. The context of this scrupulosity might cover both types mentioned above, i.e., effects of a recent conversion and some form of OCD. Judging from the revulsion he expressed earlier over his "sins of the flesh," and advice to others on "obscene and sensual" thoughts disrupting one's prayer, it could be that sexual obsessions provided at least some of the content of his scrupulous sufferings.[41]

Scrupulosity can have both psychological and religious grounds. A classic remedy for scruple sufferers like Ignatius is to find a confessor to follow blindly.[42] Ignatius did this but to no avail; the torment persisted. Pitifully desperate to gain release from the anguish and damage of this excruciatingly obsessive-compulsive pattern, he said he would even "follow a little dog" if he could find a way out.[43] Coming from a fiercely proud man, this is a profound confession of suffering, powerlessness and desperation.

Ignatius' suffering intensified. Frequent temptations often came to him "with great vehemence".[44] He was tempted to commit suicide by throwing himself down a ravine close to the place where he prayed. Ignatius' terrifying battles with scruples and severe suicidal impulses have been described as a regressive crisis.[45] This psycho-spiritual crucifixion was fiercer than any physical battle Ignatius could contemplate. No wonder he bartered with God for any other trial in exchange for this excruciating mental and spiritual torment.

A combination of grace and intense scrupulosity warded off Ignatius' "vehement" self-annihilation impulses: "But knowing it was a sin to do away with himself, he shouted again:[46] Lord, I will do nothing to offend you" which he repeated many times.[47] Still, he took on even greater asceticisms by denying himself both food and drink. He did this in imitation of something he read that had worked for a saint in need of God's favor.

The fortitude of his will to persevere in light of his intense desperation and mental anguish reveals his deep inner struggles. Ignatius decided to fast until such time that God answered him or he was near death. He knew that if he reached this state, he most likely would not have the strength to ask for food, or eat it if it was offered. For a week he fasted while fulfilling the full regimen of his spiritual disciplines, including "praying on his knees from midnight on."[48]

The following Sunday, on his regular confession day, and in the habit of reporting "very minuscule" details of his life, Ignatius informed the confessor of his new ascetical disciplines. He was "commanded" by the priest to break the fast.[49] Even though he was still "physically strong" he obeyed his confessor. His pride is evident in this declaration of "strength." That day and the next he was freed from his scruples only for them to return the third day. The same obsessive compulsive pattern began all over again. Current sins blurred with the sins of the past, so that "it appeared to him he was obliged to confess them once more."[50] This time the obsessive thoughts were followed with a strong disgust for the life he was leading and also accompanied by "vehement" thoughts "to stop it."[51]

Ignatius had reached the end of his patience. As definitively as he committed to life-long mastery of self, he all but admitted he wanted nothing more to do with any of it. Months of hard labor, severe fasts, agonizing self-doubts and fearsome psychological and spiritual trials, all linked to his scruples, ran their course. He had explored every avenue, sought the best spiritual advice, and maximized every act of will to master and control his sinful memories. Yet, he was unable to find a solution or gain release from this fearsome and damaging habit.

This very likely could have been the end of Ignatius' conversion journey. He could have given up and walked back home to Loyola or the Madrid court to resume his old life. He could have continued his rigorous asceticisms relying on willpower alone. Either choice would have made Ignatius nothing more than an historical footnote.

It is just at this point when Ignatius felt like an utter failure that graces opened his heart and mind to the most important insight of his life. This turned out to be the most vital juncture in his conversion journey. What no effort of his own could achieve came to him from the Lord "as if awakening him from sleep;" as if from a dream.[52]

Grace awakened Ignatius to investigate the "vehement" spirit of disgust compelling him to end his spiritual journey. With a profound economy of words Ignatius expressed the insight which will lead him to the most important discernment of his life: he determined "with great clarity" never again to confess sins from the past.[53]

Scruples and Narcissistic Pride

Pride is linked to neurotic suffering.[54] "The only way out of the jungle of neurotic symptoms is to enable the neurotic to acquire the attitude of humility, to forget the overmastering and grasping self, and to live for others."[55]

The neurotic's suffering and his scrupulosity is a distorted focus on the self: "The scrupulous person...concentrates continuously and exclusively on his own ego. I have never come across such people who entertain scruples with the Commandment dealing with the love for one's neighbor."[56]

Late in life Ignatius linked scruples to pride. In 1556, the year of his death, he sent a letter to Fr. Marin Valentine with this insight: "And believe me, if you have true humility and submissiveness, your scruples will not cause you so much trouble. A kind of pride is the fuel they feed on, and it is pride which places more reliance on one's own judgment and less on the judgment of others whom we trust."[57]

Ignatius receives grace to both see and cease his obsessive confession habit. In doing so, his pride is both exposed and broken. When he identifies scruples as rooted in pride, Ignatius identifies his core sin. Christian tradition has described pride or narcissism as the chief vice. Re-reading the first paragraph of his *Autobiography* with fresh eyes we hear a man describing himself in painfully stark language. He is filled with overweening pride. Pride caused his Pamplona battle "injury." Even worse, by force of his willful pride he persuaded the commander, against the opinion of "all the other knights," to engage a military campaign. It was horribly reckless—suicidal even—causing injury and one death.[58]

Ignatius' breakthrough realization that pride is his core sin headlines the *Autobiography*. It is also dominates a series of vignettes recorded shortly after his awakening. During a life-threatening fever, he thought himself a "just" man and "had more trouble with this thought than the fever."[59] He conceals his family name from a benefactor along with his plans to go to Jerusalem because a "fear of vainglory...so afflicted him."[60] Nearly twenty-two years later, Ignatius recorded in the *Spiritual Journal* that he continued to struggle with pride.[61]

The Powerless Paradigm and the Particular Examen

The resolution of the scruples crisis presents a *Powerless Paradigm*. Ignatius accepts the invitation to conversion and faced the truth of his sins and addictions. He declares they cannot give life. He must now surrender his pride and admit that he cannot save himself. Powerless to master his scrupulosity, he receives graced insight to stop his obsessive confessing. In this he accepts God's grace and love as sufficient for his salvation *SpEx* [320.7]. Ignatius has finally let go of the reins of his life and begins to live his *Suscipe*.[62]

This tipping point in Ignatius' conversion and the shift in attitude it brings is notable. All the more so in light of his prior manifest determination to conquer his sinfulness by force of his own will. His *Autobiography*'s terse narrative hides the magnitude of the spiritual and psychological transformation in Ignatius. The transformation is stark. Ignatius moves from managing his spiritual growth with the same swagger that he waged the Pamplona battle, and becomes a man of much greater humility, willing to be led like a boy at the hands of a schoolmaster.[63]

The *Examen's PE* targets root sins and vices that inhibit integrated Christian growth. Early in his conversion Ignatius' addictive, sensual, and his most manifest sinful habits are purged. Now, after his harrowing experience at Manresa he has access to the necessary personal data that enabled him to target the roots of his visible sins.

Ignatius' battle with his scruples was in effect a Pamplona of the spirit and psyche. Arising from the battle was a chastened man with a singular desire to serve God in humility and with indifference. This harrowing experience and its resolution model the "sourcing" of root sin or root vice which block spiritual progress. Such sourcing forms the core structure of the *PE*. A template of the *Powerless Paradigm* enfolding root sin and the *PE* is modelled this way:

Ignatius' struggle with scruples hiding his vainglory ⇨ ⇩	The initial confrontation with one's root sin ⇩
Ignatius' constant re-confessing to seek salvation by willpower alone ⇨ ⇩	The effort to control one's root sin ONLY by personal effort or force of will ⇩
Ignatius' suicidal impulses, disgust and the desire to walk away from his new found faith ⇨ ⇩	Despair and desire to give up faith when human effort alone fails ⇩
Ignatius' tracing the spirit of disgust to a demonic source ⇨ ⇩	Insight that desire to reject the spiritual journey is a temptation ⇩
Ignatius abandoning his compulsive con-fessing of past sins ⇨ ⇩	Admitting powerlessness to save one-self and surrendering prideful actions ⇩
Ignatius being taught as a child and receiving graces according to God's design ⇨	Allowing God to shape one's *Sacred Story* according to His will and graces

Ignatius' battle with his scruples broke through the vainglory that had characterized his personality up until that point. The self-mortification required to surrender pride became not only a defining characteristic of his life, but also a defining virtue of the *General Examen* for candidates seeking acceptance to the Society of Jesus.[64] It was this harrowing process of purification and self-mortification that opened him to the profound mystical graces detailed in his *Autobiography*.

This transformation in the structure of Ignatius' desires marks the most significant shift from the disordered spiritual and psychological traits of the past to the new man of the *Fundamentum* he became.[65] Ignatius began to serve God not as commander of his own life, but as Christ's powerless servant being led by the Spirit.[66]

Ignatius Starts Life Over as a Sacred Story

Luis Gonçalves' preface to the *Autobiography* specifies that Ignatius' liberation at this vital juncture was much more than his release from scruples. It was the conquering of his vainglory.[67] It was the sin of pride and vainglory with which he defined himself at the outset of the *Autobiography*, not sins of the flesh. But scrupulosity over his sinful lusts likely formed the nexus surrounding this harrowing episode in his spiritual journey.

The commanding personality who had emerged from Loyola castle at the age of sixteen, finally uncovered the roots of the sins that fed his disordered actions. At the age of thirty, it was his struggle with scruples that revealed these core issues. The mystical graces showered on Ignatius at this tipping point in his life are significant. For those willing to follow his footsteps, the specific mystical graces Ignatius received are not important. What is critical for *Examen* practitioners, in light of the *Powerless Paradigm,* is the spiritual indifference and new docility to the Spirit's promptings displayed by Ignatius.

The targeting and nullification of his root vice of pride and self-love, the sins traditionally viewed as more grievous and ancient, is the liberation necessary to achieve spiritual indifference. And it is this indifference that makes Ignatius able to find God in all things.[68] Success in the battle with one's core sin of pride and self-love, and the indifference success of this type produces, is the necessary foundation to build one's spiritual house according to the *Ignatian Paradigm.*[69]

The Patience Paradigm and the Near-Death Narratives

Ignatius included a trio of near-death narratives in the *Autobiography*. Taken together they seem both strangely placed and inexplicable. The narratives appear immediately after his harrowing experience confronting his scruples. The narratives are consecutively linked in the *Autobiography* yet detail specific time periods that span the remainder of Ignatius' life. The first account is from 1522; the second from 1532, and the third from 1550, about five years before his actual death. I collectively title these three accounts the *Patience Paradigm*:

> On one occasion, while in Manresa, having fallen ill with a high fever and being on the point of death, he was quite certain that his soul was about to depart his body. At that instant the thought came into is mind that he was numbered among the righteous, but this brought him so much distress that he tried everything to dismiss it and to dwell on his sins. He had more difficulty with that thought than with the fever, but no matter how he toiled to overcome it, he was unable to do so.

CR

> On another occasion, when he was traveling from Valencia to Italy by sea, the ship's rudder became smashed in a violent storm, and being in a crisis, he and many other passengers aboard concluded that, as things then stood, they would not be able to escape death. Thus, making use of his time, he made a careful examination of his conscience and prepared himself for death, but he felt no fear because of his sins nor was he afraid of being condemned, but he was especially disturbed and sorry, knowing that he had not put to good use all the gifts and graces that God our Lord had granted him.[70]

CR

> In the year 1550, he was once more gravely ill, due to a serious sickness which, in his own judgment and that of others, was to be his last.

Thinking of death at the time, he experienced such joy and so much spiritual consolation in the thought of having to die that he burst into tears. This came to be of such frequent occurrence that many times he stopped thinking of death just so as not to have so much consolation.[71]

Ignatius must have had a reason to recount and link three near-death episodes at this juncture in the *Autobiography*. The fact that they all deal with death unites them thematically. However the description of Ignatius' response to death in each instance varies. His varied reactions signify different states of spiritual growth and religious consciousness. This difference seems to be what Ignatius wanted those reading the narratives to note.

In the first instance, fear was paramount. Ignatius, having a loss of confidence possibly borne of the pride and vanity he so feared, caught himself. He knew sin still had deep roots in him. He lacked the confidence that he was among the righteous.

In the second account, grief and sadness predominate. Here he was well along in his spiritual journey and caught up in the service of God. In examining himself he felt no fear of his sins or of being condemned. Instead, he was overcome with a great grief that his love for God had issued forth in only a partial gift of self. Fear was no longer the measure. Rather, love was the measure, and serving the one he loved. Grief and sadness predominated this experience because he felt his response and his service had been so little, so late.[72]

In the third narrative, an ardent love is central. The idea of death rendered Ignatius barely able to function and dissolved him in consolatory tears. The longing for God that only death could realize is now a total, consuming fire. Ignatius strove to keep himself from thoughts of death in order to perform life's necessary tasks.

Always one to notice and take account of his spiritual progress, here he was close to his actual death recounting memories of his soul's response to three near-death experiences. It is possible to discern in this triple narrative Ignatius' progress along the mystical path from purgation, through illumination, to union. A chart of the *Patience Paradigm* is as follows:

Ignatius, justifying himself, anxiously recoils and focuses on his sinfulness ⇨ ⇩	Panic over one's salvation due to weakness and sinfulness ⇨	**PURGATION** ⇩
Ignatius, no longer fearful, regrets not having responded sooner to God's graces ⇨ ⇩	Sadness at slowness of one's response to God's love and invitation to intimacy ⇨	**ILLUMINATION** ⇩
Ignatius' intense joy at the thought of dying and being with God ⇨	An ardent, all-embracing love of God and desire for complete union with the Trinity ⇨	**UNION**

What do these three narratives tell us about Ignatius and the conversion process? Ignatius examined his conscience up to his death. If this places Ignatius in a perpetual state of purgation, all three stages of the mystical path "merge, overlap, intertwine–none can be taken in isolation from the others."[73] Ignatius' *Examen* practice so closely linked to the purgative way indicates the ancient belief that purgation lasts up to the point of death, and beyond.[74]

Ignatius' life-long examination also indicates that conversion is not a single event but a life-long process. Life-long conversion requires patience, the patience of a lifetime. However for those committed to spiritual growth significant evolution will be discernible over the course of one's life as Ignatius discloses in the near-death narratives. Purgation is always part of the journey. But progress to illumination is likely. And no more than a handful will achieve as full a union with God as is possible this side of eternity.

One of the great mystics of the Christian tradition discreetly yet humbly documents that his spiritual development lasted a lifetime. It is both a paradigm of caution and of consolation. It is a cautionary tale because the spiritual journey requires life-long commitment to a constant examination of the conscience, both general and particular, up to the point of death. Conversion, even for saints, lasts a lifetime.[75] It is also a tale of consolation. Commitment to the process of spiritual growth and conversion evolves over time. It starts in fear of God, due to one's failings and sins. It ends in total trust and love in the face of God's profound mercy.

The *Patience Paradigm* invites the realization that conversion is not a single event that can be confronted and dispatched. Conversion is instead an extended process that must be measured in decades, as this series of vignettes stretching over twenty-eight years reveals. There are no short cuts to spiritual growth, even for saints.

What is most vital is Ignatius' docility and mortification of spirit, which enabled him to be led by God "like a child at the hands of a schoolmaster." His signature sanctity with its mystical graces is made possible only because Ignatius faced the truth of his sins and addictions. He does this by admitting his powerlessness in the face of his core sins and finally surrendering control of his life to God. In truth, powerlessness, and with patience, Ignatius allowed God to lead him and shape his *Sacred Story.*

The Organic Development of Ignatius' Discernment Rules

It is worth noting the organic development of Ignatius' discernment principles and how closely linked they are to his progressive conversion. Ignatius gains graced insight, both on the nature of his temptations and how to deal with them. His insights grow in nuance as his conversion deepens and the temptations become subtler.

Ignatius has two sets or "weeks" of *Rules* for his discernment guidelines. He directs his First Week *Rules* to two kinds of people: (1.) those moving from one mortal sin to another; *SpEx* [314.1]; and (2.) those seeking to rid their souls from sin and rise in service to God; *SpEx* [315.2]. It is these types of conditions and temptations that Ignatius grappled with early in his conversion. They are unique to those in the pre-purgative and purgative states of development. It is from the sins and temptations at the pre-purgative and purgative stages that the *Truth Paradigm* emerges. Ignatius boldly declares that his sins and addictions cannot offer life—the temptations are false loves that must be denounced.

Ignatius' First Week *Rules* are directed to persons "whose lives are dominated by the capital sins, the root of whose actions are found in pride, covetousness, lust, anger, etc." as "the mode of their temptation is pleasure, operating instinctively and almost automatically on the pleasure-pain axis."[76] Ignatius' first crisis, wherein he was menaced by the thought of living without his vices for seventy years, is a classic example of these First Week "pleasure-pain axis" temptations. The *Rules* identified above signify his wisdom in confronting such crises. The *Truth Paradigm* is directly linked to those *Rules*.

The Second Week *Rules* are guidelines for those who have reined in habitual patterns of sin and the deeds associated with disordered appetites and affections. The person of the Second Week is more developed. Hence the strategies of temptation increase in subtlety, residing more in thoughts than in the sensible imagination.

For these people, temptation to turn from God comes in the form of false reasoning. Temptations create intellectual confusion, and in extreme cases, a sense of the absurdity of religion and of spiritual growth. Ignatius experienced these temptations in the disgust he felt about his scrupulous struggles. The temptations make Ignatius want to stop his faith practice. They so riveted his attention that he was "illumined" to question their source.

Ignatius realizes the initial trap was laid much earlier. It began with the temptation to constantly re-confess his sins. What appears as an admirable practice of conscientious confession becomes instead a weapon turned against him. He knows it is damaging him. But his pride, hidden from view, compels him to stay in control. By willpower alone, he seeks to manage his conversion and save himself. The *Rules* of the Second Week are for those whose progress has brought them to a place of reasonable mastery over behaviors linked to disordered sensual temptations and unruly habits. But the roots of those sinful habits have yet to be purged. It is clear that Ignatius moves from grappling with the manifest behaviors at Loyola, to struggling with the roots of those behaviors at Montserrat and Manresa.

This shift is noted by the new type of temptations experienced at Manresa. It is accompanied by new discernment techniques he "learns," and then "applies," to manage these temptations. Ignatius' *tracing* how such a spirit could 'get hold of him' signifies the Second Week *Rules*: *SpEx* [333.5 & 334.6].[77] This shift is a clear indication of the movement from the temptations of the purgative stage to the temptations of the illuminative stage of spiritual growth.

It is evident that the process of Ignatius' conversion and examination of his conscience confronts him with temptations that lead to the graced insights he needs to stay the course. Those insights, as noted, are codified in his discernment *Rules*. Ignatius, in his Introductory Observations also confirms the *Rules'* link to progressive conversion. The First Week *Rules* are more necessary for those in the purgative state while the Second Week *Rules* are more critical for those in the illuminative state of spiritual growth *SpEx* [10].[78]

The Loyola sojourn after the battle injury marks the first stage of Ignatius' conversion and is associated with the goals of the First Week *Rules*: the mastery of habitual sinful behaviors. Ignatius' journey through a harrowing struggle with scruples advances him spiritually wherein he achieves liberation at a more elemental level: exhuming from the depths of soul and psyche, the root sins that are blocking his complete offering of self to God.

The eradication of sin at the root level frees one to hear and follow the Lord in the small and large decisions of life, and this is the goal of the *Spiritual Exercises*. Ignatius expresses this goal in the opening statement of the *Spiritual Exercises*: "which have as their purpose the conquest of self and the regulation of one's life in such a way that no decision is made under the influence of any inordinate attachment."[79]

Anyone who seriously engages the *Examen*, and walks daily the path of conversion it unfolds, will confront the same cross-pressures and temptations Ignatius did. God gifted Ignatius with the wise, accurate discernment principles necessary to find his way home. This gift benefits the whole Church and everyone on the journey back to God. These principles illuminate the emotional, spiritual, physical, and psychological inspirations coming from two spiritual spontaneities, which Ignatius defines as consolation and desolation. They are accessible, understandable, and effective guidelines that clearly reveal how to discern those inspirations from a Divine source and those inspirations that spring from the enemy of human nature.

Challenges of the Examen's Narrow Path

The former soldier, with his inordinate passions purged, and his heart and life illuminated and redirected in service to his Lord, desired complete union with Christ in the work of redemption. Ignatius' own pattern of conversion and call is distilled in the *Exercises* and the *Examen*. The portion of Ignatius' conversion story that stretches from his early recuperation and purgation at Loyola to the mystical illuminations at Manresa contains four important paradigms. The paradigms clarify Ignatius' unique, progressive conversion experience and its core dynamics that we find distilled in both the *Spiritual Exercises* and the *Examen*.

The first, the *Ignatian Paradigm*, entails the spiritual structure or template of both the *Spiritual Exercises* and the *Examen's* five-point *GE*. It invites us to fundamental conversion by helping us identify and confront the manifest sinfulness and addictions in our lives.

The second, the *Truth Paradigm*, invites us to name our sins and addictions and truthfully define them as false gods that cannot save, heal, or bring us peace.

The third, the *Powerless Paradigm*, invites us to integrated conversion by targeting the spiritual and psychological matrix of core sin(s) blocking our deep surrender to God; this is the purpose and goal of the *PE*. Pride and narcissism repudiate God. They fuel dissent against the need for God's healing and love. The *PE* targets pride and promotes a humility that affirms we are powerless to save ourselves. We must pray for the graced insight to unmask the spiritual disorder of pride rooted deep in our hearts. Once unmasked, narcissistic pride can only be dismantled by God's grace. God will help us achieve the docility and spiritual indifference to be led like a child, so that our *Sacred Story* can unfold.[80]

The fourth, the *Patience Paradigm*, defines conversion as a gradual, lifelong project that requires grace, patience, and enduring commitment. There is no short cut to spiritual growth, even for saints. Each of us must honestly confront the fact that our conversion and our efforts to remain open to God's grace is a daily process. We must commit to a daily process that lasts a lifetime.

The last three paradigms reveal why the *Examen* as a spiritual discipline is often avoided, or if engaged, why people let its practice slip.

The *Truth Paradigm* details the need to name sins and addictions for what they are: false lovers, habits destructive of our physical, psychological and spiritual life. Ignatius feared that his struggle to stay sober, as Alcoholics Anonymous might term it, could last for "seventy years." It is easy to understand why so many who desire to confront sinful and addictive habits recoil in fear when they intuit a similar fight. Even to name them as sin or addiction creates anxiety. For the pleasures associated with sinful vices and addictions are hard to surrender. And pain, even imagined pain, of withdrawing from their delights, unleashes spiritual, emotional, physical and psychological cross-pressures that significantly muddy the waters of conscience.

Ignatius however received graced insights into his temptations. He was blessed with gifts of discernment that enabled him to speak truth to the power of the black noise of temptation, sin and addiction. In naming the false loves of sin and addiction as ruinous to health, hope and life, his heart stabilized. Speaking the truth always liberates the spirit. It sets us free (Jn. 8:1-38).

Ignatius' wisdom in dealing with these primal temptations, sins and addictions is encoded in his First Week *Rules* for discernment. The *Rules* are gifts of grace that result from his organic and deepening conversion. Anyone who seriously engages the Christian path will, like Ignatius, need the insights of discernment to stay the course when the journey's duration is grasped. Only discernment can enable a person to negotiate the confusing cross-pressures of emotion and spirit associated with the withdrawal from habitual vices, destructive addictions and sinful life-patterns that torment body, mind and soul.

Ignatius' *Rules* are essential for anyone engaging the *Examen.* We all live with white noise and black noise that work on us every moment of our lives. White noise and black noise are two sources of inspiration, or 'two spontaneities.' Both push and pull our thoughts, emotions, psyches and bodies. One pushes us toward blessing and life and the other toward death and curse. The person searching for his/her authentic self but incapable of discerning the different desires and dreams springing from those two spontaneities is apt to mistake a counterfeit identity as genuine; sin as life, and addiction as friend and peace-giver.

The *Powerless Paradigm* represents a far more complex and subtle aspect of our conversion journey. Viewed from Ignatius' perspective, it appears as a brief scuffle with scruples soon overcome. But it propels him into the thorny spiritual and psychological matrix anchoring his sinful pride and vainglory. The victory achieved in unraveling the matrix of these "sins of the spirit" came at the price we all must pay; admitting our powerlessness to save ourselves from the destructive narcissism that prevents our humble acceptance of God as healer, forgiver, and Savior.

The life-long combat with one's sinful vices can feel threatening. The challenge of identifying, understanding, and overcoming one's spiritual sins, which are deeply rooted in the structure of one's personality and history, raises the bar significantly. People will be reluctant to engage in such a battle. Or if they muster the courage, they may wonder how to negotiate the challenges, fears, deceptions and sufferings that posed such a dangerous and harrowing trap for Ignatius.

These deeply rooted spiritual and psychological disorders, more than the obvious sinful vices, shape one's identity and definitions of success. It is one thing to struggle with surrendering pleasures in a purgation of the senses. It is quite another to lose a meticulously crafted identity in a purgation of the spirit.[81]

It is no wonder that Ignatius would have gladly endured any trial other than this harrowing scrupulosity. The physical pain of his leg being reset without benefit of anesthetic is preferred to the crucifixion this stripping of narcissistic pride posed for his ego-identity, even though that identity was neither genuine nor authentic. Surrendering to God the control of his scruples was surrendering a carefully constructed identity, leaving him defenseless and childlike. He literally had to go back and start life over while God treated him as a schoolmaster treats a child.[82]

Spiritual surgery by the Divine Physician enables God to unfold our *Sacred Story*. It is the surgery's fruit that must motivate and give us courage. Ignatius regained his youthful innocence and along with that innocence came enlightenment like no other (Eph. 3:20-21). Ignatius' "vain and overpowering desire to gain renown" was purged of its sinful distortions, and by means of this harrowing journey back to childlike innocence, the path to true greatness was opened to him. The mysteries of the universe, hidden from the wise and clever, are only revealed to the childlike Mt 18:1-4; 11:2-26).[83]

The *Patience Paradigm* informs that deep, integrated conversion requires a lifetime of effort, patience, and ongoing daily discernment. Ignatius confronted the reality that his new Christian life required a commitment to reigning in the passions associated with his early years, and that the process might last for seventy years. This fourth paradigm gives us evidence of that time line. It acts as encouragement for us to engage the same commitment in the face of our own fears. It also invites us to a calm and patient commitment as the process unfolds, by the power of God's grace, across the arc of life's journey.

The Examen as an Ignatian Spiritual Discipline

At this point, it is helpful to sketch a vision for the *Examen*; one linked to Ignatius' conversion, and the four paradigmatic schemas his conversion enfolds. To begin, we turn first to the *Exercises* and Ignatius' many letters. Ignatius frequently promotes the various disciplines of the *Exercises'* First Week. He promotes them as the principal pastoral tools for the Society's apostolic efforts in both Europe and the mission territories.[84] The *GE, PE* and confession are central to these First Week *Exercises*.

The *Examens* might be considered the most basic tool for the conversion process the *Exercises* invite. Surely they were for Ignatius and his first companions.[85] Yet Ignatius employed the *Examens* differently than other spiritual traditions of the times, as disciplines in and of themselves.

The guidelines proposed by Cisneros that Ignatius received at Montserret introduce the *Examination of Conscience* only when a person enters the illuminative path. Ignatius presents it as the first exercise in the purgative way. In Cisneros' model, the goal of the three-fold path (purgation, illumination, union) is to prepare us for contemplating Christ, the end of which is ecstatic union. For Ignatius, contemplating Christ comes after the *First Week* exercises on purgation.[86] Their goal is union too, but conceived instead as union in following Christ on mission, which represents a mysticism of service.[87]

The extension of the *Examination of Conscience* into one's daily prayer, whether or not one ever makes the *Spiritual Exercises,* is really a mystical discipline in ongoing conversion. It is necessary for achieving what Ignatius saw as the end goal of all spiritual exercises:[88] "disposing the soul to rid itself of all inordinate attachments, and after their removal, of seeking and finding the will of God in the disposition of our life for the salvation of our soul."[89]

The *Examen*, inclusive of the four paradigms, can be understood as enfolding the graced invitation to the fundamental and integrated conversion that is characteristic of the Ignatian spiritual growth paradigm. The organic process of conversion requires ongoing discernment. The combined goal of both conversion and discernment is to identify and reject the inspirations of human nature's enemy and embrace the graces of human nature's Creator in all of one's thoughts, words, and deeds. Furthermore, according to the Ignatian Paradigm of conversion, the mastery of ones' root vices and sins is essential to achieve the spiritual indifference and docility necessary for an effective response to the Spirit's initiatives, the full measure of which takes a lifetime to achieve.

The *Sacred Story* method addresses the two critical issues that this study has uncovered thus far. First, it addresses the urgent need for discernment rules to address the crises presented by the fears of purgation (vices, addictions and sinful habits) and its duration. Second, it offers insights on how to tackle the spiritual and psychological matrix in one's life characteristic of the *Powerless Paradigm* and the *PE*. The need to link spiritual and psychological growth emerges as a critical issue for contemporary commentators on Ignatius' *Examen*.

The next step in building a new model of Ignatius' *Examen* requires analyzing its traditional structure. We will also review how the first Jesuits used the *Examen* pastorally in Europe and the mission territories.

3

The Examen and its Use by the First Jesuits

The Structure of the General and Particular Examens

St. Ignatius documents the structure of both the *General* (*GE*) and *Particular Examens* (*PE*) in his notations for the *First Week* of *The Spiritual Exercises*.[1] The *PE* is a program of spiritual growth that targets specific sins and habits needing to be highlighted and eradicated. The *Spiritual Exercises* detail what times of day and how often the *PE* is to be performed. According to Ignatius' instruction, the daily structure of the *PE* is as follows:

1) Set one's heart immediately upon rising and resolve to guard against a particular sin or defect one wishes to change.
2) After lunch, ask for the grace to know how often one has fallen with respect to the particular defect or sin, make amends, and avoid it in the future.
3) The first examination then begins: a) one demands an account of oneself hour by hour; b) marks on a chart how many times one has fallen into a particular defect or sin (diagram *A*); c) renews the morning resolution and makes amends, preparing for the next time of examination.
4) The second examination begins after supper.[2] It repeats the same process as the mid-day exercise. One marks the number of times he/she has fallen into the sin or defect on the second line of the diagram.[3]

(St. Ignatius uses the "G" to indicate each day of the week in descending order, Sun. → Sat.)

G_____

G_____

G_____

G_____

G_____

G_____

G _____

The instructions in the *Spiritual Exercises* for the *General Examination of Conscience* are longer than those of the *PE*. They offer a detailed review of one's thoughts, words, and deeds in light of the "Ten Commandments, the laws of the Church, (and) the recommendation of superiors."[4] This structure conforms more closely to the custom of the times for foundational conversion as detailed in the work of Garcias Cisneros.

The *GE* has five stages. It is proposed in the *Spiritual Exercises* as a method of preparing the soul for the Sacrament of Reconciliation:[5]

1) Prayer of thanksgiving for favors received.
2) Petition for the grace to know one's sinfulness and eradicate it.
3) A methodical review of one's *thoughts, words, and deeds* from the day.
4) To ask pardon of God for one's faults and sins.
5) To petition for the grace of amendment and to pray *The Lord's Prayer.*

The *Exercises,* the *Constitutions,* and the early *Directories* are silent on the relationship between the two methods of examination outside of a retreat context.

Rodríguez's richly detailed commentary gives instructions on the inter-relationship of the two methods, suggesting a common practice in the early Society of enfolding the two into a single prayer period.[67] Still, it is not clear even from Rodríguez's expansive text or any other early *Directories* whether the two methods are prayed consecutively or collapsed into a single structure. Rodríguez only tells us that if the twice-daily *Examen* is ignored, Jesuits will have failed in "one of the chiefest points of our religion."[8]

Rodríguez places greater emphasis on the *PE,* spending thirty-five pages on its use and practice, while expending only eight pages on the *GE.* The explanation of the *Truth* and *Powerless* paradigms give plausible evidence that regular application of the *GE* might best serve to track the more obvious sins (and addictions) of one's lower nature. The *PE* would track the more entrenched, serious sins of one's higher, spiritual nature (similar to the sinful pride Ignatius discovered in his struggles with scrupulosity, which shaped the *Powerless Paradigm*).

The divergence between Ignatius' greater emphasis on the *GE* and Rodríguez's greater emphasis on the *PE* are understandable. Ignatius wants to ensure that the foundation for conversion is solidly planted. This must happen by a courageous and accurate accounting of one's manifest sins highlighted by the *GE* in the First Week of the *Spiritual Exercises.* Rodríguez, writing as a theologian after years of spiritual direction work with Jesuits, is focused on the integrated conversion fostered by the *PE.* However, once the foundation of conversion is secure, this integrated conversion leads to an Ignatian spirituality of indifference and mortification of the spirit.

Sacred Story seeks to provide an effective daily method for both the *GE* and the *PE.* For this reason the structure used for *Sacred Story* merges the *GE* and *PE* into a single prayer unit. *Sacred Story* conforms its method to the thematic template below but in a new form that enfolds the findings of all previous research, (including the five major challenges delineated in the following chapter).

On awakening on does a daily prelude or pre-visioning. The goal is to set one's heart immediately upon rising and resolve to guard against a particular sin or defect one wishes to change. Here is the five point structure:

1) Prayer of thanksgiving for favors received.
2) Petition for the grace to know one's sinfulness and eradicate it. Ask especially to know how one has fallen in the particular defect or sin, to make amends, and avoid it in the future.
3) Demand an account of oneself hour by hour in thoughts, word and deeds on all sins, but most especially on how many times one has fallen into a particular defect or sin.
4) Ask pardon for faults and sins and renew the morning resolution.
5) Petition for the grace of amendment in preparation for the next time of examination and close praying *The Lord's Prayer*.

Challenges of Ignatius' Examen: Structure and Method

How does Ignatius incorporate the lessons he learns from Loyola to Manresa into the *Examen?* What challenges do they present to the examiner? It is worth analyzing the *Examen* as a means of conversion and transformation. We can explore how the method and repetition of the *Examen* challenges one to awaken to what Ignatius calls "inordinate attachments." Ignatius awoke to the inner dynamism of the spiritual world in the journey from Pamplona to Manresa. In his conversion experiences and struggles with scruples he discovered not only his own spiritual and psychological self but also Divine and demonic influences at the center of his heart.

Ignatian spirituality helps one attune to the voice of God, the voice of the self and the voice of the "enemy of human nature." In attuning to these three distinct personal forces or voices, one can learn how to follow Divine inspiration in all life choices and relationships. One can also neutralize the role of the enemy of human nature and the whims of one's disordered appetites while slowly gaining freedom from inordinate attachments. This, in essence, is how Ignatius described the purpose of a person doing "Spiritual Exercises" in the *Introductory Observations.* At the top of his list for effective strategies in this journey is "every method of examination of conscience."[9]

The removal of inordinate attachments is necessary to facilitate union with God and follow Divine inspiration in both the small and momentous choices of life. We see in Ignatius' own story this process begins when he identifies and ceases the disordered habits of his sinful and addictive appetites. He is then led to discover his root sin(s), admit his powerlessness, and in humility, become both flexible and docile in following Divine inspiration. Indeed, the flexibility and docility in following Divine inspirations in service of the Kingdom is the most distinctive feature of Ignatian spirituality.[10]

Five main tasks or challenges confront the examiner when joining the *GE* and *PE* in a single prayer.[11] These five tasks include: taking personal responsibility, asking for graces, consistent timing and repetition, ongoing conscious objectification of sin and inordinate attachment, and sustaining focus on particulars.

Personal Responsibility

The personal responsibility Ignatius places on engaging his spiritual disciplines is significant as these disciplines require a spirit of great generosity. Ignatius asks for no less than a total gift of self. This includes offering to God one's will and liberty as a "profitable" means of gaining the graces sought.[12]

Perseverance in the discipline of *Examen* is also difficult. Ignatius considered the *Examen* not only a front-line activity in spiritual growth, but as a necessary and life-long practice. It is a prayer that Rodríguez asserts cannot be dispensed with even in times of sickness.[13] Ignatius himself testifies to the necessity of life-long attentiveness in the work of conversion twenty-six years after his wounding at Pamplona. In advice to Theresa Rejadell, Ignatius relates that the imperfections of sin will shadow us our whole lives. Hence the efforts required for spiritual growth will never cease.[14]

Lastly, cooperating with graces offered by God to face one's defects and sinfulness is vital. The willingness to see one's manifest sins is not necessarily a product of the will, but a product of grace. The responsibility to courageously stay the course for integrated conversion is also difficult, as Ignatius' battle with scruples testifies. However the willingness to ask the questions about oneself—to ask for the grace to see—is something that requires commitment and personal initiative. Ignatius considers such cooperation with grace to be a work of singular spiritual merit.[15] As noted by Ignatius' secretary, Alfonso de Polanco, God rewards an individual with grace proportionate to their effort and diligence.[16]

Asking for Graces

Ignatius structures the *Examen* like the *Spiritual Exercises* so that the practitioner asks God for the graces and gifts that lead to conversion. The asking must be repeated and specific. The joint *Examen* prayer calls upon the examinee to attend to the graces and gifts already received; to ask for graces of enlightenment and self-knowledge so that one can see sin in its general and particular manifestations; to beg for the grace of forgiveness and pardon for sins committed; and finally, to ask for the grace to amend one's life.

Ignatius convinces us that God's response to all such requests is multifaceted and abundant.[17] His convictions align with Jesus' in the Gospels; the belief that what is requested in faith, God will provide (Mt. 7:7). Asking for specific graces in the *Examen* is a central component of spiritual transformation and change that is characteristic of Ignatian spirituality. The gifts received lead one to gratitude, sorrow, contrition, thanksgiving, and praise.

Timing and Repetition

The *Examen* requires discipline regarding both the time of day when one prays and the length of prayer. The instructional notations on the combined *PE* and *GE* method as written by Ignatius require the following steps (all of which are also included in the *Sacred Story* method):

- A moment upon rising to focus attention on a particular sin or defect.
- A quarter hour *Examen* at mid-day, including the notation of particular failings.
- A quarter hour *Examen* at night, including the notation of particular failings, with a comparison of the same from the mid-day *Examen.*
- Attention throughout the day when one falls into the particular sin or defect. [18]
- Some moments each day to compare progress in growth regarding the particular sin or defect, and also to compare progress from day-to-day and week-to-week.

The exercises detailed here total about thirty-five minutes per day. Ignatius' insistence on fidelity to this discipline is well documented. For members of religious orders and priests, the amount of time seems reasonable, but what about for laity? Here we might consider what an early Directory counseled as appropriate daily spiritual practice for laity. The suggested prayer exercises detailed for the spiritually active layperson could by their length easily take an hour, equivalent to what Ignatius wanted Jesuits to commit.[19]

Is such repetition spiritually beneficial or could a repetitious focus on sinfulness be spiritually and psychologically unhealthy? There are both spiritual and psychological challenges in constantly minding the issues and patterns where one seeks change: e.g. calling to heart upon waking the issue of spiritual challenge/growth that one hopes to notice during the day, or the physical gesture of placing the hand to the heart when one fails. Both practices cultivate a psychological attunement to thoughts, words, and deeds and make one mindful of graces needed in the daily *Examen*. Both practices require effort and reflect Ignatius' personal discipline of making every moment of the day -each thought, word, and deed - transparent and accessible to inquiry, and when needed, to graced transformation.

A constant focus on inordinate attachments or one's sinful pride is certainly difficult. But Ignatius did not think it destructive or harmful. He saw it instead as a necessary exercise for positive spiritual growth. The meditations and graces outlined in the First Week *Rules* clarify this.[20] One seeks removal of sin and defect - inordinate attachments- to facilitate openness to God's grace, love and forgiveness.

Ignatius was graced with remarkable consolations even when focusing on his sinfulness. Many of his letters speak of God's gentleness to the sinner. The section below on the use of the *Examen* in the Society's early apostolic history validates a general approach that favors a focus on God's mercy over fear of God's justice.[21] Luis Gonçalves recorded that Ignatius' experience of sin not only created an opportunity for grace, but also generated in his heart important insights on the true nature of sin and God's love:

> "Realizing how often he had sinned and offended our Lord, he had often wished that the divine Majesty might take away from him such abundant consolations to punish him for his faults.... but that, so great

was the mercy and gentleness of our Lord in his regard, that it seemed that the more he sinned, the more he understood his sins and desired to expiate them, so much the more did our Lord give Himself to him and open to him the treasure of His consolations and gifts."[22]

Everard Mercurian, the fourth superior general of the Jesuits and the individual responsible for consolidating the early commentaries leading to the *Official Directory* of 1599, views the purgative process in a similarly positive way. He echoes Ignatius' mystical language that the discovery and eradication of sin produces spiritual illumination.[23]

The *PE* still facilitates integrated spiritual development.[24] The positive growth achieved from the *PE* results from one's cooperating with grace to clear away the rubbish of sin and inordinate attachments. Rodríguez's commentary makes this point very clearly.[25]

The *Official Directory's* instruction on the gift of hope for those who enter the *Spiritual Exercises* should apply equally for those who engage the *Examen*.[26] A fundamental reason for engaging the Ignatian exercises on sin, of which the *Examen* is a paramount discipline, is to encounter the mercy and love of God.[27] Yet one can't forget the frightening neurotic sufferings and suicidal impulses Ignatius endured to achieve his more balanced and positive views towards his sinfulness. Purgation, especially of sensual appetites and addictions will, for most everyone, be both grace-filled and arduous. The same can be said for the integrated purgation of pride which is deeply rooted in one's spiritual and psychological history.

Ongoing, Conscious Objectification of Sin and Inordinate Attachments

Ignatius employs five practices in the *Examen* that together serve to render constant and conscious awareness of sins and inordinate attachments, both *particular* and *general*. These are:

(1) momentary awareness upon rising of the sin or defect;
(2) attentive pauses during the day and the placing of the hand over the heart when one fails;

(3) marking down twice daily the number of times one has failed in the particular way he/she seeks to reform;

(4) comparing and contrasting, day to day and week to week, the progress one is making on mastering the particular sin or defect; and,

(5) conscious attention to the thoughts, words, and deeds in the course of the day.

The intensity and regularity of these combined practices is challenging, as is their goal of attunement to situations that generate both temptation and failure. However, they are essential tools for seeing the interconnected patterns and trends regarding one's sins and inordinate attachments. Ignatius is a strategist who believed the effectiveness of his pastoral work hinged on helping people understand their spiritual state through the nature of their sins. When the Inquisition demanded he cease making distinctions between different types of sin, they removed his most vital pastoral tool for "helping souls."[28]

On the other hand, there are aspects to the *Examen* that are largely overlooked but integral to its function. Ignatius' *Rules* regarding the monitoring of thoughts, guarding of the tongue, and evaluation of one's deeds against the backdrop of the Ten Commandments and the Laws of the Church are rarely commented on: *SpEx* [38-41]. Are these aspects largely overlooked today for fear the examinee will become obsessive-compulsive or neurotic? If so, we must find a way to mine them for their spiritual power. They reveal Ignatius' remarkably sensitive radar for registering and evaluating the most mundane events in his own life for evidence of the Divine or demonic. These disciplines disclose to us Ignatius' own hard-won insight that for the person intent on spiritual growth, every dimension of our lives, interior and exterior, must be brought to conscious awareness and examined.

Of particular import for Ignatius, and a challenge to the examinee, is the practice of guarding the tongue to rein in intemperate speech. In the notes for the *GE*, he spends three times more commentary on sins and defects involving *words*, as he does on *thoughts* and *deeds* combined. In his biography, Idígoras sketches a profile of Ignatius regarding the importance of the spoken word.

"The naked, clear word, endowed with an enormous strength, was his greatest weapon. He spoke little, but always after much reflection. He exaggerated not at all, used adjectives and superlatives rarely, and he never uttered a gratuitous, unessential, meaningless word. The word for him meant commitment. This is why he recounted events simply, without ornamentation, suggesting directly, never obliquely. He always kept his word, and he was always in command of what he said. From the day of his conversion, he never uttered an injurious word about or scornful word to anyone. His control over this tongue was absolute. He paid a great deal of attention to what he said and to whom he said it, how he said it and when he said it. This was why his words 'were like rules.'" [29]

Idígoras' testimony is confirmed not only by the notes on the *GE* but also in many of Ignatius' letters including an early instructional letter to the community at Alcalá, written just after he was elected general.[30] The asceticism of consciously controlling one's words is a serious spiritual discipline. When practiced, it is a powerful aid in attuning the mind and heart to its inner dispositions and attitudes, both conscious and unconscious. The fact that it is not easy does not deter Ignatius from listing the control of one's speech in the *GE* as a necessary practice for spiritual growth.

There is both a negative and positive focus to these awareness exercises. The negative focus is obvious: the need for attention to failure, sin and inordinate attachments in order to elicit repentance and reform in one's life. One of Ignatius' first personal reforms was truth in his speech.[31] The positive motivation is that scrutiny of the particular sinful patterns in one's speech will in the end produce very beneficial results.

What can encourage the examinee to become constantly and consciously aware of his or her shortcomings? Diligent engagement of all Ignatian spiritual disciplines, including the *Examen*, is necessary for their fruit to be realized.[32] Perhaps the fact that there are no instructions in the text of the *Exercises* nor in the early *Directories* (for actions to be taken if the *Examen* is failing to achieve results) is significant. Ignatius instead proposes his compare and contrast method of having the person discern, day-to-day and week-to-week, where one notices improvement.

There seems to be little doubt that if the *Examen* disciplines are applied as prescribed, significant progress will result.[33] Rodríguez offers further evidence that Ignatius believed the *PE* especially would produce positive results in targeting and eradicating sin and vice if executed according to the right method.[34] Stating this in positive terms, it means growth in humility and spiritual indifference opens the heart and affirms the Divine inspirations leading to healing, spiritual freedom, fullness of life, and interior peace.

Focus on Particulars

Ignatius if anything is a strategist. The *PE's* focus on specific sins, especially those most destructive to advancement in the spiritual life, demonstrates this fact. Ignatius' natural human endowments combined with his graced conversion experiences, especially his struggle with scruples, shaped this *PE* method. The *PE* targets the root issue(s) unique to each individual that block spiritual growth and restrict response to God's grace.

The uses of the *PE* while practicing the *Spiritual Exercises* include its application for discovering faults in one's meditations. The early Jesuit *Directories* encoding the best in Ignatian spiritual practices are heavily weighted toward the *PE*.[35] However, the predominant value of the *PE* that is most frequently discussed is its efficacy in pinpointing those defects that are most troublesome to one's spiritual growth.

Some Jesuit *Directories* are less specific about what the *PE* targets. For example, Fabio de Fabi describes the removal of obstacles or "some particular fault" as the purpose of the *PE*.[36] The authors of *Directories,* who had direct contact with Ignatius and are therefore most likely to know his mind, define the utility of the *PE:* as targeting predominant sins, vices, and defects that are the principal "source" of many others.[37] The *PE* is applied to "root out" these particular defects, and it is this interpretation that the *Official Directory* of 1599 enshrines.[38]

Rodríguez illuminates the tradition of the *PE* with new language regarding these root faults. He posits that each person has a "King Vice" strong enough to carry one off course more than anything else:

> There are certain passions that are called predominant, which seem to lord it over us and make us do what we otherwise would not do. So

you hear some people say: 'If I had not this, I think there is nothing that would embarrass me or give me trouble.' This, then, we should attend to most in our *Particular Examen*.[39]

Rodríguez sees the *PE's* focus on one sin or defect, to the exclusion of the rest, as a necessary tactic that produces greater well-being for the whole person.[40] One should not dilute the effectiveness of the *PE* by examining more than one vice at a time. However, he advises that one ought to take the "King Vice" and break it down into component parts.[41]

Rodríguez advises that an individual should hold focus on only one vice or defect until it is more or less mastered. In the space of nine pages he demonstrates how to do this, indicating that a single vice manifests itself in the practice of humility, mortification, charity, abstinence, gluttony, poverty, patience, obedience, chastity, ordinary actions, and conformity to God's will. Thus, he shows the holistic nature of core sin and its effect on one's entire human nature.[42]

The singular or particular focus advanced by Ignatius is unique. Ignatius learned the necessity of this during his struggle with scruples that unmasked his pride. Yet, more than just a singular focus, the diligence with which one pursues a vice to its root or "source" is essential to the *PE's* effectiveness. It is this characteristic, best articulated by Rodríguez and in conformity with the living tradition of the founder, which most faithfully captures the resolute personality of Ignatius.[43]

How long might it take to grow in taming our core sins, addictions and vices? For Ignatius the harrowing with scruples that uncovered his "King Vice" was of short duration, a matter of months. But its successful resolution took years.[44] For others, "There are things such that a whole lifetime would be well spent over one of them, for that would be sufficient for some particular man to attain perfection."[45] We see that the focus on particulars, and tracking them over time, is a very rigorous challenge presented by the *PE*.[46]

The Examen: Its Use and Practice by Ignatius and the First Jesuits

After the founding of the Society of Jesus, the *Examen* was widely employed with every class of people ministered to by the Jesuits. The early *Directories* point to extensive use of the *PE* by "unlettered" persons and busy people who had no time to do the *Exercises*. The uneducated were to receive the same forms of the *Examen* prayer as those more experienced in religious practice.[47]

Ignatius is clear about the *Examens* as valuable apostolic tools to use with the laity.[48] The instruction to use the First Week e*xercises* in public ministry is repeated in numerous letters to Jesuits working in the European theatre and the mission territories. The phrase, "some methods of prayer," signified the Principle and Foundation, the *PE*, the *GE* and regular confession. All these disciplines were essential tools in the purgation focus of the First Week *Exercises*.[49]

The *Examen* was one of the most vital apostolic weapons in Ignatius' spiritual arsenal for religious and laity alike.[50] Ignatius even used the *Examen* as a principal tool in his training of the early companions.[51] The *Examen* was a standard weapon in Ignatius' pastoral arsenal for all Jesuits, not just the first companions.[52]

The teaching of Christian Doctrine for the early Jesuits was coupled with instructions for examination of conscience and the confession of sins. The instruction was less about theory and more about practical formation in "how life was to be led as a Christian."[53] Jesuit pastoral practice with the laity did not shy away from the *Examen's* focus on sins. The early Jesuits, however, generally sought to highlight the more positive aspects of spiritual growth and God's mercy.[54] This positive focus matched Ignatius' own graced experience of God's love and mercy as he awakened to his sinfulness.

There are important links between the *Examen* and the practice of confession apart from the obvious bonds between these two spiritual disciplines in the First Week *Exercises*. The first companions had a common practice of confession every two weeks. And the zeal of those to whom they ministered encouraged frequent confession in many early ministries of the Society. The practice of a general confession every six months to gain a greater knowledge of self, and as an "expression of conversion," is advocated by Ignatius for all Jesuits.[55]

The practice of frequent confession, which Ignatius may have learned through Cisneros' writings, evolves into a pastoral aid that the early Jesuits widely recommend to all types of people. Its goal is to help an individual "begin to make a new book of one's life." Ignatius' application of the general confession as a review of one's life to aid in spiritual growth leads to its acceptance in the wider stream of Catholic practice.[56] This focus on frequent confession unquestionably has intimate ties to both modalities of the *Examen*.[57]

Early Jesuits offered most of their spiritual direction in the confessional.[58] Many of these early Jesuits would have brought the formative experiences of the *Exercises* to their confessional ministry, where even the meditations on sin in the First Week "were contrived to elicit gratitude."[59]

It is clear that the early Jesuits understood these traditionally dreaded practices as "consolatory" and spiritually "therapeutic." Early Jesuit pastoral practice promoted the *Examen* and frequent confession as well as the other "ministries of the word," with the conviction that the average person to varying degrees is capable of directly experiencing the presence of God in his or her soul.[60] It seems reasonable to conclude therefore that many of the people to whom these early Jesuits proposed the practice of the *Examens* would have been recipients of the more mercy-focused, consolatory practice of confession.

And in the context of that confessional practice, sound spiritual advice genuinely helpful for integrated spiritual growth could have been offered.

Thus it appears that the early ministry of the Society of Jesus, as it touches on the *PE* and *GE,* and by extension, frequent confession, is about integrated spiritual growth. The formation is dedicated to bringing individuals into direct, healing, and consoling contact with the person of Christ. In this vein one needs to view the positive fruit of both *Examen* modalities as the product of a daily prayer practice, grounded in regular, sacramental confession, whose goal is a formative and healing personal encounter with Jesus Christ.

Summary

Summarizing this brief survey of the *Examen's* structure, method, and apostolic use in the early Society gives focus to the *Sacred Story* method presented in the third section of this book. Engaging the *Examen* and maintaining fidelity to its disciplines requires significant personal initiative and responsibility. First, one must engender the reason and will to be personally responsible for one's own spiritual growth. All Christian spiritual disciplines are in essence a commitment to follow the person of Christ. *Sacred Story* encourages individuals to let one's faith and relationship with Christ take center stage.

There is nothing in Ignatius' demeanor or his spirituality that invites a casual, on-again-off-again engagement with Christ. Inspired by the La Storta vision, Ignatius' life and spiritual legacy invite a complete gift of self to God. The commitment to a practice is, in essence, a commitment to a person. One has to take the time daily to engage the *Examen* and the relationship with Christ it signifies. This is no small feat. It demonstrates the narrow path the *Examen* embodies.

Second, it is critical that one understand the *Examen's* method and the specific graces one seeks. The *Examen* has a tactical quality. One has to grasp how to apply its disciplines. This includes understanding the need to ask for specific graces, why one is asking, and what to expect from the asking. For example, in praying to know one's sins, it is critical to understand what one seeks. One seeks God's love and mercy where one most needs hope and healing. One also seeks awareness of personal sins, and forgiveness for culpability. For confronting sin is in reality a remembering in light of God's love.[61]

Third, techniques that help one to appropriate a conscious awareness, throughout the day of one's thoughts, words and deeds (especially the issues of speech that were so central to Ignatius' spiritual method) receive both new emphasis and updating in *Sacred Story*. Ignatius' hourly practice of the *Examen* demonstrates how constant spiritual attentiveness can be practically applied today.

Fourth, as a spiritual diagnostic, one must realize the *Examen* will take one into the core area(s) of disorder and chaos in one's personal history. Stating this fact clearly at the outset and providing incentives for practitioners to desire and endure it is a challenge *Sacred Story* meets head-on. *Sacred Story* also provides a tactic for helping individuals access the spiritual and psychological components of what Rodríguez calls *King Vice*, and which Rickaby calls the "ancient defect". *Sacred Story* creates opportunities for examinees to see their lives holistically. A person must both see and understand how a core vice affects their entire human nature. Root sin manifesting as habitual vice, like Ignatius' pride and vainglory, compels an examinee to explore both the spiritual and psychological dimensions of their history.[62]

Ignatius' struggle with scruples is notable for both the spiritual and psychological tension it displays. Those wanting to follow Ignatius' path must likewise confront the core spiritual and psychological deficits in their lives. This is the true path to achieving breakthrough realizations and the graced mysticism of service that the Ignatian *Examen* invites. Everyone seeking sustained spiritual growth ultimately faces a harrowing descent into varying degrees of chaos, grief, anger, anxiety and distress that must regrettably accompany the conversion process and Gospel living (Lk 9:2-26). It is a process of birth that has its unfortunate agony, but also its ecstasy (Jn 16:21).

The accumulation of both and psychological baggage blocks the docility, indifference and spiritual freedom Ignatius' *Examen* invites. Docility, indifference, and spiritual freedom are not ends in themselves, but are the essentials needed to serve the King and the Kingdom. The *Ignatian Paradigm*, as a process encapsulated in the *Examen*, is an integrated call to purgation, discernment, and spiritual freedom. The *PE*, properly applied, promises to speed one along the journey that, sooner or later, all must navigate.

Fifth, *Sacred Story* incorporates Ignatius' marking technique in a constructive, integrated way. Ignatius, at the end of the *Autobiography* mentions the technique of "marking" specific failures on a daily basis. This marking has two essential functions: (1) to keep track of the fundamental issue(s) blocking spiritual progress; and (2) to encourage and engender confidence that progress is taking place. Documenting in some fashion the spiritual growth facilitated by the *Examen* provides not only hope in the times of desolation that accompany everyone's spiritual journey, but helps facilitate integrated insights about one's life. These insights in turn encourage greater growth, interior freedom and peace. They also provide excellent material for confession and spiritual direction!

Sixth, *Sacred Story* emphasizes a regular practice of sacramental confession as a fruitful and synergistic companion to the practice of the daily *Examen*. Groups who tested *Sacred Story* and combined the practice of confession with regular practice of the *Examen* advanced measurably faster in understanding their core life issues. Also, they experienced God's mercy where they needed it most and were generally more faithful in the daily spiritual disciplines of *Sacred Story*.

Sacred Story proposes regular sacramental reconciliation as an integrated way of marking one's spiritual progress, reviewing one's life, and inviting the healing graces that Reconciliation affords; in essence, to make always "a new book" of one's life, and to discern a path in service to the King and for the Kingdom.

4

Five Challenges Point to the Examen's Future

Introduction: Third Millennium Challenges for the Examen

The Ignatian *Examen* proposes a narrow path to spiritual growth that is demanding yet effective. Because it is demanding, many avoid it. Many others avoid it because they can't reconcile feelings and attitudes towards religious beliefs and practices in light of the pressures and biases of modern culture. The dominant culture has reshaped our expectations on what is obligatory, healthy, and personally beneficial for a Catholic Christian's spiritual journey. The individualism of the age encourages us to pick and choose whatever is appealing to our immediate desires. This further complicates faith commitment, prayer and discernment.

The Church, in every age, must find a way to make both our Faith and Christ relevant amidst the all-encompassing changes in global consciousness. The mission today, as in the past, requires developing effective and dynamic evangelization strategies while holding fast to the anchors of Scripture, Tradition and the Magisterium. Jesuits have achieved great success historically in this mission of dynamic fidelity.[1] The Society's mission in this regard is simplified by the incredible legacy of St. Ignatius' spirituality.

Many of the deepest fault lines running through our contemporary, globalized culture and also through Catholic Christianity can be confronted by praying St. Ignatius' *Examen*. It is remarkable that Ignatius' spiritual genius anticipates and embraces those fault-lines. An *Examen* method faithful to his vision can respond to them.

The following section highlights the insights of eight commentators on the Examen - their appraisal of its problems and possibilities for our day.[2] All eight are faithful to the unique form of *Examen* framed by the *Ignatian Paradigm*.[3] Collectively the eight uncover issues Ignatius had not explicitly addressed, though the issues and effective responses to them are implicit in both Ignatius' spirituality and the *Ignatian Paradigm*.

Previous Themes

Common themes surface in the writings of these eight commentators. They detail rationales, methods, and challenges presented by the Ignatian *Examen*. For example, the *Examen's* focus on sin must also be inclusive of God's grace and mercy. This integrated character of the *Examen* has been missing at times. The *Ignatian Paradigm* compels this integrated approach. An *Examen* faithful to the Ignatian model should incorporate the full paradigm beginning in gratitude and culminating in a heartfelt contrition that leads to service.[4]

The *Examen* must also function as a vehicle for discernment. This is evident in the analysis of Ignatius' progressive conversion as he learns discernment techniques while undergoing integrated spiritual growth. In the *Examen*, discernment operates on two levels: first, discernment is necessary to separate the Divine spontaneities from the demonic in all the discreet moments of daily living; second, discernment is necessary in commitment to the *Examen's* life-long purgation. The life-long journey encompasses the purgation of manifest and root sins. Spiritual, psychological and moral confusion can reign supreme as one seeks spiritual docility and indifference to hear God's will and stay the course in the here and now. The *Examen* and discernment become "inseparable disciplines in one's spiritual journey."[5]

Five New Themes

Sacred Story method addresses five critical issues unique to our times. The five issues have roots in the *Examens'* structure and require analysis: (1) narcissism and individualism; (2) narrow moralism; (3) the interplay between sin and psychological compulsions; (4) the social dimensions of sin;

and (5) modern secularizing trends and their impact on God-mindedness or God-consciousness.

Narcissism and Individualism

The words "narcissism" and "individualism" are not common to Ignatius' milieu, however, pride and vainglory certainly were. There is a long tradition in both ancient and contemporary literature warning about the cancerous influence of pride and vainglory. Saint Augustine's majestic Book Ten of the *Confessions* speaks to pride's control of his inmost thoughts.[6] Augustine's confession of pride mirrors Ignatius' "overpowering desire to gain renown." Diadochus of Photice, writing in the fifth century, pointedly notes that self-love and love of God are mutually exclusive.[7] Rodríguez too gives evidence that from early in the Society's history, pride and vanity were corrosive to the Ignatian *Examen*.[8]

Individualism and narcissism were revealed as dominant cultural trends in the 1980's when the *Examen* commentators critiqued these "isms" as poisonous for spiritual growth. The social critic Christopher Lasch views individualism as a form of reactive narcissism linked to the overwhelming global problems of modern society.[9] He relates the book of Genesis' thesis in contemporary categories: that personal sin expressed as narcissism facilitates the individual's retreat from the sphere of social concern and relationship. The predictable outcome, historically viewed, is the chaos in our world which the Christian tradition reliably identifies as wholesale evil.

The American Psychiatric Association (APA) first listed narcissism as a personality disorder (NPD) in its fourth Diagnostic Statistics Manual (DSM IV) catalogue in 1980.[10] The APA estimates that only one percent of the general population and about fourteen percent of the clinical population has NPD as a serious pathology. In examining the nine NPD characteristics indicative of the characterological disorder identified by the APA, one can conclude that most people manifest many of these traits—in thoughts, words and deeds—which can be deemed sinful. The APA is not in the business of identifying sin. They describe narcissism as a clinical disorder with purely psychological origins. As a "serious pathology" it accounts for a mere one percent of the population. Yet contemporary researchers have documented an explosion of narcissistic tendencies, especially among the younger generation.[11] The Christian tradition would view many of the behaviors and actions of a narcissistic personality as objectively sinful, e.g. "envy," "lacking empathy," or being "interpersonally exploitative."[12]

Ignatius' vainglory would be noted by Ecclesiastes' Teacher, Augustine, Diadochus, Lasch, and even the APA. Many of Ignatius' personality traits are visible in the APA's categories. Pride and narcissism both have equivalent personal, spiritual, psychological and social consequences. What may be new and worth noting is the clinical use of narcissism to describe this ancient spiritual malady first documented in the Book of Genesis (Gen 3:1-7).

A modern bias favoring scientific categories over their moral counterparts might explain the new terminology. Or perhaps science is just now recognizing this ancient defect. Whatever the reason, narcissism appears to be the word of the moment for defining the root sin that tore through Ignatius' early life.

The word narcissism has a greater wince factor than either pride or self-love. The latter have positive connotations denoting self-esteem and personal self-worth necessary for proper human flourishing. And in an age of public obsession with celebrity the word vanity is more virtue than vice. But to invite someone to examine her or his narcissistic tendencies carries a clinical and moral gravitas that provokes serious self-reflection, even shame.

Pride was Ignatius' Achilles' heel. Pride is the vice more commonly linked Christian tradition to Original Sin than the other six vices. The advantages provided by semantics to induce self-reflection need to be seized. Consequently the word "narcissism" is used in *Sacred Story* to help people better understand the cancerous aspects of egoistic pride. Narcissism is the principal element the *Examen* targets. Individuals must identify it in their thoughts, words and deeds to advance spiritually. Life as *Sacred Story* begins when narcissism can be targeted and neutralized by God's grace.

Narrow Moralism

Narrow moralism is an undue, exclusive and non-integrated focus on moral acts. The *Examens*, especially the *PE* with its marking system, can prove detrimental to spiritual growth by creating obsessive anxieties as each new instance of some sin is catalogued and marked. This is especially true in scrupulous persons like Ignatius himself. A narrow focus prevents one from gaining a holistic view of one's life and history. When this happens, spiritual growth is limited.[13] The *Examen* has been a damaging exercise for some by fostering neurotic, obsessive/compulsive behaviors.

It is not necessary to eliminate the Commandments and the moral code they embody from the *Examen's* purview in the hopes of preventing an *Examen* from devolving into a narrow moralistic exercise. Ignatius had no such qualms, neither in his practice of the *Examen* nor in his public ministry.[14] Still, narrowly focusing on an action by extricating it from both a specific context and a wider life-story effectively prevents access to the higher perspective necessary to see the sin and/or a behavior's root cause, which are the major goals of the *PE*.[15] Access to the interconnected life-patterns and narratives to which sin, addiction, vice, and grace are tethered is central to the *Examen's* function. The spiritual and psychological data needed for effective discernment is eliminated without them.

The philosopher Charles Taylor highlights narrow moralism in another context that invites reflection and comment.[16] By framing the call to holiness reductively, with an exclusive focus on moral conduct, a belief system forms that views human effort alone as sufficient for benevolence, happiness, and human flourishing. The need for God and God's grace to reform lives is displaced: a major contributor to modern secularism.[17]

With the widespread belief that persons can both confront and master their darker impulses and attain happiness unaided by grace, two additional challenges are presented for *Sacred Story Examen*. The first is expanding the meaning of discipleship beyond the narrow righteousness achievable solely by human effort (Mt 5:20), as the Ignatian *Examen* invites. The second is to ensure the method is faithful to the Ignatian model, i.e., that it conforms to the full demands of the Commandments. *Sacred Story* invites the constant petitioning of God's grace to open one's eyes and heart to see and feel the effects of God's mercy in light of one's sinfulness, narcissism, and addictive vice.

Both an awareness of sin's corrosive effects plus a felt understanding of the role God's saving grace plays in light of personal sinfulness must be experienced. This is necessary to convince us that it is not possible to achieve Gospel benevolence and righteousness unaided.[18] Such experiences can further shatter the "dignity" of the self-sufficient, buffered identity.[19] In addition they open the self-enclosed to the transformative power of the personal God.

Taylor identifies another cultural issue *Sacred Story* method must address, related to the narrow moralism just discussed. He traces a strong negative bias against orthodox Christianity in secularism's rise during the Enlightenment. At times the anger devolves into hatred.[20] The modern expression of this anger may well influence attitudes toward the ascesis required by the *Examen*. This would include striving to master vice and reign in disordered passions that is part and parcel of the *Examens'* discipline.

A Christian discipline too passionate and enthusiastic in seeking holiness is highly suspect in an age that values a detached and rational intellectualism.[21] Religious practices that aspire for a more transcendent moral order beyond mere human flourishing are seen as proposing goals that deny some the right to happiness.[22] The suspicion of a Christianity that demands perfection and moral zeal over and above what a polite, enlightened society deems appropriate has subtly evolved in our age. It is demonstrated in those whose passion for tolerance and inclusiveness stands in opposition to those who reproach anything that falls short of tradition's moral codes and Commandments. This skirmish between the "tolerant" and the "intolerant" is found as often within religious confessions as it is between a specific confession and society's secularists.

A way forward must be found that fosters the quest for the transcendent moral and spiritual values demanded by the Ignatian *Examen*. It needs to confront and disarm both the rigid ideologies of the "intolerant" and the "tolerant." The call to conversion must invite the tolerant beyond the fear and anger they believe the Commandments and the received Tradition demand, which at times, leads these people to outright rejection of them. For the intolerant it means going beyond a rigid and narrow application of the moral code that fosters scrupulosity, zealotry and fanaticism.

The *Sacred Story Examen* invites practitioners to honestly identify the moral dimension of their life narrative according to the normative standards of Tradition. Its methods avoid promoting the Pelagianism, obsessive worries, reactive angers, and monocular vision fostered by narrow moralism. *Sacred Story* is a merciful discipline leading to genuine and integrated human flourishing. It is geared to benefit the practitioner no matter his or her stance toward authoritative tradition.[23] The means for achieving this balancing act in *Sacred Story* is a process fully engaging Ignatius' "sourcing" method that impels one to search for the root causes of sin and dysfunction. It is these "unexamined" core sins and wounds, and the anger, anxiety and grief linked to them, that can generate most of the unreasoned, reactive ideologies that short-circuit any conversion process.

The sourcing method of *Sacred Story* is supported by other Ignatian inspired disciplines. *Sacred Story* has a narrative introduction and "Rules of Engagement" incorporating wisdom from the Introductory Observations of the *Spiritual Exercises*. The Rules of Engagement challenge the reactive ideologies of both right and left, while the narrative addresses potential biases before one engages the discipline.

Sacred Story emphasizes that the *Examen* is rooted in the Church's tradition and not simply a legalistic obligation imposed by an outside authority. The narrative avoids any impression that its goal is the counting of moral peccadillocs. Doing so holds the interest of the religious skeptic who might not affirm traditional moral categories. It also helps mitigate the anxieties of the conscientious traditionalist who may tend toward scrupulosity. Consequently, the *Sacred Story Examen* can help diffuse tensions and fears associated with both poles along the "narrow moralism" continuum.

Sacred Story addresses one final issue that is clearly present in Aschenbrenner's work and implicitly in Campbell's writing. Both wrote their articles on the *Examen* at the height of the Cultural Revolution in the late 1960s and early 1970s. It is the period of history Taylor defines as the "Age of Authenticity" and is characterized by a revolution in changing attitudes and sexual mores.[24] The meaning of language shifts in this epoch. Words like "genuine," "freedom," and "authenticity" are appropriated to define the evolving ethic of free sexual expression and self-fulfillment. This new definition of authenticity imprisons many traditional Christian (and specifically Catholic) sexual teachings in a cage of narrow moralism.[25]

Contemporary Western culture attributes positive virtues, or at least a stance of 'non-judgment,' to a liberated expression of instinctual desires. Yet Ignatius rejected the free expression of his instinctual desires as antithetical to his truest human nature. For contemporary individuals, an evolving sense of authenticity in human self-expression easily compromises the "genuineness" Campbell ascribes to the *Examen* as an ascesis or "discipline of authenticity."[26] Also compromised by the new interpretation of authenticity are Aschenbrenner's insights faithful to Ignatian discernment principles distinguishing between two spontaneities; one Divine and one inspired by the enemy of human nature.[27]

The dominant culture prefers that desires remain undifferentiated in regards to spiritual and moral categories of right and wrong. In practice this means that undifferentiated desires bypass the measurement of truth or authenticity of the Decalogue and the laws of the Church that anchor the *Exercises'* considerations on sin, *SpEx* [42].

Those faithful to Ignatius' discernment methods must demand such differentiation, or risk stripping the spirituality of its power to change lives. For in today's milieu, a call for desires to be examined and tested for authenticity in light of Ignatian principles can lead to serious charges of intolerance. In a life of undifferentiated desires, one is adrift with an ever-evolving description of human nature that can't be easily measured against the definition of desolation Ignatius defines in his *Rules* as coming from human nature's enemy.

In a milieu where 'freedom' and 'authenticity' have become so wedded to expressions of instinctual desire (viz. Freud), one is subject to the reproaches of 'narrow moralism' in favoring the received (moral) Tradition as guide and norm for living. When culture ascribes a positive value to the expression of instinctual desires, the moral ascesis fostered by the *PE* is seen as unnecessary. Or more negatively, it will be viewed as promoting spiritual and psychological damage.

In his *Rules,* Ignatius suggests (tangentially supported by Campbell and Aschenbrenner) that the genuine Divine inspirations of God lead one to reject definitions of the self, inspired by the "enemy of human nature." One is instead to labor under the banner of grace and allow God to heal one's authentic human nature hidden by sin, wounds, narcissism and psychic dysfunction.

Ignatius discovers an instinct of purity and selfless service during his conversion. The new man God revealed is antithetical to the old man who freely indulged instinctual desire that defined his first thirty years. The fantasies and desires of the old man are rooted in a pre-purgative imagination. The release from instinctual compulsions, sins and addictions, the shattering of his pride, and his humble, obedient service to Christ and the Church are his new benchmarks for defining true freedom and authentic human nature.

The challenges presented by the contemporary readings of "narrow moralism" in light of the Age of Authenticity are not easily solved.[28] Additionally the Church is confronted today with pressures in advancing a morality consonant with Ignatius' own instinct of purity, weakened as it is by sexual scandals. Moreover, we live in an age where pleasure and physical intimacy are equally or more highly valued than procreation as the end goal and ultimate purpose of genital sexual expression.

Four small steps are taken in *Sacred Story* to address these challenges. First, the *Sacred Story Examen* incorporates, as did Ignatius' original *Examen*, considerations of the Commandments and teachings of the Church in its discernment method. Second, it re-appropriates the language of "genuineness," "freedom" and "authenticity" for those unique Divine inspirations that Ignatius himself discovered as the true expression of his human nature. Third, it invites the direct, personal encounter with Christ, the individual to whom one's life must conform. This personal encounter is crucial. For the graced encounter which transforms one's emotional, intellectual, and spiritual horizon is not a law or an institution, but the person of Christ who exemplifies authentic human nature. This direct, personal encounter with Christ is a signature element of the *Spiritual Exercises* and of all Ignatian Spirituality.

And finally, *Sacred Story* defines the positive and negative boundaries of Ignatian discernment. For Ignatius, authentic consolation is always consonant with the Decalogue and received Tradition. Attraction to, and indulgence in pleasure is described by Ignatius as "low and earthly," as both a temptation and one of the principle signs denoting spiritual desolation.[29] The spontaneity inviting surrender to such passions—passions that symbolize a core value of the Age of Authenticity—constituted the first serious temptation Ignatius experienced after his conversion, and it is this temptation that frames the *Truth Paradigm*.[30]

These four small measures incorporated in *Sacred Story* help those living in the shifting paradigms of contemporary culture. *Sacred Story* is addressed both to those who for whatever reasons have strong feelings against an external authority as well as those who cling to laws as their sole security and identity. The disciplines of *Sacred Story* invite individuals to set aside prejudices. The program demands that a person open one's heart to an experience of integrated conversion like that of St. Ignatius.

The Matrix of Sin and Psychological Compulsions

The description of Ignatius' conversion experience highlights the matrix of sins and vices he manifested and confessed. It also identified psychological influences that likely contributed to them and/or acted at least in part as their fuel. The study also identified the integrated spiritual and psychological growth documented by the *Autobiography*.

Ignatius' spiritual and psychological maturity after his recuperation at Loyola is manifest in his mastery of sinful behaviors and addictions. His maturity deepens with the identification of, and commitment to eradicate, the root sin of pride in the struggle with scruples during his harrowing experience at Manresa. It is also manifest in his balanced calm after an intense period of dangerous, neurotic mood swings that characterize his spiritual torments. Ignatius' struggle at Manresa is a battle with both the sinful and psychological root issues— deep-seated concupiscence—necessary to achieve integrated healing. Using both classical theological formulations and modern psychological categories the *Powerless Paradigm* is elemental purgation.[31] The *Spiritual Exercises* that Ignatius was living facilitated this integrated, spiritual-psychological healing.[32]

Many *Examen* commentators discuss the importance of identifying the interplay between sinful habits and the makeup of one's psychological character. It is essential to identify the life events and traumas that can act as sin's source and accomplice.[33] The examinee must source sin's origins and its evolutionary character in his/her family. Cognizant of theorists who trace life's fixed patterns, for good or ill, to the first five years of life, we are invited to examine, "across our being," issues that might be spiritual, biological or psychological.[34] The biological and psychological play their part but sin finds its habitation in the spiritual. In this, what is sinful must be examined and resisted.

The *Examen* practitioner must see the familial roots of Original Sin and learn the difference between "sin, my sin, and sin in me."[35] In order for purgation to promote transformation, an *Examen* practitioner must discern his complicity in the sinful compulsions, neuroticisms, addictions, and negative self-image he experiences. Taken together, these form the 'dark night of the senses' typical for the common person. Using psychological challenges to scapegoat sin is not satisfactory. A person must accept responsibility for working against sin that manifests as psychological complexes. Individuals must confront the shame, embarrassment, and humiliation that admitting sin requires. Rationalizations and defenses can act as impenetrable armor preventing the awakening of one's conscience.[36]

Recidivism in the *Examen's* practice should be noted. The recidivist might simply blame her constant failures on psychological problems or neuroticisms. Thus, she is not responsible for her behaviors.[37] One might conclude that this particular problem emerges most often when a deep, integrated exploration of sin and its spiritual and psychological roots has been avoided.

One easily affirms that the matrix of sin, combined with what our commentators define as sinful, psychological compulsion, has characterized every individual's spiritual struggles since time immemorial. It is a cosmic struggle that has evolutionary dimensions:

> Sin, we begin to see, is more than a violation of a law. In the Byzantine liturgy, before receiving the Eucharist both the priest and people pray together for forgiveness of all sin, deliberate and inherited. Sin is anything that prevents God from being God in our life. It is as much the brokenness of our ancestors that we have inherited as our own willfulness. It is the "sin of the world" or a sharing in original sin. We open ourselves to the cancerous, cosmic influences of sin by being born into this world. And to this inherited evil we add our own deliberate sin. Our whole being shudders at the fragmentation. We feel caught in a prison of darkness and yet we see a delicate ray of light leading us out through the crack of *metanoia,* a conversion to the Lord.[38]

Ignatius indirectly addresses the distinctively psychological, familial and developmental elements of the spiritual journey. His compendium in the *Exercises* of *Rules* for dealing with scruples, and the psychological insights woven into the *Rules* for discernment are easily interpreted as a response to his acute awareness of the psychological dimension of integrated spiritual growth necessary for authentic wholeness and holiness. One can make the case that for Ignatius' day, a psychological method of sorts is encapsulated in the rules for scruples.[39] The *Sacred Story Examen* provides a technique that takes the spiritual and psychological elements of the personality into account. The method allows for personal responsibility in the face of sin. It also provides strategies for helping examinees access and disarm the psychological stresses and cross-pressures that can fuel sinful patterns and passions.[40]

An integrated approach that encompasses both the spiritual and psychological dimensions of human experience is important for everyone. Perhaps it is especially imperative for those whose principal experience in life is being sinned against. Original Sin that is generational and familial generates significant static in the form of fear, anger, and grief. Early memories of innocence betrayed and trust broken make the project of self-examination and the discussion of sin radioactive. They block the process of reflection, acceptance, and forgiveness that the Ignatian *Examen* encourages.[41]

Sinful passions and habits whose roots in early developmental experiences might be repressed or forgotten pose unique challenges. Maté, Allers, Horney, Idígoras and Meissner focus on the shaping influence of early life experiences. Of the *Examen* commentators reviewed, English takes the presence of early childhood traumas seriously and is the most helpful in providing constructive ways of approaching these early childhood wounds. He understands that the memory can provide access to life's significant events, and be a channel for graces and healing.[42]

Sacred Story provides a method for accessing memories and experiences that have interrupted or injured one's spiritual and psychological maturation. This is done in much the same way that the *PE* helps "source" those sins and vices that are the origin of many others. Today, Ignatius would consciously seek the source events—both spiritual and psychological—that form the basis of his narcissism and the manifest sins disguising it. He has already done this for us by sourcing his root sins in the tripartite shield of "riches, honors, and pride." According to Ignatius, it is from these "three steps" that "the evil one leads to all other vices." These are Satan's signature in the Ignatian meditation on the Two Standards *SpEx* [140-142].[43]

A Return to Childhood Innocence

In the *Exercises*, the "Consideration of Different States of Life" immediately precedes the meditation on the Two Standards.[44] In his "Consideration," it is telling that Ignatius recaps previous exercises of the Christ child's spiritual and moral development: 1) from his foster father and his mother he learns to observe the Commandments and the life of obedience, and; 2) from his eternal Father he learns the life of evangelical perfection.

The juxtaposition of these exercises and their summary in the Consideration's introduction with the Two Standards reveals more clearly Ignatius' comments in the *Autobiography* intimating a return to his own childhood to learn aright what it means to be man. He learns this not from his father Don Beltrán, nor his brother Martín García nor any father surrogate. Instead, he learns this lesson from God, who "treated him as a schoolteacher treats a child...because he was thick and dull of brain."[45]

The meditation on the "Standard of Satan" reveals the negative spiritual influences that work directly on the human subject. In the modern-day application of the Ignatian *Rules*, it is common to perceive such influences flowing directly from spiritual powers and also through the history of family, clan and nation. Ignatius affirms that the Standard of Satan was dominant ('king'), in his first thirty years of life.[46] Yet his conversion amply demonstrates that malformation of spirit and/or psyche, and lack of love or proper example of Christian living early in life, is trumped by God's grace in the individual who submits to graced conversion. Simplicity, obedience, and innocence of heart transform a heart divided by pride, addictive passions and disobedience.

Ignatius' story also reveals that to begin afresh, one must work with grace and the Spirit's illuminations. One does this not only to identify the roots of one's maladaptive behaviors, but also to allow them to be uprooted so a new life can take hold. Using Ignatius' own story, and adding what we know of human psychological development, the search for root causes should include those formative events and life situations—both suffered and committed—that fashion desires and lifestyles eroding of childhood innocence.[47]

Spiritual and emotional archaeology is absolutely essential for spiritual insight and growth. It is congruent with Ignatius' own strategy in searching out every source blocking the free activity of grace, especially ones that are the "cause of many others." A diagram that reveals Ignatius' progressive enlightenment on the nature of sin in his life, as well as the element of psychological/family history, is used in *Sacred Story*:

Sacred Story Integration and awareness template

VISIBLE SINS

The Fruit or Ornamentation
(Ignatius' addictive gambling, reactive anger,
and sexual self-indulgence)
*Manifest fear, anger, and grief, moral weaknesses, vices, addictions,
and sinful habits that are the most visible to you.*
↓   ↑

CORE SINS

The Trunk or Superstructure
(Ignatius' arrogance, blinded conscience, and narcissism)
*Disobedience and narcissism, along with its fear, anger, and grief,
that forms the trunk or superstructure of your daily life,
feeding on originating sins and events.*
↓   ↑

ORIGINAL SINS

The Roots or Foundation
(Original Sin and concupiscence that wounded Ignatius' heart and soul;
distinctive family/clan sin and/or early life-events that wounded him
spiritually, psychologically, and physically)
*Ancient, originating events that rooted the patterns of disobedience
and narcissism, along with its fear, anger, and grief.*

Sacred Story's Examens methodology provides tactics for moving in both directions along this continuum, from root to branch and branches to root. This gradual awakening is necessary in order to facilitate an integrated "reading" of one's life, much in the same way Ignatius appears to have done during his own awakening.

A Broken Heart as a Paradigm for Lost Innocence

The dogma of Original Sin is abstract and difficult for most people to grasp easily. New categories and paradigms for describing the effects of sin's evolutionary impact on the human family are helpful. Original Sin can be better understood if identified not only by a constitution weakened by Original Sin, what the Tradition has described as concupiscence, but also of a heart broken by a world of sin.[48]

Simply put, sin breaks relationship with God, the self, others and creation. And broken relationships break hearts. Broken hearts in turn lead to the loss of faith, hope and love -all principal characteristics of spiritual desolation. A broken heart and crushed spirit—cut off from faith, hope and love, and thus cut off from meaningful relationship—seeks anesthesia for its pain and sorrow in pleasure, material acquisition, addiction and reactive violence, as Maté documents. The reality of a wounded, broken heart as a symbol of sin's impact makes the dogma of Original Sin immediate, personal, and heartfelt. Accordingly the image and language of a broken heart is used throughout *Sacred Story* to illumine sin's impact.

The Social Dimensions of Sin

Ignatian mysticism has been depicted as a mysticism of service. The purgation facilitated by the *Examen* leads to a union with God that expresses itself in labor for the Kingdom on behalf of Christ and his Gospel. Sin and dysfunction block a person's freedom and availability for this service.[49]

Sin's impact therefore is not only an inner reality but also a social reality. Sin is social because it hinders availability for service and also harms those in one's "life-world"; the milieu in which one makes her way in the world.[50] The socialization of sin in the Ignatian *Examen* also includes the fractured relationship between the human person and creation.

An individualized understanding of sin as a principal focus of the *Examen's* ascesis is shortsighted. For sin is both personal and social. We have come to understand that engaging our Catholic Christian faith entails an integrated responsibility to advance justice on all fronts. Ascetical disciplines like the *Examen* are suspect if practitioners are led into a privatized spirituality disconnected from the world's suffering and pain. *Sacred Story* highlights the *Examen's* innate dynamic as a discipline both personal and *social*.

A fully realized *Examen* enables and encourages one to see the links between thoughts, words and deeds in one's own life; the links with the persons in one's social milieu; and the links to the situation of the poor and the environment. A fully realized *Examen* emphasizes the interconnected dimension of creation and the personal responsibility each individual possesses, either for adding to Church, community and societal problems, or becoming part of the solution.

Expanding our view of the *Examen's* social dimensions—a view of creation's interconnectedness—is rooted in the Ignatian *Contemplatio*; *SpEx* [235, 236]. Ignatian spirituality reveals a mysticism of God's in-dwelling and laboring in all creatures and elements, both on earth and in the heavens. After all, Ignatius' mysticism is about finding God in all things.[51] We remember that Ignatius' early conversion at Loyola opens him to the beauty of a starry night.

Praying the *Examen* invites God into our lives to reveal our sinfulness, addictions and dysfunction. In so doing, God heals us, and opens our hearts to loving service, allowing us to see the world around us both in its beauty and in its suffering. The *Examen* leads to interior freedom for our self-donation in service to the Kingdom.

Pierre Teilhard de Chardin expands on Ignatius' themes of cosmic mysticism in reflections on sin in the world. Even in evil's destructive and atomizing force, Teilhard discerns an inevitable and intensifying understanding of the person's inherent unity with others and all creation:

> Every new war, embarked upon by the nations for the purpose of detaching themselves from one another, merely results in their being bound and mingled together in a more inextricable knot. The more we seek to thrust each other away, the more do we interpenetrate.... Moreover, being each exposed at the core of their being to the countless spiritual influences emanating from the thought, the will and the passions of all their fellow-creatures, they find themselves constantly subjected in spirit to an enforced rule of resonance...—there is only one way the tide can flow: the way of ever increasing unification.[52]

Teilhard's mysticism compels us to see that even the most cancerous aspect of Original Sin, signified by the violence that isolates and separates people from each other, will conspire to force individuals and societies to confront their dependence and interconnectedness as it increases. Joseph Ratzinger acknowledges that Teilhard's Ignatian-influenced mysticism shows clearly that man and cosmos "belong to each other" and will "become one through their 'complexification' in the larger entity of the love, that…steps beyond and encompasses bios."[53] Using Teilhard's template, he reveals how it "renders comprehensible" St. Paul's vision of all things being *one* in Christ Jesus.[54] It reflects Paul's image of Christ as the first born of creation (Col. 1:15-22).[55]

This understanding of the interconnectedness of human networks in both sin and grace naturally expands to the *Examen's* focus on the natural world. We now understand environmental ecosystems are vital to our survival.[56] Degradation of ecosystems is increasingly viewed by the Church as "sin" that violates the commandment of love because of the human threat they occasion.[57] Individual and cultural expressions of narcissism and pride manifested as excessive consumption need to be linked to such exploitation that affects people and ecosystems. They are "sin" because they threaten and destroy life.

This does not necessarily mean one's examen prayer focuses on whether or how one is working directly with or on behalf of the poor or fragile ecosystems. But it does mean examining greed, waste, indulgence, overconsumption, and selfish "use of creatures." It also means inviting graced insight to help see how our choices and lifestyle lack freedom, and how these are connected to our addictions and sins. All of us need to awaken to choices and lifestyles that have destructive consequences not just for "me," but also for all of God's people and creation.

This holistic world-view creates a greater sense of urgency in the use and practice of the *Examen*. But it also directly challenges those who facilely disconnect personal lifestyle choices and consumption habits—narcissisms and addictions of all kinds—from their impact on the earth and humanity. It may have been understood in the past, however, that the "individual" conversion process facilitated by the Ignatian *Examen* as life-prayer is not a monadic exercise focusing ultimately on "my sin," "my personhood," or "my life-story." It is not an isolated instance of the creation/redemption work of Christ. Understanding it in this narrow sense violates its purpose and makes it irrelevant to the mission of universal reconciliation promoted by the Gospel, the Church, and the Society of Jesus. The personal responsibility of one's labor in the practice of the *Examen* must instead be framed as collaborative effort joined with God's grace, reconciling oneself with God, self, others, and creation.[58]

Sacred Story facilitates this higher perspective and the communal dimension it signifies by inviting us to labor in awakening to our sin, addiction and dysfunction. It invites us to accept responsibility for our share of sin's devastation in our lives and in our larger social universe. It allows Christ to heal us and transform the way we labor in our own *Sacred Story* with his Sacred Story in the work of universal reconciliation.[59] Personal transformation is an intrinsically social act, and Ignatius' *Examen* is at its core an exercise in communal prayer.

Secularization and Its Impact on God-Consciousness

We began with reflections from Lewis and Pieper. Both men identify an intentional strategy by forces aligned against human nature, making awareness of God in the-here-and-now difficult, if not impossible to achieve. Ignatius would concur. The forces leading us to distraction—to a world of "total work"—render it impossible hear God's voice and our consciences in the present moment. This distraction and separation is the goal of the enemy of human nature.

Most *Examen* commentators are aware of the difficulties secular culture presents to persons seeking to cultivate self-awareness. Aschenbrenner hints that undefined pressures make it difficult for persons to achieve the daylong attentiveness the *Examen* invites. Townsend highlights the materialistic bent of modern society that erodes one's awareness that "all is gift," the fundamental gratitude so central to Christianity, and expressly highlighted in Ignatian spirituality.[60] English decries the market culture's "drive to success" as an embodiment of the anti-Christ, fostering the self-indulgence that is so cancerous to the spiritual life.[61] Tetlow sees modernity's false freedom as individualism and narcissism, turning a person away from honest assessment of his/ her life, away from others in his/her life-world, and ultimately, away from God.[62]

These pressures and challenges act to constrict one's heart and imagination. They make it difficult to desire engagement with the Ignatian *Examen* (what can it do for me?), and also difficult to continue once the practice starts to take bites out of our time and our egos.

Any self-discipline poses challenges. What usually motivates action, however, is a compelling belief, personally experienced, that makes a discipline worthwhile. We must possess a frame of reference that gives value to engaging a practice like the *Examen* and staying the course once a commitment is made. Certainly Ignatius provides compelling reasons to stay the course, which address some of modernity's threats to 'God-mindedness.' An effective and enduring practice of the *Examen* requires these reasons.

The discipline and ascetical effort Ignatius invested daily and hourly to achieve docility and the spiritual indifference the *Examen* cultivates is manifest in the *First Principle and Foundation.* His insights draw on the energy generated by his passionate belief in, and his desire to be united with the Trinity in the eternal Kingdom of the saints and blessed. For Ignatius, these transcendent and eternal goals are the purpose and end of human striving. We see evidence of this in both his letters and the *Constitutions'* General *Examen*. In these sources we hear Ignatius address the theme of the Christian life in light of this "eternal" horizon.[63]

It may be true that Christians today affirm an afterlife as part of the creedal inheritance of their faith. Yet the concept that the journey of life is but a step to an eternity with God in the Kingdom of the righteous—an operative and vital belief capable of shaping attitudes and values for daily living—has lost ground. Replacing it are more powerful market-driven, self-help forms of Christian spirituality that compel us to focus on instantaneous success.

Taylor offers an explanation for this loss of transcendence in modern culture and specifically in Christianity. Very few act on the belief that that actions in the here-and-now link to an eternal and transcendent realm. The consciousness of life events grounded in "higher time" has given way to viewing events in "vertical time-slices." The assorted unrelated incidents of daily living cohere only in one-dimensional perspectives of "profane time."[64]

His narrative on the migration of human consciousness from belief in a "demon haunted world" requiring the holy powers of saints, angels, and miracles, through "disenchantment" and, finally, "excarnation," is multi-dimensional. One of Taylor's so-called "modern social imaginaries" facilitating this migration deserves comment. Along with a flattened time-consciousness, comes the "innovation" to conceptualize the business of daily life as exclusively intra-human. All aspects of daily commerce, labor, and exchange can be "disengaged" from any reference to God.

This hermeneutic allows human imagination to unchain itself not only from God-consciousness but from all meaning making that relies on God as source and end. This imagination revolution opens the way for exclusive humanism and atheism. For the non-believer, this "disengaged" stance is associated with rationality and freedom from the confining and odious aspects of religiosity. It grants dignity, meaning, and prestige to its adherents. This disengaged stance once confined to cultural élites is now the principal hermeneutic for whole societies in the world today.[65]

The majority of religious believers easily adopt this temporal/secular world-view. We can all consciously or unconsciously operate on its terms in the business of daily life. To varying degrees all of us are "buffered" from both the transcendent and the world of "higher time." It is not that Christians do not believe in God or an afterlife. Rather, what generates passion, energy, interest, and meaning is skewed in favor of the visible, material world, not the Kingdom-to-come.[66] In this anthropocentric shift, people easily lose sight of the relational dimension of faith. What is lost is the awareness that intercommunion with the Divine is not only possible but also transformative in this life.[67]

Sacred Story's method does not rely on denunciations of materialism and hyper-activism, at least not as a first strategy. It can't because these realities are consciously or unconsciously operating as principal meaning-makers for engaged Christians. Contemporary formulations of the Christian kerygma have unwittingly led many to associate more work, more donations of time or money, more social engagement, more action on behalf of justice—more investment of effort in the material realm—as the signature of the modern apostle.

Sacred Story follows the advice of Ignatius and uses through-the-day awareness disciplines and the *Examen* periods of contemplative rest to attune our hearts to both God and "higher time." This is what Pieper and Lewis invite: that we step into the contemplative stream where the present touches the eternal, the place where the personal God can be encountered and the place where the world as a whole can be glimpsed. *Sacred Story* is framed as a conscious-ness-altering activity that grants its practitioners a higher perspective by offering disciplines that ground them firmly in this "present-eternal" realm of the God who is yesterday, today and forever.

With this grounding comes the ability to discern what is and is not of value. In this way, our judgments are not based on the limited, rationalistic assertions of a "buffered identity." They are rooted in a heart and mind that by grace have become attuned and vulnerable to all of creation and to the Presence—the One who is the Way, the Truth, and the Life—who invites us to produce fruit that endures to eternal life (Jn. 14:6; 6:27; 15:5).

Scripture provides multiple stories valuing the contemplative pause, possibly the most familiar is Martha and Mary (Lk. 10:42). Jean-Pierre de Caussade highlights the value of contemplative rest in defining the "present moment" as a "sacrament."[68] Buddhists call it mindfulness. In our age, Eckhart Tolle[69] and Michael Brown use techniques of grounding consciousness in the present to achieve breakthroughs in perspective.[70]

Ignatius, by his hourly *Examen*, anchored his heart and consciousness in the present moment. In so doing he seemed always to know his final end, his final home. But more than just awareness of eternity, Ignatius gained a wisdom grounded in a holy and holistic awareness of the material, political, human and spiritual worlds. His genius and holistic perspective compelled the Russian mystic and hermeticist Valentin Tomberg to see Ignatius' spirituality as the perfect melding of intellectuality and spirituality, a conjoining that holds faith and knowledge in balance.[71] Ignatius embodies The Fool of the twenty-first Arcanum in that "he succeeded in attaining to the wisdom of perfect equilibrium between the world of the mystical revelations and the world of human task and actions:" as a fool, he is a "man placed as an intermediary between two worlds—the divine world and the human world."[72]

This "practical mysticism" of Ignatian spirituality, specifically the *Examen*, joins the transcendent and eternal with the imminent world of action. Ignatian spirituality has been defined this way in the past: as "contemplation in action."[73] Tomberg suggests it has an even more universal reach, encompassing Eastern religious modalities.[74] It is, he says, a spirituality that unites the consciousness of the Divine with that of the human, transforming the "schizophrenia of two consciousnesses not in harmony with one another—into wisdom."[75]

The *Examen*, more than any other spiritual discipline anchored Ignatius' heart and mind in this present/eternal realm where he encountered the mystery of God in his daily faith journey. It can still serve this purpose, and must, especially in our catastrophic loss of *Kairos*—of transcendence—and the suffering and boredom it creates in our time-flattened *Chronos*.[76]

Sacred Story revitalizes innate aspects of Ignatius' *Examen*, especially those aspects that correspond to our age's deep hunger for religious transcendence. Its method responds to those individuals whose only alternative for transcendence has been secular presence awareness techniques or the mindfulness principles of Eastern spiritual disciplines. Remarkably, Ignatius' spirituality and his *Examen* encompass all of these techniques and disciplines. *Sacred Story* invites awakening to the higher consciousness a less "buffered" experience of the Divine promises. It facilitates an escape from the malaise of immanence where the sheer force of a time-flattened, disenchanted world blocks our path to religious transcendence.[77]

Part Two of this book will outline the rationale for the *Sacred Story* method and explain its various components in light of the insights and challenges discussed. *Sacred Story* uses equivalent structures and disciplines as Ignatius' original *Examen*. *Sacred Story* opens a path to this mystical discipline of gratitude, discernment, reconciliation, and Christian decision-making. The goal is an ongoing pledge "to labor for fruit that endures to eternity."

Part Two

Recovering the Examen's Vitality and Relevance

There are very few who realize what God would make of them if they abandoned themselves entirely to His hands, and let themselves be formed by
His grace. A thick and shapeless tree trunk would never believe that it could
become a statue, admired as a miracle of sculpture...and would never consent
to submit itself to the chisel of the sculptor who, as St. Augustine says, sees by
his genius what he can make of it. Many people who, we see, now scarcely live
as Christians, do not understand that they could become saints, if they would
let themselves be formed by the grace of God, if they did not ruin His plans by
resisting the work which He wants to do.

—Spiritual Teachings of St. Ignatius Loyola

5

Contemporizing Ignatius' Discernment Rules

The Need for Discernment

Those engaging in the daily *Examen* practice of *Sacred Story* will regularly experience blockages to integrated growth that are spiritual, psychological and emotional. This will be true even as they awaken to avenues for integrated progress. Ignatius encountered the same types of blockages and opportunities on his conversion journey. A process of conversion facilitated by an effective and strategic *Examen* practice is always accompanied by the push and pull of consolations and desolations. As Ignatius' progressive conversion illuminates, these two spontaneities indicate paths to positive growth or blockages to integrated growth.

It is essential for those engaging *Sacred Story Examen* to understand basic discernment principles. If the *Sacred Story* practitioner awakens to the consolations and desolations of conversion without a roadmap, they will be lost. The feelings and choices that are inspired by experiences of consolation and desolation can lead one to mistake the light for the dark, the dark for the light, and a counterfeit identity as authentic.

Adapting Ignatius' Classic "Rules" for Sacred Story

The *Spiritual Exercises* are the usual forum for discerning major vocational choices. Major vocational choices are usually single acts that oftentimes alter the fundamental course of our lives. Ignatius intended the *Examen* to be used by those who never engaged the full *Exercises*. It too requires discernment methods. The focus of a daily *Examen's* discernment is not a vocational state per se but the thoughts, words, and deeds of one's life, whatever one's chosen vocation. Its strategic purpose is to examine whether those thoughts, words, and deeds express quest and tendency towards God and the Kingdom, or towards the enemy of human nature and his realm.[1]

Sacred Story contemporizes Ignatius' *Rules* to make them accessible for a self-guided process. The inspiration for updating the *Rules* comes from Ignatius' progressive conversion as detailed in his *Autobiography*. The very crises caused by his faith commitment are the tools God uses to illuminate discernment principles and allow him to negotiate the crises.

Sacred Story creates new paradigms for expressing Ignatius' *Rules* and facilitates discernment encompassing holistic, integrated growth that is both spiritual and psychological. The *Rules* anticipate the relativism that disconnects human desire and action from Christian norms of right and wrong. *Sacred Story's* goal is to help people reflect on desires and choices in light of Ignatius' definitions of consolation and desolation, and in light of the Divinely crafted human nature both those spontaneities seek to influence and inspire.

The Boundaries of Ignatian Discernment

The *Autobiography* reveals that Ignatius discovers the First and Second Week *Rules* organically and progressively as his purgation unfolds.[2] Some distinguish between Ignatius' "first" conversion at Loyola and his "second" conversion at Manresa, implicitly supporting the idea of Ignatius' organic, progressive conversion and congruent development of the *Rules* with this two-tiered conversion.[3]

The temptations Ignatius confronted early in his conversion process— temptations distinctive to those discussed in his First Week discernment principles—unfold in the purgation of his more manifest sins and vices. He was still lured by the pleasure of instinctual satisfactions that characterized his life up to this point. What Ignatius describes in his *Autobiography* are First Week temptations and consolations typical of the purgative stage of spiritual growth.

The temptations unique to Second Week principles are those temptations that Ignatius encountered deeper in his conversion journey. The scruples crisis fed the good or holy illusion of his rigorous confession habit. Ignatius had gained mastery over the manifest sins of his former life. Evil had to insinuate itself in a more subtle and nuanced way—under the guise of "good"— one that hooked into his root sin of narcissism and pride. It is this root struggle with pride (manifest in his scruples, obsessive confessional practice and its successful resolution) that forms the *Powerless Paradigm* and the signature elements of the *PE*.

The *Rules* of Week One and Two are inspired and originate during the very purgative process that gives birth to Ignatius' unique habit of general and particular examen. *Sacred Story* reimagines the *Rules* with the dynamic fidelity characteristic of St. Ignatius. A first step in framing the *Rules* for a self-guided process is helping users understand discernment's boundaries.

Discernment is difficult and Ignatius gifts the Church with clear discernment boundaries. One of those boundaries is a benchmark for spiritual consolation. The other is a benchmark for spiritual desolation. Together they furnish *Sacred Story* practitioners with two clear signposts for their progressive conversion journey.

First Benchmark:

A Definition of Consolation: *Inclinations, Inspirations and Choices that:*
1. *Enflame the heart with love for God,*
2. *Increase docility and humility and,*
3. *Align the heart to truths proposed by the Scripture, Tradition and the Magisterium.*

The foundation for the first benchmark comes in a congruent reading of Ignatius' definitions of regular consolation and consolation without previous cause; consolación sin causa (CSC/CSCP) *SpEx* [332.2].[4] There are diverse readings of what Ignatius means by CSC; its purpose, frequency and signature characteristics. Ignatian scholars have debated the differences.[5] What is CSC?

Ignatius says that it "belongs solely to the Creator to come into a soul, to leave it, to act upon it, to draw it wholly to the love of His Divine Majesty," *SpEx* [330.2]. This "quality" of activity by God and the "type" of effects it produces in the soul are congruent with Ignatius' preliminary definition of consolation in Week One:

> I call it consolation when an interior movement is aroused in the soul, by which it is enflamed with love of its Creator and Lord, and as a consequence, can love no creature on the face of the earth for its own sake, but only in the Creator of them all. *SpEx* [316.3].

A consolation of this type is "prompted (sine causa) in a person by some influence beyond his or her affectivity and awareness."[6] The heart "enflamed" is paradigmatic of all consolation. It is the direct consequence of the Holy Spirit's most profound actions in the human subject moving one toward self-less charity. Consolation of this type can only come from God: "The CSCP (CSC) therefore, sums up that Father-initiated 'flight from self-love, self-will, and self-interest' [Ex 18]…and corresponds to the exercitant's basic dynamic for fulfillment…arising from a gratuitous and purely disinterested love…The CSCP is emphatically Christocentric."[7] The role of Spirit, Father and Son in the impact of CSCP is a Trinitarian grace unique to Ignatius' mysticism.[8]

There is a third dimension to CSC apart from being "enflamed" with love for God and led toward selfless charity. This third element is its "ecclesial" context, a dimension that is both a quality and a confirmation of the consolation's character as "sin causa"[9]. Such consolations never contradict received Tradition. Ignatius' letter to Dominican sister Theresa Rejadell is the clearest example to confirm this characteristic of CSC.[10]

Consolation without previous cause is a graced encounter that draws one wholly to God, and to selfless love, without contradicting the truth of received Tradition. It can be conceived as the grace of fundamental conversion that reorients one in the direction of the Divine. In this Ignatian context, CSC provides "illumination" but not in the sense of private revelations. Instead, it facilitates a wisdom revealing one's authentic personality before God; one's sins, yes, plus the evidence of things in one's life that are opposed to God.[11] Most importantly, one's authentic self is revealed in light of God's fundamental and all-embracing love for God's creature.

This form of consolation is what Ignatius receives while recuperating at Loyola. It propels him into the desert of his first purgation of the senses, his First Week exercises, temptations, consolations, and insights into discernment in light of these desolations and consolations. The CSC is also evident in Ignatius' illumination at Manresa; his "great clarity of mind" enables him to "see" the wrong in his scrupulous habit so destructive of his spiritual goals and also to surrender "control" of his life entirely to God.

The trials at Manresa, followed by his illumination and "great clarity of mind" vis a vis the compulsive confession habit, constitute Ignatius' more integrated "second" conversion that led him to a deeper selflessness, docility to the Spirit, obedience, and the mystical graces.

Consolation without cause is rightfully viewed as the fundamental reorienting grace of conversion.[12] It is made possible by Christ's supreme sacrifice, a sacrifice that is visibly and invisibly, with deliberate intention and relentless love, repairing the damage to human nature wrought by Original Sin and the enemy of human nature (1 Cor. 15:25-8; 2 Cor. 5:16-20; Col. 1:15-20; Phil. 3:21).

The subject who receives it might not be aware of consolation as a reorienting grace, but consolation is operative nonetheless. It becomes more thematic as the subject's conversion deepens. It is operative because Christ wishes all to be saved. Definitions of CSC and regular consolation are thus always one and the same: grace. The effects of those graces are progressive, deepening as one advances on the path of purgation, through illumination, to union.

The effects of consolation always enflame the heart with love for God, compel growth in selflessness and charity, and increase docility and obedience. And the obedience is to the Truth of the one whose Spirit and Presence confirms the faith of the Church (Mt. 16:17-19, 28:16-20; Jn. 20:19-23). It is not a rigid adherence to rules and norms, or a blind conformism to the law of external authority. Instead, it is the harrowing and hallowed surrender in freedom of one's life to the One who is the Way, Truth, and Life.[14]

The meeting between the soul and Christ denoted by the CSC has the effect of fostering the integrated conversion signified by the *Ignatian Paradigm*. It initiates a new consciousness of life's possibilities that leads to an awareness of one's visible sins in light of these holy stirrings of grace. As one's conversion deepens, the touch of God penetrates to the roots that fuel those sins and the intellectual and psychological defense structures that support those roots. The further one moves towards God, the more one can accomplish for Christ's work of universal reconciliation. At these critical points of conversion, there is more reason for the enemy of human nature to do everything possible to disrupt a life that is oriented to the glory of the Divine Majesty.[13]

In summary, the signature characteristics one uses to determine the authenticity of genuine spiritual consolation are these: genuine consolation will always open and enflame the heart with love for God; it will increase one's docility of spirit and one's humility; and the inclinations and choices inspired by authentic consolation will not contravene Scripture, the received Tradition or the Teaching Church. For the Spirit of God, which inspires each of them, is not divided or contradictory.

Second Benchmark:

A Signature Definition of Desolation: "Inclination to Things Low and Earthly"
  1. Defines Appetites Dissimilar to Scripture, the Received Tradition, and the Teaching Church.

St. Paul in his letter to the Colossians encourages his listeners to "put to death" those actions and aspects of self that are opposed to Christ.[15] St. Ignatius defines these Pauline attributes of the "old self" more succinctly as "inclinations to things low and earthly."[16] The Age of Authenticity celebrates and elevates such instinctual desires as benchmarks of human freedom and expressions of individuality. This would include not just sensuality but also lusts for material gain and comforts that far exceed the basic necessities of life. Inclinations and appetites that contravene Scripture, received Tradition and the Teaching Church (STTC) are, according to the measures used by Ignatius, indicators of spiritual desolation.[17] Ignatius provides guidelines for those trying to navigate the radically individualistic waters of human desire in our contemporary world.

St. Ignatius calls Satan "the enemy of human nature." Ignatius' distinctive use of human nature in his *Rules* and his definitions of desolation as "darkness of soul, turmoil of spirit, inclination to what is low and earthly," signifies an understanding of human nature that is consonant with STTC upon which his *Examination of Conscience* in the *Spiritual Exercises* is based.[18] Ignatius' own struggles with "things low and earthly" prior to his conversion—addictions to gambling, undiscriminating sexual behavior and a violent temper—are in part what ground his graced insights into the meaning of spiritual desolation and dysfunction. And together, Ignatius' strategic identification of inclinations and actions contravening the three pillars of the Church (STTC) as symptoms of desolation, create significant dissonance in an age of quieted conscience.

Ignatius' *Rules* link spiritual desolation with actions based on instinctual desires and pleasures that contravene STTC norms of truth.[19] Ignatius says that desolation is "entirely opposite" consolation and that the "thoughts that spring from consolation are the opposite of those that spring from desolation" *SpEx* [317.4]. If consolation's thoughts lead to inclinations supporting STTC, then desolation's inspirations lead one in entirely the opposite direction.

Linking desolation's "low and earthly" inclinations to the objective norms of Gospel and Ecclesial-sanctioned righteousness guarantees through the ages the reliability of Ignatius' *Rules* for Christian decision-making. Shifting the ground-rules based on the objective rightness or wrongness of moral inclinations and actions-according to individual whim compromises Ignatian discernment as a system. It dissolves and renders it useless.

Greed, materialism, anger, sexual lust and all inclinations to things "low and earthly" are things Ignatius defines as enemies of true human nature. For discernment to be effective and strategic as Ignatius intended, all such inclinations must be examined as indicators of inordinate attachments, and signs of one whose interior spiritual freedom is compromised. Helping individuals accurately identify inclinations and behaviors that fail to align with STTC and revealing them as indicators of spiritual desolation will lead the willing to probe much more deeply into their emotional, spiritual, personal and psychological history for the roots of those inclinations. The goal of Ignatian discernment is to identify "inordinate attachments" so that one can gain the freedom to more fully engage their new life in Christ and like Ignatius himself, allow God to draw out their *Sacred Story*.

Applying Insights on Ignatian Discernment Rules to Sacred Story

Purgation is the school in which Ignatius learned to discern the various spirits. *Sacred Story's* new reading of his principles employs the *Rules* as they develop organically in the *Autobiography* through his progressive purgation to illumination. The *Rules,* called "Guidelines" in *Sacred Story*, retain their basic structure as Ignatius wrote them. Cast in a semi-narrative format, they complement *Sacred Story's* introductory narrative of Ignatius' spiritual and psychological development condensed from his *Autobiography.* Detailed here are attributes that are unique to the *Rules* (Guidelines) and their application to *Sacred Story*: spiritual and psychological maturity, authenticity, inspiration, desolation and consolation as lifestyles, heart and mind illumination to new consciousness.

Spiritual and Psychological Maturity: Spiritual and psychological aspects of growth are incorporated into the language of *Sacred Story* Guidelines. The language fosters the more integrated approach to self-awakening and spiritual development vital for an effective *Examen*. The framework of two "Weeks" has been replaced with two "foundations," to distinguish the progressive dimension of spiritual/psychological maturity denoted by Ignatius' spiritual growth from Loyola to Manresa—from purgation to illumination. In the daily practice of *Sacred Story*, one moves from understanding manifest sinfulness to discovering the more subtle and nuanced dimensions of sin and temptation at the root of one's personality. This process of spiritual growth is a life-long task.

The language of fear and anxiety Ignatius employs in the *Rules* to convey the actions and marks of the "enemy," are expanded to capture the psychological aspects such fear triggers during the purgation process. This helps to mine the more therapeutic aspects of Ignatius' wisdom. The words "panic," "menacing fear" and "dread" are incorporated to help practitioners better identify the states of desolation that can actually have both spiritual and psychological manifestations.[20]

Authenticity: The word "authenticity" has been inserted into the *Sacred Story* language of "human nature." This is done to address: (1) the complications arising from surrender to the instinctual pleasures that the "Age of Authenticity" defines as normative for human flourishing and (2) the fluidity of human self-identity typical of a relativistic age. Authenticity is used to denote only those aspects of consolation that according to Ignatius' norms, spring from a source clearly distinguishable as Divine and as validated by the congruence between consolation without previous cause (CSC)- by Scripture, Tradition and the Teaching Church (STTC).

Inspiration: Today the words "consolation" and "desolation," do not readily reveal the meanings Ignatius wanted to convey. Consolation and desolation actually denote "inspirations" coming from either divine or demonic sources. What people consider the "spontaneous," the "authentic," the "real" etc. can actually spring from either a divine or a demonic source. The new *Rules* define such spontaneities as "inspirations," i.e., as people actually register them. *Sacred Story* uses the language of "inspiration" (Divine-Inspirer, counter-inspirer; divine inspiration, counter inspiration) to render Ignatius' wisdom of two spontaneities more accessible and intuitive to those using a self-guided process of discernment.

Desolation and Consolation as "Lifestyles:" Desolation and consolation as depicted in the *Exercises* are spiritual "states." They might also be considered lifestyles.[21] Consolation and desolation do not always align along the "pleasure-pain" axis. Life is not a collection of disconnected, isolated events; "time-slices" in Taylor's illustration. Life is a progressive 'story' whose purpose is a trajectory pointing toward the Divine or demonic. There is no static state in life. A person is either moving toward or away from God. People living by the "low and earthly" appetites defined as spiritual desolation have chosen a trajectory that shapes a life narrative or story. The same is true for those choosing to live by selfless love and faith.

Defining the 'states' of consolation and desolation as lifestyles is an effective way to personally apply Ignatius' insights of spiritual discernment. The *Examen's* commentators clearly delineate the challenges and pressures that the lifestyles of success and materialism pose in market-driven cultures. John English uses the biblical term "anti-Christ" to define these market forces contrary to Gospel values.[22] Another Jesuit, Bernard Lonergan, prefers to identify individual and societal progress systematically undermined by false intellectual systems and ideologies as unconsciousness or a collective blindness, but the impact is identical.[23]

It is difficult to be objective about anti-Gospel lifestyles when one's culture is in decline. The influence of a dominant culture weighted against Gospel values can be intensified by similar self-selected sub-cultures. The combined effect clouds one's ability to gain objectivity or to discern effectively. Anti-Gospel sub-cultures can be economic, political, artistic, ethnic, intellectual, sexual, athletic, addiction-based, Internet-based and so forth. An individual cocoons in these cultures, allowing its definitions of happiness, success, the good, the beautiful, and the moral to isolate that individual from the data coming from deep in their heart or from any other source. This process of cocooning marks the impenetrable individualism of the age. For these reasons, consolation and desolation have been described more comprehensively as lifestyles so one can measure the arc of one's life—one's life-style—against the traditional categories Ignatius defined as originating in either the Divine or the demonic.

The standard definitions of consolation and desolation (as Divine Inspiration and counter inspirations) have been expanded to include a broader array of words than Ignatius used, such as "single-hearted" and "cynicism." The goal is for individuals to better identify embedded attitudes and tendencies, both positive and negative, linked to prevailing life narratives and/or lifestyles.

Heart and Mind—Illumination and Awakening to New Consciousness: Ignatius awakened to new levels of consciousness as he sought the sources of the disorder in his life. The *Autobiography* recounts his initial awakening to "manifest" sins while recuperating at Loyola. The harrowing struggle with his scruples is resolved when Ignatius awakens "as if from a dream" to his damaging habit of confession and to pride—the core sin fueling it.

The *Examen's* commentators expect that the psychological dimension of sin be sourced. Ignatius would likely concur today. Along with the corruption caused by Original Sin we can only surmise the "originating sins" of the Loyola clan. In his early life, experiences that in part shape his desire for riches, honor and pride, lead him to immoral, aggressive and addictive passions that characterize his first thirty years.

The discernment narrative below compels this three-level "sourcing"—visible disorders, hidden vices and pride, and the originating sins—that can

lead to both the spiritual and psychological wounds fueling one's visible disorders. The goal is to help *Sacred Story* practitioners form an integrated and
holistic picture of their lives for effective spiritual growth.

A broken heart, lost innocence, dissolute passions and sinful pride result
from events both inflicted and chosen. We first feel the afflictions of Original
Sin through the evolutionary surge of corruption in family, culture and other
life events that distort our human nature, our physical capacities and the innocence of our hearts. Once afflicted—infected might a better word—we end up
cooperating to one degree or another with the sin and dysfunction that sickens
body, mind, and heart. In the end, there is no one without guilt and no one
without need for redemption.

An integrated picture of life can help one move beyond a narrow moralism
to understand, along with our inherited concupiscence, the "original" events
that may have helped one turn from God and make oneself a god.[24] To understand patterns, to retrace steps, to remember where one has been and how one
got to be where one is or how one is deifying oneself and things over God,
requires God's grace and enlightenment, but also an effective and strategic
method.

The terms "enlightenment," "illumination," "lost innocence," "broken
hearts," and "awakening," are used in *Sacred Story* to reinforce the sourcing and searching that await the engaged practitioner; a process that God's
grace must support.[25] The new consciousness that *Sacred Story* holds forth as
a reward is the awareness signified by a full and honest apprehension of one's
life and the need for redemption in light of God's love. *Sacred Story* offers
hope for integrated healing that leads to higher consciousness, both as positive
inducement to begin the search, and to stay the course once engaged.

Additional Reflections on the Second Foundation Choices

Ignatius' Second Week *Exercises* are dominated by "rules" "meditations"
and "considerations" that point toward life choices and the values to be sought
in making those choices. Ignatius intended the purgative process of the First
Week to initiate a dynamic during which one is asked to consider anew the
pattern of one's life and to further consider whether a "reform" of sorts is
demanded by the spiritual and psychological growth that one experiences.

The discernment method developed for *Sacred Story* is conceived as a practical application of Ignatius' *Rules* for those who daily engage the purgative path of *Sacred Story*. The individuals are not discerning life choices but rather patterns of thoughts, words and deeds that express "quest and tendency" towards or away from God. Those who engage *Sacred Story* with serious intent, however, are liable to ponder life choices and decisions as the growth process stirs up new inspirations, similar to dynamics in the *Spiritual Exercises*.

Anticipating this, an additional reflection is added in the Guidelines stressing the developments leading one to ponder new directions in life, principally the particular tensions created by opposing "inspirations" at such times. This additional reflection draws on the *Rules* appropriate to Second Week dynamics in light of those who, during the course of *Sacred Story*, are inspired to consider new lifestyles, career changes, or vocational commitments.

6

Discovering the Examen's Supernatural Powers

The Challenge of the General and Particular Examens

The *Examen's* general and particular focuses provide *Sacred Story* practitioners with the tools necessary for fundamental and integrated spiritual and psychological growth. More can be done to uncover the supernatural power of each method. The *GE* is a mystical discipline that facilitates the purgative stage of spiritual growth and the *PE* is a mystical discipline that facilitates the illuminative stage of spiritual growth. The mystical path is not glamorous but it is highly accessible to those who allow God to lead them gracefully through the narrow door. Both *Examen* modalities taken together as a single prayer discipline pull a practitioner into the supernatural world of the mystical path.

The General Examen and the Truth Paradigm

The *GE* and the discernment implicit in the *Truth Paradigm*, faithfully applied, lay the foundation for all future spiritual growth and mystical enlightenment. This is their indispensable role in Christian conversion and in Ignatius' spirituality. For the *GE* and the *Truth Paradigm* to have this power the boundaries of both the Decalogue and normative Church teachings must be respected. But sinful habits, addictive behaviors, and destructive compulsions, all of which Ignatius experienced, can have deep roots in the ecology of our soul, brain, and body.

We all have difficulty honestly naming these destroyers of soul and body as the killers they are. Finding the will or energy to resist them is part of the mystery of iniquity Merton alerted us to decades ago.[1] It is the "super-nova" of unbelief Taylor identifies today. In our individual and collective loss of vision, we erase the rules for spiritual growth and mystical enlightenment that have produced saints for the Church in every age. There are no short cuts to authentic spiritual growth and mystical enlightenment, no matter the personal freedoms permitted by the times.

For the *GE* and the *Truth Paradigm* to offer the grounding and foundational conversion with the power Ignatius envisioned, *Sacred Story* practitioners must hold to Tradition and the time-tested rules of spiritual growth and mystical enlightenment that they enshrine. This is especially true at the foundational level of conversion, identified by Ignatius and other saints schooled in the mystical journey as the "purgative" stage of development. Unless our sensual appetites and sinful, addictive passions at this purgative stage are accurately named and specifically targeted, advancement toward knowledge of our core sin and dysfunction—and the interior freedom Ignatius holds forth as the signature of his spirituality—is blocked.

It is one thing to accurately name and target these sins and addictive passions. It is quite another to work with grace for their uprooting. Christian tradition identifies Original Sin's byproduct as concupiscence. Concupiscence muddies reasoning and weakens the spiritual constitution and our will-power, making fundamental purgation particularly arduous. Sin at this level of purgation operates almost instinctually and automatically along the "pleasure-pain" axis. It operates like an addiction or a compulsion.[2]

Emerging brain science helps us understand bio-chemical factors that predispose people to sinful and addictive passions that complement the weakening of the spiritual constitution. We explored Ignatius' addictive and sinful passions in view of theories on childhood development and early trauma described by Allers, Maté, Horney and others. Maté shows how anxiety and stress are "salient in the ecology of addiction."[3] Addiction is "often a misguided attempt to relieve stress."[4] Many do not fit the clinical definition of an "addict." Everyone is afflicted with addictions of one sort or another, just as Tradition affirms that everyone is scarred by Original Sin.[5] Fundamental conversion requires the searching that Tetlow clarified, discerning "sin, my sin and sin in me." The "sin in me" is every form of Original Sin and weakness—spiritual, biochemical, cellular, psychological, physical—that fractures my being and facilitates the free choice involved in "my sin."

Advancement in the spiritual life demands the strategic and accurate naming of sins and sinful addictions whether they are "sin in me" or "my sin." Specifically targeting these sins and addictions for "purgation" is critical. Yet spiritual growth also demands merciful compassion, patience and intelligence if purgation is to succeed.

Sins and sinful addictions at the fundamental stage of conversion—lust, greed, envy, angers, laziness, gluttony and pride—wear deep ruts in our hearts, souls, and biochemical/psychological make-up. These ruts act as default drives in our lives. They are our automatic response to the emptiness, wounds and sin that have fractured our hearts and souls. As such they are not easily surrendered or uprooted (Mt 13:24-30). We all fear the emptiness in our lives without their comforts. The mystical tradition calls the byproduct of this surrender the "dark night of the senses." The addict and the sinner both weep when drugs and sinful vices are surrendered.

The strategy outlined by Ignatius in the *Truth Paradigm* (which forms the core of his First Week *Rules*) reflects a spiritual acumen closely allied to the five-level strategy Maté proposes for naming, targeting and defusing the biochemical and psychological roots of addiction. Maté's five steps are: (1) relabel; (2) re-attribute; (3) re-focus; (4) re-value and; (5) re-create. These five steps complement Ignatius' confrontation and naming of his sins and addictions as "false" sources of life and peace.[6]

Ignatius regains stability of heart when he confronts his "tempter." Similarly, Maté's research reveals that with arduous work, addictions similarly confronted and minimized can balance the brain's biochemical structure, helping to rewire its neural networks. Destructive addictions afflict people like Ignatius who are spiritually poor. Recovery demands disconnection from false lovers and reconnection with what is eternal.[7]

Sacred Story expands Ignatius' first week *Rules* (called Guidelines for Fundamental Conversion and Spiritual Growth in *Sacred Story*)) with Maté's insights, allowing Ignatius *Truth Paradigm* and his *Rules* for week one to reveal their full spiritual, psychological and physiological dimensions. The following template highlights the method:

Declare to Christ that the specific sin, addiction, or destructive compulsion is a false lover.

Describe to Christ that the specific sin, addiction or destructive compulsion comes from the enemy of your human nature.

Descend with Christ into your memory to "see" and "feel" your first experience of this specific sin, addiction or compulsion, asking him to compassionately reveal the stress fractures, loneliness and wounds in your heart that it promised to satisfy.

Denounce with Christ as your witness the sin, addiction or destructive compulsion for its ruinous effect in your life.

Decide for Christ to heal this wound, diffuse the stress, anxiety and fear feeding it, and transform its damaging effects on your life into a *Sacred Story*.

Christ tolerates nothing that destroys human nature. The incarnation has secured human nature. It has provided ample grace for the law's complete fulfillment (Mt 5:18). Christ's compassion is infinite for contrite hearts that seek him, no matter how slowly they advance along the mystical path. Most of us will labor all life long, seeking greater and greater freedom from the sinful passions and addictions that afflict our spiritual growth and erode our human nature. The sinner like the addict is always in recovery. But as Ignatius indicates, precision in naming and confronting sinful passions and addictions is absolutely essential if spiritual growth, interior freedom and enlightenment are ever to be achieved.

The Particular Examen and the Powerless Paradigm

Ignatius' marking method for a particular sin or vice includes a physical gesture (hand to the breast, etc.), to be employed during the day when one falls into its grip. Ignatius intended these exercises to compel a conscious recognition of our most damaging and oftentimes unconscious habits and patterns.

The practice can be difficult because it confronts an individual with that which is most fearful and/or humiliating and therefore not easy to face. This practice, whose goal is spiritual growth and perfection, can devolve into a narrow moralism that undermines its effectiveness.

Ignatius' "particular" discipline is absolutely indispensable for an effective *Examen*. *Sacred Story* eliminates the superficial counting system that defeats its purpose. *Sacred Story* focuses a practitioner's attention on the particular events—core sins, addictions, vices—but compels a more integrated awareness around these particulars. The goal is the same goal as the *PE*; helping practitioners awaken to the particular circumstances when such failures and/ or temptations occur, noticing their source and context in one's emotions, key relationships, and personal/family history. The goal of the *PE* is to target and eradicate "root" issues; what Rodríguez identified as "King Vice" and Rickaby the "ancient defect." A successful integrating strategy also entails awakening to and targeting originating events that Maté and others indicate helped form and fuel these destructive and disordered vices. We might call them source disorders.

Insights from Maté helped uncover intrinsic characteristics of the *GE* linked to the *Truth Paradigm* and Ignatius' First Week *Rules*. A method akin to Ignatius' *PE* developed by Michael Brown helps uncover the *PE's* intrinsic power to source formative and/or root events leading to signature weaknesses, failures, addictions and sins.[8] Brown's *The Presence Process* (*TPP*) "method" follows the same arc of discovery as the Ignatian *Examen*. *TPP*:

(1.) begins in gratitude;[9]
(2.) moves into areas of personal disorder in thoughts, words and deeds, and seeks to restore order and balance;[10]
(3.) reconnects the heart to its source of innocence in God (Inner Presence);[11]
(4.) demands surrendering arrogance that refuses to forgive others who have caused grief, anger and fear in one's life, and to acknowledge how one has passed on that grief, anger and fear to others, and;[12]
(5.) calls one to discover creation's interconnectedness[13] and insists that one embrace freedom in responsibility to become a source of love and creativity for others.[14]

The Presence Process: Perceptual Tools and the Examen

The Presence Process helps illumine the integrated human and spiritual growth that the *PE* demands. Brown's method is a ten-week process of interconnected awareness exercises that anchor a person in the "present moment," exactly like the *Examen* intends. *TPP's* principal focus is attending to negative events experienced in the immediate present to achieve awareness of "originating" events that initiated patterns of thoughts, words, and deeds blocking emotional growth. This is similar to the *PE*'s targeting of negative "root" sins and vices that block spiritual growth. The *TPP's* perceptual tools are designed to help a practitioner achieve affective awareness of these destructive patterns in the same way Ignatius wants an exercitant's awareness and emotions stirred and roused in the contemplations of sin in the *Exercises* of the First Week.

Brown focuses an individual to attend to a trinity of emotions—anger, fear (anxiety-stress) and grief—when these are triggered by some event in the course of the day. Conscious awareness of anger is central for Brown but fear (stress) and grief are also crucial.[15] Brown's method demands heightening one's emotional awareness in much the same way that Ignatius' is focused on attuning to one's affective states. Both men invite an awakening to the real state of one's mind and heart. Indeed Ignatius wants one to pray for an authentic response to the real events of sin in the world and in one's life. It is emotional memory and affective awareness that moves one toward understanding and from understanding, to conversion.

It is this affective connection to the impact of sin and vice on one's heart and soul that leads to deeper understanding and conversion. This is what the *PE* lacked when it was distorted by inviting practitioners to focus only on cataloguing sins and life events in an isolated fashion. Brown helps us re-imagine the *PE*'s strategic goal of sourcing root events for their emotional and affective content. Only an affective and emotional dynamic linked to the *PE* can help practitioners discover the key connections between their core/root sins and their emotional/psychological dysfunction. It is necessary to connect the dots for integrated growth, wholeness and holiness to be achieved.

Sacred Story's "daily exercise" augments Ignatius' daily awareness technique. It invites affective awareness of root issues blocking spiritual and emotional growth that holistic development requires if it is to be sustained. The daily exercise in *Sacred Story* marries Brown's psychodynamic process of reflective memory with Ignatius' *PE* "hand to the chest" discipline. When events in the course of the day "trigger" one's negative emotions of "grief, anger or fear (stress-anxiety)," but especially anger, the event or person that triggered the event is a "messenger." The event might "legitimately" draw one's ire, but asking for the grace of "why" one's ire, stress or grief is triggered eventually uncovers one's root sin(s) and dysfunctions. The idea of a "messenger" as valuable spiritual tool has its complement in the Western Christian tradition as well.[16]

Narcissism and Pride: The Roots of Sin and Dysfunction

Brown posits that the upset caused by a triggering event or encounter reminds one of an original event that set a pattern. The pattern causes emotional imbalance. Until one gets to the root issue, the imbalance continues to be acted out in drama where one plays the victim or the victor. Brown's intuition on the importance of these events and encounters fits well with Horney's 'resistances' revealed by anger and upsets.[17]

Horney further posits, complementing Brown that the development of neurotic trends takes on two different characteristics in those who have early life trauma. For one group, the hurts of early life develop into neurotic trends of resignation, boredom and cynicism. Horney says they turn to life's periphery. This is not unlike the reaction of victims when original points of vulnerability are touched, as described by Brown. For the second group, the hurts of early life develop into highly successful neurotic trends (impenetrable to analysis) that render one a victor. The victors refuse to make themselves vulnerable to anything or anyone that can threaten their success.[18] Maté also details a form of this dual neurotic/narcissistic structure.[19]

Brown invites the difficult process of briefly stopping in the course of the day when one encounters events and persons that touch vulnerable spots, engendering anger and upset. He further invites the awareness of how one "acts out" as a narcissistic victim or victor. He invites one to cease acting out. There are compelling similarities here to Ignatius' *Examen* mandate to gain control over one's words. Instead of acting out, Brown invites one to take the energy normally used in blaming others or seeking power over them, and turn it inwards.

The goal is to "name" the feeling (anger, hurt, fear, grief, etc.) so that healing can take place. To be healed, he says, one first needs to feel what needs healing. However, feeling oftentimes brings one back to the painful originating events that caused the failed pattern of attention getting (victim and victor) to begin with. The goal is to constructively move on with one's life.[20] *Sacred Story* takes this integrative process for events that happen during the day outside of the set time of the formal *Sacred Story* prayer sessions.

The *Sacred Story* application enlarges Brown's concept of 'victim' and 'victor' with the language of narcissism.[21] In place of the victim and victor, *Sacred Story* uses the phrases passive narcissism and aggressive narcissism. The new language allows real events during one's day that trigger anger and irritation to act as 'portals' to one's spiritual and emotional narrative. This helps individuals source the root of narcissism (pride) fueling his or her most destructive spiritual and emotional patterns. This targeting and identification is critical for integrated conversion.[22]

The narcissism people uncover in this process is congruent with the root vices the *PE* is designed to target. The process in *Sacred Story* approaches root sin and vice not in an isolated fashion but from the perspective of one's whole life narrative. The goal is to help people guide their consciousness to the 'root' origins of vice, where it exists. The goal is for these destructive emotional, spiritual and psychological superstructures, or "dramas" as Brown calls them, to be gradually dismantled by conscious attention and grace: the ultimate goal of the *PE*.

Sacred Story asks a practitioner to identify ten neuralgic events and persons from his or her past. The individual is called to 'watch' these events/ persons dispassionately and 'without condition,' 'feeling' them till they reveal to the heart the reason(s) why they create stress, pain and discomfort. Brown invites conscious awareness of significant memories (persons/events) that symbolize and signify blockages preventing emotional/spiritual growth. His technique is analogous to Ignatius' use of imagination in the *Exercises*. *Sacred Story* incorporates this persons/events exercise with additional exercises on the capital sins and the Decalogue. Allowing the *PE* to source both emotional and spiritual triggers in real time enables practitioners to see life holistically and identify the stress fractures undermining integrated spiritual growth. This is the *PE's* principal role.

Brown has "confirmations" presented before his detailed ten-week process to help people prepare for challenges of self-discovery.[23] Thumbnail wisdom from Ignatius' *Rules* (called *Affirmations*) is provided at the beginning of the *Sacred Story* process to serve this same purpose.

7

Ignatius' Life as Sacred Story

Introduction

Sacred Story enfolds the *Ignatian Paradigm* and the traditional five points of the Ignatian *General Examen and Particular Examen*. *Sacred Story's* five chapters—Creation, Presence, Memory, Mercy, and Eternity—are detailed below. The narrative of Ignatius' life, placed ahead of *Sacred Story*, gives the new five-part method context and focus. It is especially beneficial for those unfamiliar with Ignatius and his spirituality.

The paradigm of a story—a *Sacred Story*—for framing the traditional Ignatian *Examen* prayer is used for two principal reasons. First, it transforms the *Examen* from a mechanistic, solo exercise—life lived in vertical time slices—into a conscious engagement with one's entire life story encountered in the present moment. Second, it frames one's life, creation as a whole, and salvation history as interwoven narratives that have a beginning, middle and end.

The Narrative

The narrative of Ignatius' life as *Sacred Story* integrates the four paradigms (Ignatian, Truth, Powerless and Patience) with insights on confronting the challenges in praying and understanding the *Examen*. The narrative's first section tells the story of Ignatius' conversion through the lens of those four paradigms. Ignatius' initial illumination reveals the framework of the *Ignatian Paradigm*. This includes both the template for the *Spiritual Exercises* and the arc of the five-point *Examen* structure. The *Truth Paradigm,* as fundamental conversion, recognizes sin and addiction as death dealing not life giving. The *Powerless Paradigm* that describes Ignatius' battle with his root sin of pride— framed as "narcissism" in the narrative—and his evolution towards docility in stopping the scrupulous confession habit, reveals the path to integrated con- version. The *Patience Paradigm* reveals conversion not as a single event but as a daily process of surrendering control of one's life to God.

The *Sacred Story* narrative outlines a mystical path of awakening to higher consciousness that all are invited to engage. The path leads through purgation and illumination eventually to union with God. This schema of the *Examen* is in fact a condensed version of the *Spiritual Exercises*. *Sacred Story's* goal is to facilitate the dynamic process they invite.[1]

Sacred Story narrative introduces Ignatius prior to his conversion. The portrait of Ignatius exposes his matrix of sin and psychological challenges. This helps readers have a realistic context for understanding spiritual growth as a holistic process encompassing both spiritual and psychological dynamics. The stark portrayal of Ignatius' family and his personal struggles demytholo- gizes the holy card image of saints.

By not glossing over his problems, Ignatius becomes a model for all who need hope that life's difficulties can be transformed by grace. Ignatius believed that of all people in history, no person had sinned more than he, nor been given more grace. Beginning with Ignatius the proud sinner, the narrative then traces his trajectory through the first stirrings of graced insight, the awareness of his sin and disordered passions, to atonement and finally to his life of transforma- tive service.

The *Sacred Story* narrative of St. Ignatius' life directly confronts the life- long nature of the spiritual struggle towards wholeness and holiness revealed by the four paradigms. The narrative's core feature is an exploration of Ignatius' narcissistic patterns. It reveals how they are linked to the spiritual and psychological deformities in the saint's life that controlled his disordered thoughts, words, and deeds. The story consciously links the spiritual and psy- chological dimension of his personality to demonstrate that holistic growth is a process that is spiritual, emotional and psychological. The objective is to help practitioners understand the depth, complexity, and integrated character of conversion.

This integrated view of conversion intends to diffuse two types of reductionism. The first naively denies the existence of evil. It views sinful habits as merely developmental problems, dismissing both personal culpability and the moral quality of the actions. The second naively detaches evil and immoral habits from the psychological and emotional life of the examinee, seeing these habits only through a spiritual lens. When the traumas of spirit and psyche which often generate the sinful habits are left undetected and unhealed, they continue to provide the fuel for recidivistic patterns so characteristic of a stalled purgative process.

The narrative suggests that Ignatius sourced the origins of his visible sins, and progressively discovered their source in his narcissistic pride. The narrative takes this progressive dynamic one step further. It imagines that a third millennium Ignatius would source roots of his narcissistic pride in earlier childhood events and sinful family dysfunctions. Understanding the pervasive nature of Original Sin that gave rise to the unholy history of the Loyola clan, he would discover how the enemy of human nature's trinity of "riches, honor, and pride" had evolved into a family legacy.

Confronting the narcissistic matrix leads one to the roots of the visible sins. This allows God's illuminative and healing graces to uncover and slowly heal the hidden wounds of spirit and psyche fueling them. The language of "wounded heart" and "wounded innocence" compels the sourcing of early-life events to help people seek God's grace, healing and peace. When successfully confronted, the path leading to greater authenticity, renewed innocence, and higher consciousness is accessible.[2] That which can cause the most dread and anxiety for the *Sacred Story* practitioner, the matter covered in the *Powerless Paradigm*, is revealed as the means to enlightenment and peace, and the holiness of a fully integrated personality. This elemental conversion is proposed as a return to the creativity of childhood.[3]

The two crises Ignatius confronts early in his conversion, which are symbolic of the core principles of discernment from the First and Second Week *Exercises*, are discussed in the context of Ignatius' gradual awakening to the different spiritual forces at work in his life. This helps practitioners hear in Ignatius' own story the background that led to his discovery of these discernment fundamentals. This elucidates their real-life context in ways that provide practical insights for personal application.

Discernment principles are introduced into the narrative by highlighting the two sources of inspiration and the different influences these two sources produce in the heart. Utilizing Aschenbrenner's language of "two spontaneities" for describing consolation and desolation, *Sacred Story* narrative reframes Ignatius' classic categories of God and the enemy of human nature with the titles "Divine-Inspirer" and the "counter-inspirer."

The word inspiration, and the concept of "Divine-Inspirer" and "counter-inspirer," better capture the "felt experience" of both divine and demonic influences in daily life. Most people expect the Divine to be inspirational. Most do not associate the "spontaneous" feelings inspired by the demonic to "feel" right, good, natural and even holy. But they often do. Consolation and desolation are augmented with the words "white noise" and "black noise" to make them more intuitive.

Using inspiration for First Week *Rules* reframes the free expression of instinctual drives as the form of temptations Ignatius discerned in his own life that demanded conversion. These temptations are encapsulated in his definitions of desolation. Using inspiration for the Second Week *Rules* reveals that the enemy of human nature can mimic an "angel of light." The ultimate goal in using inspiration in *Sacred Story* narrative is to introduce a habit of critical reflection, forcing analysis of all "spontaneous" and/or "positive" feelings, and inviting people to investigate their source.

The social dimension of thoughts, words, and deeds is discussed, and shown to have consequences for oneself, others, and the whole created order. Every discreet thought, word and deed has significance, even if its significance is invisible to the actor involved. The dynamism of this interconnected order of creation is linked to Christ. Christ is revealed as the One who bears the burden of every malicious thought, word or deed throughout time. Christ is the one who makes a *Sacred Story* out of individual lives, creation, and all of salvation history.

As the Son of God, Christ's vulnerability to the evolutionary force of evil present in thoughts, words, and deeds, throughout history, makes him the source of salvation. He asks others to share in his reconciling work by their directing every thought, word and deed toward the same work of reconciliation.

Personal responsibility is paramount in choosing a path that produces fruit that endures to eternity, as Ignatius modeled.

The *Sacred Story* narrative proclaims that life on this earth is short. An urgent response to accept Christ's invitation to conversion is required. One is called to work wholeheartedly for universal reconciliation in this "final act" of history. This urgency addresses the *laissez faire*, time-flattened consciousness of contemporary materialism and secularism. The project of reconciliation is pressing, and one is invited to engage it daily and fearlessly. Individual decisions—thoughts, words, and deeds—all shape history's final arc. One need not fear to follow. God will provide what is needed each step of the way. The work-a-day world, business decisions and the incidentals of daily living are all inextricably wedded to eternity.

Sacred Story is an integrative process that invites one to see the world as a whole, and one's life as a significant part of salvation history. *Sacred Story* is a process that leads to a relationship with God that is heartfelt and real. The holistic perspective of *Sacred Story*, combined with deepened personal relationship with Christ, nullifies a trending toward narrow moralism (the result of an atomistic and obsessive focus on individual acts). It fosters the personal connection with Christ so central to Ignatius' spirituality.

Christ is the authority one is responding to in one's choices and decisions. In turning from the matrix of one's narcissistic, sinful vices and towards authenticity, innocence, and selfless service, it is Christ one is obeying. Christ, as foundation of the Church, transcends time and history. Christ embodies all laws. He shows us by his actions the true meaning of our human nature. Christ is the first principle of creation, sacrificial lover, and first-born from the dead in whom the universe past, present and future coheres.

Sacred Story narrative addresses those who have excused themselves from the legal requirements of Christianity. They have ignored these guidelines because they have been blinded to the Person who embodies the laws of human nature. This is an appeal to those who consider themselves "spiritual but not religious" and have buffered themselves from the objective norms of Christian discipleship. It is likewise an appeal to those whose identity and security come from a strict adherence to the rule of law and who have may never have encountered this same Person who embodies the law.

8

Sacred Story Practice and Structure

The New Examen Method: Sacred Story

Sacred Story daily practice begins each day like the *PE* with a "previsioning."[1] Ignatius devised this means to anchor his awareness in the present moment to aid discernment. The previsioning on waking takes advantage of the silent moment before rising to be aware of God and one's affective state. It is an opportunity to begin the day with an awareness of the integrated framework of *Sacred Story*: Creation, Presence, Memory, Mercy, and Eternity. One is invited to pay particular attention to upcoming events that might upend spiritual progress or erode peace of mind and heart.

At day's end there is an update of Ignatius' "marking" method. Practitioners are invited to write two short words or phrases that identify a consolation and/or desolation of the day. Writing daily but briefly reinforces *Sacred Story* practice and encourages an integrated awareness of the spiritual and psychological content of one's life. Practitioners are encouraged to focus on the day's unique failings and angers, i.e., the content specific to the *PE*. The marking exercise reinforces the awareness of Creation, Presence, Memory, Mercy, and Eternity that serve as *Sacred Story* frames. Practitioners should be mindful of all these themes when noteworthy experiences happen.

The day concludes with a bookend exercise to the morning's previsioning. In his additional directions for prayer in the *Exercises'* First Week, Ignatius highlights the moments before falling asleep and after waking to call attention to what one is seeking *SpEx* [73-74].[2] Incorporating this evening exercise in *Sacred Story* stimulates a conscious pattern to pay attention to the critical event of the day, bring it before God, and invite God to work in one's heart in the unconsciousness of sleep.

At week's end the *Sacred Story* practitioner is requested to review the week's "markings" and to discern any patterns that emerge. Of particular interest are patterns that deal with the core matrix of spiritual and psychological issues discerned to be most detrimental to integrated spiritual growth. The exercise is repeated each week, and at months end. The weekly summaries are culled for insights that might bring hope, consolation and awareness of integrated growth. This adaptation of the *PE* marking method respects Ignatius' original intent. He wanted an individual to source and track root vices. *Sacred Story* method incorporates the necessary spiritual and psychological dynamic of a "life-story," retaining sourcing as an integrated exercise leading to insight and growth.[3]

The application of *Sacred Story* prayer method is just like the practice of the *Examens*: it can be done daily; at mid-day and in the evening. Practitioners are invited to bring the issues of annoyance and the strong emotions that surface during the half-day prior to each prayer (this is the data relevant to the classic *PE*). Two options are given for praying *Sacred Story.* Both correspond to methods of prayer Ignatius suggests in the *Spiritual Exercises.*[4] To foster an integrated reflection process and real-time discernment, the practitioner is to open and close each session of *Sacred Story* prayer with an inward recitation of each word: "Creation, Presence, Memory, Mercy, and Eternity."

Two options are given for closing prayers: the traditional *Our Father*, as suggested by Ignatius, and his *Suscipe*. The *Our Father* is highlighted as the traditional prayer and placed first. The *Suscipe* is offered as an alternate prayer for those who may prefer it or find prayer to God as Father difficult.

Sacred Story: Five-Point Examen Structure

The *Sacred Story* structure itself incorporates the *Ignatian Paradigm* and the combined *GE* and *PE*:

CREATION	A graced experience of God's love opened Ignatius to: ⇨ ⇩	**GIVE THANKS FOR FAVORS RECEIVED** ⇩
PRESENCE	A dissatisfaction with vain fantasies which led to surrendering to holy day-dreams, characterized by consolation, which in turn: ⇨ ⇩	**PRAY FOR GRACE TO SEE CLEARLY** ⇩
MEMORY	Caused him to review his life and actions leading to: ⇨ ⇩	**GIVE A DETAILED ACCOUNT OF CONSCIENCE: GENERAL AND PARTICULAR** ⇩
MERCY	Grief with yearning for penance and repentance for his past sins, culminating in: ⇨ ⇩	**ASK PARDON FOR ONE'S FAULTS** ⇩
ETERNITY	Ignatius' passion to amend his life and a desire to love God wholeheartedly. ⇨	**RESOLVE AND AMEND TO SERVE GOD**

Creation, Presence, Memory, Mercy, and Eternity

Each of the *Sacred Story's* five points or chapters (Creation, Presence, Memory, Mercy, and Eternity) unites thematically with the traditional five points of the combined *PE* and *GE*. The five-point structure elucidates each element of the method in three ways: (1) a single word that can be easily remembered; (2) a single sentence that defines the theme and specific graces sought; and (3) a longer narrative that frames the particular theme, similar to a typical Ignatian meditation in the *Spiritual Exercises,* with a prelude and a request for the specific graces sought.

Sacred Story's milieu is transcendent, reaching from creation to eternity. Each person's life history is situated in this transcendental template as an integrated component of the whole created order; every thought, word, and deed, energetically linked by creation's intimate and deliberate design. So-called private, discreet acts—all thoughts, words and deeds—are framed to have both social significance and consequence. Detailed below is a brief synopsis of each of *Sacred Story's Examen* components:

CREATION:

(The Context*)* A personal, loving God made everything in the cosmos, including each individual person. Everything coheres in Christ, through whom and for whom everything was made. All is a gift, given by the God of Love who desires to share love with others. One should express gratitude for the gift of life, the gifts of creation and the Love that brought all into being. This is the Love that Ignatius awakened to while recovering from his injuries at Loyola. Each person prays to understand the Love through whom one is "fearfully and wonderfully made" (Ps. 139:14). Each person prays to see they are physically and spiritually linked through Love in Christ to all of creation, and to all of humanity.

(The Sacred Story Method) Creation is viewed as an interconnected web, i.e., all life is social, and all individuals are brought into being by Love and for love. One prays for gratitude and for a personal, transformative experience of God's love for "my unique creation," and to see my unique creation as a vital component of the entire Divine cosmic order.

PRESENCE:

(The Context) The gifts of life and the God of life are found in the present moment, not in the past or the future. One's awareness of God, and of the state of one's life and heart, can only be discovered by anchoring both in each and every moment of the day; in every thought, word and deed. This was Ignatius' discovery as he awakened to both holy and narcissistic daydreams during his convalescence at Loyola. Ignatius' awareness of the spiritual movements that created consolation and desolation resulted from his close attention to his thoughts and moods in the present moment. Reflecting on his reflections, he discerned the true self from the false self once the feelings and inspirations dissipated. Ignatius always lived in the present moment.

(The Sacred Story Method) Inviting practitioners to anchor mind and heart in the present moment challenges the time-flattened consciousness of secular and materialistic mindsets. It proclaims that one's awareness, rooted in the present moment, activates the place of privileged encounter with the Divine. It allows one to experience life, open one's heart to God, and be blessed with a heightened consciousness of God, self, and the whole created order.

MEMORY:

(*The Context*) Ignatius awoke to his lost innocence reflecting on his past deeds. He was allowed to feel the real impact of those deeds on his heart and in his life. Anchoring one's heart and mind in the present moment provides access to one's memory of deeds committed both by and against oneself. One seeks the grace to awaken to and feel the difference between "sin, my sin and sin in me." Violations against love done to me and by me, all form part of sin's evolution. The evolution of sin is what the Incarnation, life, death and resurrection of Christ has definitively conquered. The most public face of sin's evolution is narcissism and pride that wounds God, self, others and creation. Narcissism shields one from seeing life honestly. It cripples each person's ability to hear and freely respond to the unique role God urges them to embody for Christ's work of universal reconciliation.

(The Sacred Story Method) The matrix of sins and injuries—spiritual, psychological and physical—whose evolutionary imprint one receives from family and society, are the prime target of the *PE*. Graced awareness is sought to remember, name, and perceive any destructive spiritual and psychological events whose injury to one's human nature reverberates to the present day. This nexus of sin and psychological compulsions experienced as a "loss of innocence," left unlinked and unexplored, blocks spiritual growth. It will lead to recidivism, voluntarism, a narrow moralism, and finally, a failed purgation. The *Sacred Story* method is designed to link these two realities: (1) sins committed against a person and; (2) sins committed by a person. This dual reflection is offered to better assist those whose radioactive memories of being "sinned against" have effectively blocked reflection or consideration of one's own personal sinfulness. It is designed to help practitioners link critical events in their life narrative. It is essential that we as individuals understand the evolution of sin in our lives and ask for forgiveness for our own "trespasses," while offering to forgive those who have "trespassed against us."

MERCY:

(The Context) Remembering his loss of innocence, in ways both particular and general, Ignatius felt both remorse and a desire for reconciliation. Ignatius "knew" God's love for him even in the very depths of his sinfulness. Through his weaknesses, he had a personal encounter with Christ in whose mercy, forgiveness and love he was spiritually reborn.

(The Sacred Story Method) Events that damage hearts, destroy hope, and mar our true human nature become, through God's mercy and forgiveness, the cornerstones of a new life—they become our *Sacred Story*. The acceptance of God's mercy for one's trespasses, and offering that same mercy to others who have "trespassed against us," unlocks the heart's imagination to see the world as a whole. The social dimension of sin is disclosed, as are the social ramifications of forgiveness and redemption. All creation is affected by our personal acceptance of God's forgiveness for our trespasses, and when we extend that same gift of forgiveness and reconciliation to others who trespass against us. Accepting this mercy, and granting it to others, opens our hearts and minds to the experience of the world as a whole and the higher consciousness this bestows. It sets the stage for opening our hearts and imaginations so that we may hear and feel Christ's invitation to work with Christ for universal reconciliation.

ETERNITY:

(The Context) The mercy and forgiveness Ignatius received reshaped his entire life vision. The energy released by forgiveness and reconciliation gave him the freedom to follow the unique path God opened to him. His anti-story became *Sacred Story*, contributing mightily to God's universal work of reconciliation. Ignatius' journey began with a desire to give his life to God. It was expressed first in the Jerusalem sojourn and concluded in Rome with the birth and growth of the Society of Jesus.

(The Sacred Story Method) Christ seeks out those who are lost: the broken hearted; those whose lives are shattered; those who "labor and are overburdened" (Mt 11:28). To those who have become childlike through forgiveness, he reveals the mysteries of the Kingdom of Heaven. In this knowledge, one gradually learns, through grace, how to make each thought, word, and deed serve this eternal King and his Kingdom. Everyone dreams his or her life can make a difference - not for just fifteen minutes of fame, but for a life producing fruit that endures to eternity. One longs for authenticity. The path of Creation, Presence, Memory and Mercy opens one to Eternity. Eternity represents the hope, love, joy, meaning, peace, authenticity and union with God, heart-to-heart, that every person has sought since time immemorial.

Part Three

Writing Your Sacred Story

Enter through the narrow gate; for the gate is wide and the road broad that leads to destruction, and those who enter through it are many. How narrow the gate and constricted the road that leads to life. And those who find it are few.

ଔ

Come to me, all you who labor and are burdened, and I will give you rest. Take my yoke upon you and learn from me, for I am meek and humble of heart; and you will find rest for your selves. For my yoke is easy, and my burden light.

—Matthew 7:3-15; 11:8-30

9

Sacred Story Introduction

Rules of Engagement

The *Sacred Story Examen* is modeled on St. Ignatius' classic spiritual discipline and is a proven path to spiritual growth. It is the narrow road but the one taken by many saints in the Church's history. If you feel ready to make your faith and Christ the center of your life, you will find no better daily spiritual prayer discipline. Divine love is an abiding relationship that God invites you to share daily. Here are some things to help you discern whether this prayer at this time in your life is right for you when it comes to entering into a daily, abiding love relationship with God.

cs If you are looking for quick fixes to spiritual or psychological problems you will soon lose heart. The full healing of your wounds, and the path to complete peace, only begin on this earth. You will achieve no final victory for what ails you this side of eternity but you will find the path to that final victory.

cs If you seek confirmation of religious or political biases you will be frustrated and possibly angry. Surrendering fixed ideologies and a judgmental heart is required fare on your *Sacred Story* journey.

ᏅᎦ   If you live principally by rules and laws or if you eschew all rules and laws, you will be terrified. For those who live only by laws will confront the fierce Love that exceeds all laws. And those who scoff at laws will discover that Love has unambiguous boundaries of right and wrong.

ᏅᎦ   If you are being asked to do these spiritual exercises to fulfill someone else's agenda, or for any sort of program requirement, kindly tell your sponsor, "no thank you." Tell your sponsor that the author of the exercises affirms that unless you engage them in complete free-dom you will fail in their practice and ruin their purpose.

So how can you tell if you should engage this prayer? St. Ignatius believed his exercises worked best for those who have a generous heart and who are aware that they need God's help.

✠   Jesus proclaimed that the sick needed a Physician, not the well (Mk. 2:17). Of course we are all sick but only those willing to see their spiritual ills will submit to the Divine Physician's healing embrace in these exercises. So if you know you are ill and believe you can't get better without God's help, welcome.

✠   Jesus calmed the storm that terrified his disciples (Mk. 5:35-41). You should engage these exercises if you are frightened about the chaos in your life, and believe God is calling you to the shore and to security.

✠   Jesus can heal chronic illness but he has come to forgive us our sins and open to us eternal life (Lk. 5:17-26). You should engage in these exercises if you have yet to experience Jesus' power to forgive your sins.

✠   Jesus encouraged John the Baptist and his followers not to take offense at him when their faith in Christ brought them suf-fering and threats (Mt. 5:2-6). You should engage these exercise if the practice of your faith is causing you to suffer persecution for

Christ's sake. Hold fast to belief in him as the Son of God and take no offense.

✠ Jesus invited the weary and the overburdened to find rest in Him (Mt. 11:25-30). You should engage these exercises if you are weary with your life and find yourself overburdened.

✠ Jesus invited the rich young man to surrender his possessions and follow Him (Mk. 10:17-25). You should engage these exercises if you are ready to let go of what is holding you down and are willing to follow a new path.

✠ Jesus invited Zacchaeus to come down from his tree and follow Him home (Lk. 19:1-10). You should engage these exercises if your privilege, position and honors have not brought you the peace, security and hope they promised.

✠ Jesus invited the woman of Samaria to drink the living water that wells up to eternal life (Jn. 4:4-42). You should engage these exercises if you are ready to surrender the cynicism of failed love and relationships, are ready to forgive and to move forward with your life.

✠ Jesus chided the work-anxious Martha to allow Mary to sit at his feet (Lk. 10:38-42). You should engage with these exercises if you are ready to sit still awhile each day and listen to the Kingdom within.

✠ Jesus invited Peter to join him in his work (Lk. 5:10-11). You should engage these exercises if you trust that your sins, addictions and failures do not limit Jesus' desire to take your hand in discipleship as he writes your *Sacred Story*.

✠ Jesus invited the Gerasene Demoniac to tell him his name (Mk. 5:1-20). You should engage these exercises if you are weary of your spiritual, psychological, and material demons. You should engage these exercises if you are willing, with Jesus by your side, to name them and allow him to exorcise and heal the spiritual and psychic darkness—the habits, sins, and addictions—that rob you of freedom and peace.

✠   God invited Mary not to fear but to say "yes" and participate in the eternal plan of salvation (Lk. 1:26-38). You should engage these exercises if you are ready to let your heart be Christ's home and so labor with Him for universal reconciliation.

✠   Jesus invited his disciples to dine with him (Jn. 15:1-17). You should enter *Sacred Story* if you desire unbounded love, joy, peace and a share in Jesus' glory—and his sufferings—that endure to eternity.

✠   Jesus invited anyone wishing to follow him to deny themself, pick up their cross daily, and follow him (Lk. 9:23). You should engage these exercises if you can willingly submit to letting Christ reveal your narcissism, and with his grace, daily confront its negative impact so he can transform your life into *Sacred Story*.

✠   Jesus invited his disciples to keep a vigilant heart and reject carousing and drunkenness as well as entrapment in the anxieties of life, lest they be surprised and assaulted on the day of the Son of Man (Lk. 21:34-36). You should engage these exercises if today is your day to hearken to the Son of Man, and to return to God with all your heart.

ભ

Creating Sacred Space

Sacred Story—Sacred Space: Choose one or two times each day when you can honor a fifteen-minute space of contemplative rest and reflection. Be specific about the time of day, and maybe the place, or places you can find these moments of reflective quiet. Everything you do with *Sacred Story* from this moment forward will be sustainable when you make a decision to step away once or twice a day. Those who have diligently practiced the *Sacred Story* method to its full potential and benefit have proven this to be true.

You will receive further guidance on how to structure these times of quiet and what to do with them. For now it is sufficient to choose the time of quiet and to ask God daily to strengthen your resolve and desire for these times of reflection. Your fidelity to *Sacred Story* depends less on you and more on your decision… to ask God… to help you… to be faithful.

❧

Sacred Story Affirmations

The *Sacred Story Affirmations* sketch out most of the spiritual dynamics you will encounter in your journey with *Sacred Story* prayer. As your first spiritual disciplines in the journey take some days to reflectively contemplate the *Affirmations* for your *Sacred Story* practice. Use your fifteen-minute *Sacred Story* discipline for this purpose. Take as many days as you desire to listen to them. Don't limit the number of days or sessions you spend with them. Your heart, by its peacefulness, will lead you forward to the next exercises at the right time. Trust your heart to lead you.

As you awaken to *Sacred Story Affirmations*, listen also for all the persons, events, and issues in your life that cause fear, stress, anxiety, anger or grief. When these feelings/emotions surface, notice how and if they connect with the affirmations that you are contemplating. Always listen with your heart to the events, issues, and persons in your life story. Listen to how or why these events, issues, and persons may be linked to the spiritual, emotional and moral dimension of your experiences of grief, anxiety, stress, anger and fear.

Remember, *Sacred Story* often focuses attention on things that are difficult and sometimes painful to experience. But it is vital to focus attention on difficulties in your life history that rob you of hope, joy, love, and freedom so you can achieve greater peace. Take as long as you desire to reflect on the affirmations of your *Sacred Story*. The affirmations are on the following pages.

❧

SACRED STORY AFFIRMATIONS

My *Sacred Story* takes a lifetime to write.

Be Not Afraid:
Fear comes from the enemy of my human nature.

The pathway to God's peace and healing runs through my heart's brokenness,
sin, fear, anger and grief.

God resolves all my problems with time and patience.

☙

I will have difficulties in this life.

There are just two ways to cope with my difficulties.
One leads to life, one to death. I will choose life.

☙

"Impossible" is not a word in God's vocabulary.

Sacred Story leads to my freedom and authenticity,
but does not always make me feel happy.

☙

My life's greatest tragedies can be transformed
into my life's major blessings.

Times of peace and hope always give way to times of difficulty and
stress.

Times of difficulty and stress always give way to times of peace and
hope.

☙

I will not tire of asking God for help
since God delights in my asking.

The urge to stop *Sacred Story* practice
always comes before my greatest breakthroughs.

ভ

God gives me insights, not because I am better than others,
but because I am loved.

The insights and graces I need to move forward in life's journey
unfold at the right time.

ভ

My personal engagement with *Sacred Story* accomplishes, through Christ, a
work of eternal significance.

Inspirations can have a divine or a demonic source. I pray for the grace to
remember how to discern one from the other.

ভ

Christ, who has walked before me, shares my every burden.

Christ, who has walked before me, will help me resolve every crisis.

Christ, who has walked before me, knows my every hope.

Christ, who has walked before me, knows everything I suffer.

Christ, who walks before me, will always lead me home to safety.

ভ

I will strive to curb temptations to react to people and events.
I will ask myself what causes my anger and irritation at people and events.
I will seek to identify the source of my anger and irritation.

121

I will give thanks for what angers and upsets me;
for identifying their source will help to set me free.

I will strive to listen, watch and pray; listen, watch and pray.
I will listen, watch and pray!

CR

Everyone has been mortally wounded spiritually, psychologically, and
physically by Original Sin and the loss of paradise.

Journeying with Christ to the roots of my sins and addictions
will help break their grip.

I will not waste time worrying about my sins and failures.
I will use my time wisely and ask God to help me
understand the source of my sins and failings .

I will trust that Christ came to heal all my wounds.

CR

I alone control Christ's ability to transform my life into a *Sacred Story.*
The process begins when I ask for the grace to
honestly name my sins and addictions.

The process continues when I invite Christ to illuminate my narcissism.

Only God's grace and mercy can write my *Sacred Story.*

CR

I will strive daily to pick up the cross, for it leads to my life.

The closer I get to holiness, the more I will see and feel sin's disorder in my
life.

The more I experience sin's disorder, the more tempted I will
be to disbelieve my life as *Sacred Story.*

The way through the temptation is to surrender my powerlessness to God.

ɞ

It is never too late to open my heart to Christ
and live my life as *Sacred Story.*

Christ, who is close to the brokenhearted, restores my lost innocence.

The path to my *Sacred Story* is
Creation, Presence, Memory, Mercy, and Eternity.

ɞ

Your heart is prepared and you have awakened to the path you are to take.
Trust it. Remember: Do not read ahead. Do not exercise ahead. Awaken to
the present moment. Take each day, and each exercise as it comes.

ɞ

I am starting a Relationship that will carry me
for the rest of my life.

I will learn the fundamentals and strive to
open my heart to God.

I trust that God will lead me.

I believe that my *Sacred Story* will unfold in truth,
in powerlessness and with my patience.

I believe that Jesus awaits me with His grace, mercy and forgiving love.

What do I need for this journey?
a generous heart;
the willingness to take 15-minutes to pray daily
and the humility to always ask God for help.

ɞ

Now your heart is set and you have awakened to the path you are to take. Trust your heart. If the path leads to the *Sacred Story* practice, following a single Rule during these preparation weeks will help you immensely. The Rule: Do not read ahead—do not exercise ahead. Stay in the present moment. Take each day, and each exercise, as it comes.

In fact, spend more days than suggested on each exercise if you so desire. The exercises are incremental and build on each other. Doing them slowly and in order will help you stay better focused and live in the present moment. Listen to your heart in the present moment. God is in the present moment. By anchoring your heart in the present moment the *Sacred Story* prayer will by God's grace and your free submission lead you to the deepest desires of your heart. Trust and don't read or exercise the disciplines out of their natural order in *Sacred Story*.

You are starting a relationship.
The Relationship will carry you for the rest of your life.
It is best to learn the fundamentals.
It is best to strive for a heart open to God.
It is best to stay focused on the present moment.
It is best to trust that God will lead you.
It is best to believe that your Sacred Story will unfold.
It is best to trust it will unfold in truth, powerlessness and in patience.
It is best to trust God on how quickly or slowly this process takes.
It Is Best To Trust God.

CR

SACRED STORY SPIRITUAL GUIDELINES

Distinguishing Divine Inspirations from the Enemy's Counter-Inspirations and How to Act in Each Case

Introduction

You will have days, weeks, months and years to read and benefit from the wisdom and guidance of Ignatius' *Rules for Spiritual Discernment*. The *Guidelines* below are modeled on Ignatius' classic *Rules* and in order to help you navigate the spiritual journey of discovering your *Sacred Story*. They summarize the emotional and affective experiences linked to your integrated human growth that is both spiritual and psychological. You will soon discover that inspirations coming from a Divine source do not always make you feel good and that inspirations from an unholy source do not always make you feel bad. Divine <u>and</u> unholy inspirations do not conveniently line up along the pleasure/pain axis we would normally expect. Discernment requires a consciously attuned heart and mind capable of listening for the deeper meaning and true source of any and all inspirations.

Take a week to slowly and reflectively read over *Benchmark One* and *Benchmark Two Guidelines*. They form a thumbnail sketch describing differences between inspirations that come from a Divine source, and those that come from an unholy source—what Ignatius calls "the enemy of human nature." The benchmark rules may not make sense at the beginning of your *Sacred Story* journey. By reading them now, you will awaken your heart to a habit of deep listening. In time you will discover profound spiritual forces at work. The Latin root for the word "obey" means to "listen deeply." What you are awakening to is a habit of deep listening and seeking to obey the most authentic inspirations of your human nature—your heart.

Come back to the full set of *Guidelines* once you have been engaging in the daily practice of *Sacred Story*. This begins in Week Twelve to Eternity. Let the *Guidelines* be a resource and tool when you find yourself getting confused and/or frustrated. You will find in them the guidance you need to figure out what you are experiencing—and what to do about it.

Creation and Salvation

God willed that human nature be spiritual and physical. We are a unity of body and soul. The gift of this blessed unity of human nature in paradise made us immortal. The turning from God we call Original Sin broke the perfect unity of human nature: body and soul. As a result, we lost the perfect control over our physical nature that resulted from our complete spiritual unity with God—lusts and other physical desires of our lower nature (concupiscence) battled with our higher spiritual nature, distorting our authentic identity as children of God. Our conscience was clouded and we lost sight of right and wrong. Disease, strife, suffering and death resulted.

The Original Sin also broke our perfect unity with God's loving will. Broken too was the harmony between male and female and their relationship with creation. Paradise was an ecstasy of harmonious relationships. Original Sin broke all relationships and broke our hearts. The Ten Commandments, revealed to the people of Israel, are one of the most significant gifts from God to help us re-learn "right relationships." In the New Covenant, Christ is the ultimate revelation of God. Christ's life and message is the most perfect expression of how each of us is called to live. This is why Judeo/Christianity is a "revealed religion." We did not come to the truth by our own reasoning processes. It had to be revealed to us. The authoritative interpreter responsible for guaranteeing the meaning of "right relationship" according to revealed truth is the Teaching Church. It is the Church that Ignatius served and loved.

It is no wonder that Ignatius' discernment rules are spiritual boundaries that help us understand the revealed truth of "right relationships" in our own lives. Ignatius' rules are discovered by our paying close attention to inspirations that we register as affective feelings. The inspirations affecting our human nature (spirit-body) can originate from three different sources according to St. Ignatius.

1) They can originate from our own human nature, as a unity of spirit/body.

2) They can originate from a Divine source that Sacred Story names the "Divine Inspirer", or

3) They can originate from a demonic source, the one Ignatius names "the enemy of human nature" and that *Sacred Story* names "the counter inspirer".

Two Benchmark Guidelines for Spiritual Discernment

To help your awakening and initiation into spiritual discernment two benchmark guidelines are offered below that you will find helpful in many life situations. It is important to understand that Divine inspiration called consolation does not always feel good. Equally important is to realize that an unholy inspiration called spiritual desolation does not always feel bad. We will explore this seeming paradox in a later lesson. For now, learn the two benchmark guidelines and realize both are intended to influence the direction of our life towards or away from God in every thought, word and deed.

Benchmark One:

Authentic divine inspirations called consolations will always have specific features. They will:

1) Increase in your heart love for God and others.
2) Increase your heart's docility, humility and selflessness.
3) Never oppose truths and teachings proposed by Scripture, the Tradition and the teaching Church, for the same Spirit guides both your life and the Church.

Consolation can be the consequence of the Divine Physician's Spirit working in you. This form of consolation helps strengthen your heart and soul, helping and encouraging you to turn to God. Consolation helps you to choose thoughts, words and deeds that express your authentic human nature made in the Divine image. Consolation can also be the consequence of the body/spirit aspect of your Divinely-shaped human nature. God created your human nature as a gift in the Divine image and likeness. Yet in spite of Original Sin's impact, cooperating with God's grace activates embedded life forces of your Divinely-shaped human nature helping heal biochemical, physiological and emotional imbalances; energizing you, and increasing thoughts, words, and deeds that express your authentic human nature.

Benchmark Two:

Authentic counter-inspirations called desolations will always have specific features. They will:

1) Increase in your heart narcissism, displacing God and others.

2) Decrease your heart's docility and humility but increase your pride and self-satisfaction.

3) Stir in you hungers and desires that, although they feel good, will frequently contradict the truths and teachings proposed by Scripture, Tradition, and the teaching Church. This is because the spirit that brings counter-inspirations is opposed to Christ and will always lead you away from life and truth. You are led away from God and truth with counter-inspirations. The desires produced feel authentic because they are linked to fallen human nature's physical lusts and spiritual pride.

Desolation can be the consequence of the enemy of human nature working in you. This form of desolation helps weaken your heart and soul, discouraging you from turning to God. Desolation helps you choose thoughts, words and deeds that are opposed to your Divinely-shaped human nature. Desolation can also be the consequence of your own fallen human nature. God created your human nature as a gift in the Divine image and likeness. Because of Original Sin's impact, not cooperating with God's grace erodes embedded life forces of your Divinely-shaped human nature. This helps diminish biochemical, physiological and emotional balance; de-energizing you, and increasing thoughts, words and deeds that are the opposite of your authentic human nature.

Guidelines for Fundamental Healing and Spiritual Growth

The practice of *Sacred Story* prayer brings to consciousness spiritual forces at work both in your life and in the world. Ignatius became a master discerner of these spiritual movements. He left us guidelines for understanding how they work. You have learned already that there are three distinct sources influencing your thoughts, words, and deeds: (1) your own emotional, psychological, and intellectual make-up shaped by concupiscence and your unique history; (2) the Divine inspiration of consolation working to draw your thoughts, words, and deeds in the direction of your authentic human nature; and (3) the counter-inspirations of the enemy of your true human nature, seeking to pull you away from your authentic self.

God as Divine Inspirer, and the enemy of human nature as counter inspirer, both seek ultimate influence over how your history unfolds: one for eternal love and life, one for eternal despair and death; one for eternal relationships, one for eternal loneliness. They both work through your strengths, weaknesses, wounded memories, hopes, dreams, and fears. God seeks to stir your conscience towards light. The enemy of human nature seeks to silence your conscience and hide it in shadows.

We identify and distinguish Divine inspirations from counter-inspirations by their intellectual and affective signatures. Ignatius defines two affective or emotional states. The first state caused by Divine inspiration of the Spirit he calls "consolation". The second state, caused by the counter-inspiration of the enemy of your human nature, he calls "desolation".

Divine Inspiration

The signature characteristics of Divine inspiration called consolation mark a healing heart returning to God and/or residing in God. God always seeks movement towards reconciliation and union. The signature characteristics of Divine Inspiration include being passionate about God and loving all things in God. They include tears of remorse and sadness when you fail, but feeling loved by God in your failures nonetheless. Also included are tears of love for Christ who suffered the consequences of all sin, including your own and every increase in love, hope and faith that magnetizes your heart towards holy things (salvation and complete reunion with God). It also includes all experiences of peace and quiet in the presence of your Creator. The Divine inspiration of consolation is manifest in humility that views eternal life, lasting love, and faith in God as the hope of the single-hearted, and the ultimate goal of those willing to risk seeing reality as it truly is.

Counter-Inspiration

Counter-inspiration, also called spiritual desolation, is characterized by real inspiration, though of a type opposite creative Divine inspiration. Counter-inspiration promotes the darkness and turmoil of a broken and wounded heart, soul, and spirit; magnetic and compulsive attractions to sensual, base and animalistic appetites. Counter-inspiration causes restlessness, anger, cynicism, and temptations that make all things geared towards faith, hope and love appear dull, absurd and destructive to your heart. Your spirit will feel lazy, lukewarm and sad, as if separated from God. The counter-inspiration of desolation is everything that magnetizes a broken heart towards cynicism, lusts, isolation, anger, despair and aloneness. The counter-inspiration of desolation is manifest in an unyielding pride that views eternal life, lasting love, and faith in God as the illusions of the simple-minded, and the result of those unwilling to risk seeing reality as it is.

Interpreting Your Feelings

Divine inspirations called consolations can make you feel bad even if they move you toward your authentic human nature. This is valid for both our lower physical nature and our higher spiritual nature. If you are trapped in illicit physical pleasures of one type or another, the spiritual inspiration to cut loose from those pleasures can make you feel distress and anxiety. Remember how Ignatius felt distress when he realized that he would have to live without the pleasures of his first thirty years for the rest of his life? He panicked. What is true of your lower nature is also true of your higher nature. For example, if you are trapped in illicit spiritual pleasures, say a false definition of success has shaped your life, you may similarly feel distress and anxiety in letting your sense of identity be transformed. You know it is a false identity but it is a familiar identity.

You are likely to feel bad in contemplating a change in how you define success. Why? Because of the uncertainty of what lies beyond the false definition of success. It may feel like a frightening void. In these instances, the inspiration to change can create distress and anxiety. Nevertheless, the fear aroused in your heart by the invitation to change needs to be strongly confronted. Why? You have to confront the fear because you are being invited towards life, not death. In these cases, you must learn to go in the opposite direction of the fear and confront the false pleasures.

Counter-inspirations, called desolations, can make you feel good even if they move you away from your authentic human nature. If you are trapped in illicit physical pleasures of one type or other, the spiritual inspiration to stay committed to those pleasures can make you feel comforted—feel good. The inspiration will be to "stay just where you are," and will most likely be supported by all manner of logical justifications for why it is the best thing not to make a change. What is true of your lower nature is also true of your higher nature. For example, if you are trapped in illicit spiritual pleasures, say a false definition of success that has shaped your life, you may feel comforted—feel good—staying committed to that false identity. You will be persuaded to "stay just where you are" in the false identity and to commit to its values with all manner of logical justifications for why it is best not to make a change. You have learned consciously or unconsciously not to go in the direction of fear. Nevertheless, the fear that the invitation to change stirs up in you needs to be strongly confronted. Why? You have to confront the fear because you are being invited towards life, not death. In these cases you must learn to go in the opposite direction of the fear.

It is critical to understand that inspirations caused by the Divine-Inspirer, and also those of the counter-inspirer, can both feel good or feel bad, depending on the state of your heart and soul. So always keep an eye on the direction the inspirations lead, more than whether inspirations make you feel good or feel bad. Do they lead toward an increase of faith, hope, and love, or the opposite? Take Note!

Examining Lifestyles

Divine inspirations and counter inspirations can manifest as lifestyles. We can be invested to a greater or lesser degree in lifestyles aligned with life or death. The book of Deuteronomy captures this reality. The people of Israel are presented with two choices; two narratives or plot lines:

> See, I have today set before you life and good, death and evil. If you obey the commandments of the LORD, your God, which I am giving you today, loving the LORD, your God, and walking in his ways, and keeping his commandments, statutes and ordinances, you will live and grow numerous, and the LORD, your God, will bless you in the land you are entering to possess If, however, your heart turns away and you do not obey, but are led astray and bow down to other gods and serve them, I tell you today that you will certainly perish; you will not have a long life on the land which you are crossing the Jordan to enter and possess.

I call heaven and earth today to witness against you: I have set before you life and death, the blessing and the curse. Choose life, then, that you and your descendants may live, by loving the LORD, your God, obeying his voice, and holding fast to him. For that will mean life for you, a long life for you to live on the land which the LORD swore to your ancestors, to Abraham, Isaac, and Jacob, to give to them (Dt. 30: 15-20).

Divine Inspiration as a Lifestyle

Are you evolving under the Divine inspirations aligned to thoughts, words and deeds harmonious with the Scripture, Commandments and the Teaching Church? If so, the Divine author of your human nature provides heart verification to alert you to thoughts, words and deeds that can move you off the true path. He does this through awakening your reason and conscience. You will feel sadness, anxiety, grief and remorse from thoughts, words, and deeds leading away from God. God grants these feeling if you are moving towards the counter-inspirations of anti-love—anti-Christ. Such feelings can be difficult, and at times very intense. Yet they are a gift and a sure sign that engaging the Gospel values grounding your faith practice and belief will result in the peace and hope you seek.

Counter Inspiration as a Lifestyle

Are you are evolving under the counter-inspirations opposed to Love? Are your thoughts, words and deeds opposed to the Commandments, Scripture and the Teaching Church? The enemy of human nature is able to hold you in the grip of your disordered appetites by deceit and false appearances. What leads you away from God and Love appears pleasurable; it is presented as good and life-giving. Leading away from the sheltering safety of God's love and your authentic human nature, these extravagant appetites, are aptly named false loves. But they are false loves that speak powerfully to broken hearts. If you are in the grip of the counter-inspirations of these false loves you will feel aversion to engaging the Gospel values or be hostile to the Commandments and guidelines of the Teaching Church. Or, if in the grip of counter-inspiration, you will experience difficulty in the practice of faith and persevering in it.

Think of Divine inspiration (spiritual consolation) as a healthy lifestyle that may not feel healthy because it is not supported by the culture or subcultures in which you live. Think of counter inspiration (spiritual desolation) as an unhealthy lifestyle that might not feel unhealthy because it is supported by the culture or sub-cultures in which you live. So always keep an eye on the direction the inspirations lead, more than whether inspirations make you feel good or feel bad.

If you want to map some of the influences in your life, make a small chart of the various sub-cultures where you spend most of your time each week, such as: work environments, online, groups/associations, athletic/exercise, arts/entertainment, political parties, television/radio, etc. Next to each sub-culture, write what you believe is its signature characteristic regarding its overall influence on your lifestyle.

Most of the sub-cultures will be a combination of both light and dark. You can ask yourself some questions to determine how they impact you. Does the sub-culture, on balance, help you choose according to Divine inspiration or counter-inspiration? In other words, is the sub-culture generally congruent with the values of Scripture, Tradition and the Teaching Church or not? Some of these sub-cultures may be fixed parts of your life and you may not have a choice but to be part of them. If this is the case, you can develop awareness of how to be "in it but not of it" . Other subcultures you may be affiliated with by personal choice. Do some of the sub-cultures force you to conceal your religious beliefs? Do you have what St. Ignatius defines as an inordinate attachment to any of these sub-cultures? Does your affiliation with the sub-culture move you further along in your *Sacred Story* or not?

Diffusing Counter-inspirations

Personal sin, addictions, and your emotional and psychological wounds render you vulnerable to spiritual desolation. When in the grips of spiritual desolation, you are robbed of faith, hope and love. Ignatius offers indispensable guidance when you are under the influence of counter-inspirations and are spiritually desolate, discouraged, hopeless and frustrated. If you pay close attention to these guidelines and act on them, you will avoid much pain and grief in your life. Do not despair if you don't understand the guidelines now, there will come a time when this wisdom will make sense and help you. Ignatius offers four main ideas of how we are to act when troubled by the counter-inspirations of desolation. Please read carefully:

1) When you are spiritually desolate and feeling a loss of faith, hope and love, NEVER change course away from positive resolutions and decisions you reached while under the influence of the Divine inspiration of consolation. Never change course in desolation!

During times you suffer the anxieties and the pressures of counter-inspirations' desolations, **absolutely never change course!** Human nature's enemy feeds on spiritual/emotional wounds and broken hearts. His counter-inspirations may seem logical but they **never lead to freedom, peace, or your heart's healing.** None of the choices and decisions influenced by the counter-inspirations of desolation, **no matter how logical they might appear,** will increase your faith, hope or love. Always be on the alert when you feel an urgent or compelling need to act immediately. The presence of an anxious urgency to reach a decision or take action is a clear sign of counter-inspirations at work.

2) During times of desolation, redouble your efforts to open and orient your heart to God. Use the means at your disposal: prayer, examination of conscience, and perhaps some simple penance or fasting (Mk. 9:29).

Counter-inspirations make it difficult to see and feel your authentic human nature. Redouble your positive spiritual efforts during these times of counter-inspiration. Redoubling efforts on these spiritual fronts might feel incredibly difficult. You will need to exercise both your spirit and body to counter them. A determined spirit is called for during such times. Be alert to thoughts, words, and deeds based on false readings of your authentic human nature. Do not be afraid, just be wise and alert. God is with you.

3) God provides the essential support and grace to withstand these times of trial and purification.

The support provided comes from your natural abilities, assisted by divine grace. You may feel completely overwhelmed by temptations or the darkness of spirit associated with disordered attractions and compulsive behaviors.

Have faith! There is sufficient grace for salvation, even if the logic of the counter-inspiration indicates otherwise.

Jesus, the Divine Physician, is very close to you during these purifications. When you encounter the full force and darkness of counter-inspirations, God is present to you but you may feel God is absent. Do not be fooled by the feelings, no matter how strong or mocking they might appear. This is especially true when your weaknesses, shame and failings are painfully highlighted. Ignatius, through trial and error, learned that God is not absent. Trust his wise counsel and affirm your faith in God during times when you do not feel the Spirit. Thank God for the fidelity He promises you.

4) Strive consciously to cultivate patience and persevere in the religious practices of your faith, especially when you are influenced by the desolation of counter-inspiration.

The Divine inspiration of consolation always returns. In the interim use the means of prayer, penance, and self-examination to resist and gain the most from these times of trial. You will learn much and grow significantly during these trials. Don't waste the opportunity! Considerable spiritual and human progress, as well as illumination, will result from your patient and persevering heart during these trials. You will discover that these times of stress, endured in faith, can produce the greatest enlightenment. Therefore, do not fear them.

Three Reasons for Spiritual Desolation

This is so important, it bears repeating: personal sin, addictions and your emotional and psychological wounds make you vulnerable to spiritual desolation. When in the grips of spiritual desolation, you are robbed of faith, hope and love. Ignatius offers indispensable guidance when you are under the influence of counter-inspirations and are spiritually desolate, discouraged, hopeless and frustrated. If you pay close attention to these guidelines and act on them, you will avoid much pain and grief in your life. Do not despair if you don't understand the guidelines now, there will come a time when this wisdom will be crystal clear.

God allows us to experience the desolation of counter-inspirations only to orient our hearts toward genuine love and our true human nature. We experience counter-inspiration's desolation for one of three reasons:

1) Desolation is directly related to wrong choices in thoughts, words, and deeds made under the influence of the false logic of counter-inspirations.

God removes the divine inspiration of consolation to warn that you are straying from your authentic human nature. God acts this way to stir your conscience so you turn back. God allows loss of consolation so you can feel the thoughts, words, and deeds associated with counter-inspirational choices. Such false choices will in due course destroy relationships, creation, human life, faith, hope and love; in essence, the very things God provides so you can find fulfillment, communion, and peace in this life, as well as eternal joy in the next. In this instance, it is our own choice that leads us to experience the desolation resulting from counter-inspiration.

2) God allows desolation, which is directly linked with your human growth and spiritual progress, to awaken your whole being—spirit, mind and body—to all spiritual, emotional and psychological wounds.

Desolation can awaken you to the destructive appetites and habits that have taken root in your being. Your being has been divided by those wounds. Spiritual progress is only possible when you awaken and confront this damaging pattern head-on. The process to identify and uproot these appetites can be likened to spiritual surgery. This awakening and spiritual renewal— spiritual healing—can at times be painful and intense making you feel hopeless and/or abandoned.

It is essential to allow these deeply rooted tendencies to surface so that a new consciousness and freedom can be born. Giving God permission to move forward with your spiritual growth is the only way these habits, grounded in counter-inspirations, can be uprooted.

Ignatius says that God supports us most especially during these times, even though we can feel lost. We might at times even feel condemned by the darkness we experience in our heart, mind, body and memories y. Ignatius, based on his own experiences of these intense moments, advises that there is always sufficient grace for our salvation.

You can have feelings of desolation associated with the awareness of your disordered appetites and human nature wounded by sin. These feelings do not in any way indicate how God views you. Instead, they offer a false reading of your authentic human nature. Do not be fooled into believing God does not love you and cherish you because you feel and experience these periods of darkness. You are not the darkness or the disordered, shameful appetites you experience. God loves you and supports your most authentic self as you suffer the stripping away of the pain, sin, narcissism and wounds that hide your authentic human nature.

The feelings of darkness are linked to your false self: the false loves, the broken heart and dreams, the narcissism and pride, the extravagant appetites, and the destructive drives associated with your spiritual and psychological wounds. With your cooperation, God is gradually uprooting these from your heart.[1]

3) Third, counter-inspirations of desolation may also make their appearance during times of spiritual advancement.

After a period of purification from the counter-inspirations of desolation, your heart finds peace in the Divine inspiration of consolation. During these graced rests, you may be tempted to believe the illusion that you have arrived and reached the end your spiritual growth. You experience this state of calm and peace as definitive, and feel that you have achieved sanctity, completion, and holiness.

During these times, and almost imperceptibly, a spirit of pride and self-sufficiency takes hold in your heart. When this happens (when, not if) the counter-inspirations of desolation return as a warning. This happened to Ignatius once. He felt that he was among the just and that his spiritual growth was complete, but when he experienced desolation, he realized that he was actually just beginning on the road to salvation.

Everything achieved up to this point is due to God's grace. Only by grace has your heart begun its reunion with God, characterized by childlike humility, trust, and dependence. It is upon the foundation of God's grace and your heart's childlike humility that spiritual progress is achieved. God allows a flood of the desolations of counter-inspiration to warn you of the narcissism and destructive pride that will halt all of your progress towards union with God. It is typically at the first sign of this narcissism and pride when an individual starts to fall away from spiritual disciplines and other practices of faith.

Therefore, cultivate humility during the consoling times of divine inspiration. Use the time of consolation as preparation for the time of desolation. Be aware and awake and always anticipate the return of counter-inspiration's desolation. Plan your actions ahead of time for when desolation returns. During your time of consolation, remember how helpless you felt during the counter-inspiration of desolation. This will remind you that God is indeed the only one who stabilizes your heart with the Divine inspiration of consolation.

When the counter-inspiration of desolation returns (when, not if), pray to understand which reason from the above three is the cause. When under the influence of the counter-inspiration of desolation, hold steady! Cultivate humility and be patient, doing everything possible to orient your thoughts, words, and deeds towards an awareness of God's presence in your life; of Creation, Presence, Memory, Mercy and Eternity. God holds you fast during the Divine inspirations of consolation. God holds you in His heart especially during the counter-inspirations of desolation. Affirm your faith in God by holding fast to spiritual disciplines and the other practices of your Faith, seeking stability and fidelity in good times and in bad.

Three Strategies of the Enemy of Human Nature: to Confound, Frighten, and Deceive Individuals Committed to Spiritual Growth

When you engage your faith practice daily, three subtle and malicious lines of attack can be employed by the enemy of your human nature to discourage you. The enemy will use the weaknesses associated with your vices, extravagant appetites, compulsive drives, spiritual and psychological wounds, and broken heart. Strategies and lines of attack include:

1) Fear and panic attacks strategically employed to block growth.

If you stay committed to the process of uprooting of vices, sins, addictions and destructive habits from your life and heart, you can be menaced with waves of fear and panic to turn you away from the healing process. If you waver even an inch in your commitment to the healing process, the fear and panic will intensify exponentially, acting to paralyze your heart with unrelenting terror and withering dread.[2] If the menacing fear is directly confronted, and you hold steadfast to the commitments associated with your spiritual and psychological growth, the panic and fear will eventually abate. If you consistently confront the fears

138

and hold fast to the healing process, you will notice that the strategy of "fear and dread" is just that, a strategy. The fears and the dread are never realized. They are only a ploy but maliciously effective if and when you surrender to them.[3]

2) Narcissism and false values masquerade as true love and authentic values.

Those committed to uprooting vices, addictions, sins and destructive habits from their life and heart will confront clever deceptions portraying narcissism as authentic love, and vices as positive values. The enemy of human nature knows that every heart searches for true love. But every heart to varying degrees is also divided and broken by the effects of its spiritual and psychological wounds. The counter-inspiration of desolation blinds your heart's perception of what is genuine—of what leads to eternal life. So your heart is easily fooled and tempted by false promises of true love.

All false loves are illicit because they are lusts masquerading as love. All false loves are like mirages for parched and anxious hearts hoping to quench their thirst and find comfort. Instead of providing lasting peace, these illicit loves—mirages—merely intensify longings, deepen self-deception, self-preoccupation and narcissism, which lead to spiritual and psychological death. It is easy to observe the corrosive effects of sins and addictions in other individuals and other groups. But when you are the person in their grip it is almost impossible to feel them as anything but a precious lifeline. God clearly sees the corrosive and poisonous effects of false loves on persons, families and societies. But those in their grip only see beauty and salvation, for all false loves appear as good, life giving and natural.

The varieties of seduction are as varied as the ways a heart has or can be broken. God won't sanction these lusts because they issue from a violated heart and lead to your heart's further violation. Once acted upon you will most assuredly violate the hearts of others. God is Love. God is the origin, the end, and the defender of the human heart. God is infinitely merciful with our struggles.

Yet God cannot sanction what destroys your authentic Divinely modeled human nature, breaks your heart, or anything that will lead to your spiritual death.

Bring all false loves to full consciousness. Examine them in light of the writings of saints, doctors of the Church, and the mystical traditions of East and West.

You will find nothing that supports their claim of authenticity. Name these sins, addictions, and habits truthfully as false lovers. Manifest these false loves to a spiritual guide who holds sacred the tradition and the Gospels. You can be convinced of their unholy origin if you resist fully manifesting them to yourself or others. Examine them in the light of day, not by the cover of night. By day they will be revealed as neither true servant of the heart nor pathway to the Divine. By exposing them, your heart will not lose love and life as you fear. You will find, eventually, the path to the only love worthy of your total devotion and self-surrender.

When you are in their grip, activate Ignatius' *Truth Paradigm* and with Christ at your side, consciously take these steps:

> **Declare** to Christ the specific sin, addiction, or destruction compulsion and name it as a false lover;
>
> **Describe** to Christ the specific sin, addiction or destructive compulsion as coming from the enemy of your human nature;
>
> **Descend** with Christ into your memory to see and feel your first experience of this specific sin, addiction or compulsion. Ask Christ to compassionately reveal the stress fractures, loneliness and wounds in your heart which it promised to satisfy;
>
> **Denounce** with Christ as your witness the sin, addiction or destructive compulsion for its ruinous effect in your life, other's lives and society;
>
> **Decide** for Christ to heal this wound, diffuse the stress, anxiety and fear feeding it, and transform its damaging effects on your life into a *Sacred Story*.

3) If you stay committed to allowing, sin, addictions, and vices to be uprooted from your body and soul, you will be assaulted by attacks directed at the spiritual and psychological wounds that make you most vulnerable.

The enemy of human nature will viciously attack where you are wounded and weakened morally, psychologically, emotionally and spiritually. Core spiritual and psychological injuries to your being affect your capacity for self-transcendence, higher consciousness and selfless love. The injuries themselves are defended by fortress-like emotional and intellectual counter-inspirations that darken your conscience, hiding your authentic human nature from view. The enemy of human nature reinforces these emotional and intellectual defense structures. His goal is to conceal from conscious awareness not only your human nature made in the Divine image, but also your heart's core wounds.

The enemy's purpose is to keep your emotional and intellectual defenses firmly in place: to keep your conscience dark, and your true human nature hidden. The enemy's assault is felt as a bolstering and intensification of the powerful emotional and intellectual defenses leading you deeper into self-centered, self-absorbed, self-defensive, self-justifying and narcissistic thoughts, words and deeds. You become ever more proud and adamantly convinced, hardened in your judgments about the meaning of life, truth, and beauty—convictions that often contradict the Scriptures, received Tradition, the Teaching Church and even Western and Eastern mystical traditions.

The hardened convictions these defense measures produce share the various qualities of desolation's counter-inspiration already mentioned.[4] The enemy of human nature's strategic attacks are designed to harden your heart, solidify your judgments, and keep you firmly committed to self-oriented, defensive measures of thoughts, words, deeds, habits, rigid reasoning systems and disordered attachments. The enemy of human nature's chief goal is to permanently camouflage your heart's spiritual, emotional and psychological wounds, so that they cannot be discovered—to hide them from an awakened conscience—so that you never notice where or why you need healing. These are the same defensive structures that Jesus says keep people from believing in him, even if he should rise from the dead (Lk. 16:31).

ॐ

Guidelines for Integrated Healing and Spiritual Growth

The Guidelines for integrated healing and spiritual growth are essential for discerning counter-inspirations of a more subtle nature. They should be applied when you have grown to the point where the vices, habits, addictions, and extravagant appetites that used to control your life and dominate your passion, are no longer effective strategies, in and of themselves, for turning you from God, your *Sacred Story*, and the practice of your faith.

When you have achieved a certain level of spiritual, emotional and psychological maturity, the enemy of human nature can best deceive you with seemingly good and holy thoughts and feelings. He mimics the Divine-Inspirer. The counter-inspirer, no longer successful in undermining your authenticity and innocence with temptations to false pleasures and discouragements of an obvious nature, nor direct appeals to narcissistic pride, must use the undetected roots of your narcissism to deceive. He will use these undetected roots of your narcissism in conjunction with your new holy inspirations and habits as weapons against you.

The enemy of human nature will then mask counter-inspirations by making them appear as Divine inspirations. Ignatius first discovered these new, subtler temptations in the midst of his fierce battle with the crippling guilt of his scruples. The obsessive habit of re-confessing his past sins appeared as a good idea from the Divine-Inspirer. It appealed to someone serious about his spiritual growth. But Ignatius was miserable and experienced the constant re-confessing as damaging. Yet he would not even relinquish the habit when told to do so by his spiritual director. He was in the grip of a habit that appeared pious and holy, but wasn't. It had all the signature marks of the counter-inspirations of the enemy of his human nature. And he was blinded to this fact.

Ignatius discovered that the enemy's tactic is to inspire desires and choices that, based on their nature as either neutral or objectively good, appear as if they will evolve towards Love and life. Thus, scrupulous confession would appear to genuinely help root out past sins and vices. Spiritual and religious persons are especially vulnerable to these more subtle temptations. A partial conversion does not sufficiently targeted the narcissistic pride that guides one's life. Those not sufficiently purified parade about like just and righteous person but instead are proud and arrogant. Jesus reserved some of his harshest attacks for these people (Lk. 18:9-14).

Some things that are good or appear to be good can, if acted upon, gradually lead you away from the good you intend, and away from God. In actuality, they lead to disintegration, separation, and death. This is exactly what happened to Ignatius. He got so disgusted with the trials and traumas of his obsessive re-confessing of past sins that he was suddenly inspired to be done with the new life he was living—to "stop it!"

When he awoke to the counter-inspiration "to stop" living a life that had revealed itself to him previously as the authentic path of holiness, he began to wonder how this spirit gripped him. He realized it was his constant pattern of re-confessing. The habit that seemed noble was silently, slowly, and maliciously eroding his confidence in himself, God, and the new way of life he had chosen. If the enemy of human nature could not get Ignatius to succumb to the obvious vices and sins of his former life, then the enemy would take his new holy inspirations, link them to his as yet undetected narcissistic pride, and grind him into the earth with it. How effective it was!

How can you know the difference between Divine inspirations and counter-inspirations, especially if a counter-inspiration appears to be positive, or feels authentic?

First, the Divine-Inspirer works to give you true joy and happiness by eliminating all sadness and upset caused by the enemy of your human nature. The counter-inspirer works against such joy and happiness most successfully by use of false reasoning, subtleties and layer upon layer of deceptions.

Second, the Divine-Inspirer alone can work directly on your heart and soul, freely entering it and leaving it but always acting to promote love of God and love of innocence. The Divine-Inspirer promotes humility, selflessness and your surrendering control of your life to God. He gifts you with an obedient spirit that accepts and affirms as true and noble the Commandments and precepts of Christ and the received Tradition of the Church. Inspirations with these signature characteristics can be verified as coming directly from the Divine-Inspirer.

Third, both the Divine-Inspirer and the counter-inspirer inspire but with opposite goals. The Divine-Inspirer seeks to promote genuine human freedom, authenticity, and spiritual and psychological growth consonant with your authentic human nature. The counter-inspirer seeks to erode genuine human freedom and to disintegrate your spiritual and psychological health. The goal is to damage your authentic human nature.

Fourth, the counter-inspirer can mimic some of the influences of the Divine-Inspirer in thoughts, feelings, desires etc., but always with the purpose of leading, you little by little, in the wrong direction; just like Ignatius with his damaging habit of confessing old sins.

Fifth, to learn the difference between false and true inspirations, you must develop the habit of examining the trajectory of your thoughts and desires. If the beginning, middle, and end are all directed to values Divine inspirations represent, they are from the Divine-Inspirer. If the trajectory of the desires and thoughts point to something contrary to the Commandments or the precepts of Christ, or they are distracting, or they weaken your aspirations for selflessness, or in some way diminish the good plans and goals you had previously established, then it is clear they are a product of the counter-inspirer. He leads you away from genuine progress, authenticity, innocence, humility, obedience and peace. Ignatius was distracted by his confession habit, and his aspirations for following the path of conversion were undermined by it. This is how he awoke to the influence of the counter-inspirer and to his crippling, narcissistic pride.

Sixth, it is critical to develop a habit of tracing the trajectory of your thoughts and desires when you have been falsely led in the wrong direction. Do not worry. You will fall for the bait countless times. When you do, examine the lead inspiration and follow it through the whole course of your deliberations. Notice how you were at first inspired, but then gradually, step by step, lost your peace of soul. Notice how your former commitments and resolutions were undermined. In this way you will learn to detect the strategy of the counter-inspirer and develop spiritual radar for these deceptive tactics. You will also learn the personal vulnerabilities you possess that are so easily manipulated by the enemy of your authentic human nature. At this level of conversion, the enemy's tactics always work on your concealed pride, vanity, and narcissism - your desire to be powerful, to not need God, to be in control of your own life, to be your own savior, like Ignatius tried to be.

Seventh, when you are progressing towards authenticity, innocence and genuine human freedom, the effects of the Divine-Inspirer are gentle and produce delight. Absent is a sense of electrical energy or anxious excitement. You will not have a restless need to make hasty decisions. Instead, you will experience calm patience and tranquility. When making spiritual progress, you can detect the effects of the counter-inspirer by the rush of electrical energy, anxious excitement, or restlessness to make hasty decisions. When you are straying from the path of authenticity, innocence and genuine human freedom, the patterns of inspiration are precisely the reverse as just mentioned. Ignatius learned when his life-trajectory was contrary to the one inspiring. The effects of that inspirer on his heart and soul were noisy and obvious. When his life-trajectory was aligned to the one inspiring, the effects of that inspirer were silent, calm and tranquil, "as one coming into his own house when the doors are open."

For example, if you are moving towards God, the enemy of your human nature will inspire black noise and create anxious thoughts and urgent feelings. If you are moving away from God, the enemy of your human nature will inspire with thoughts that are quiet, peaceful and designed to conceal your movement away from God and your authentic human nature, etc.

When the inspiration produced in your heart and soul comes directly from the Divine-Inspirer; i.e., when the effects on your heart and soul produce an intense sense of devotion and love of God and of innocence, of selflessness and willing surrender of your life to God's control, you cannot be deceived or led astray. However, you can be led astray in the after-glow of these inspirations and graces, either by your own ideas, or by the influence of the counter-inspirer.

Therefore be highly attentive during the afterglow following these Divine inspirations. Make no revisions, commitments, or plans unless you are quite clear on the source of the inspiration. The Divine-Inspirer will always pull you further along the path of love, innocence, humility, self-surrender. The counter-inspirer will always work toward disintegration, and a lessening of your previous commitments and holy resolutions.

Do you now understand how Ignatius' Divine inspiration to reform his life, and make resolutions for his past sins, was corrupted and devolved into a damaging habit of confessing old sins? The counter-inspirer accomplished this by manipulating Ignatius' intemperate, narcissistic nature, and long-standing vulnerabilities. Had Ignatius not been inspired to see the deceit, and walked away from his conversion journey, the Church would have lost the gifts of his spirituality and the many saints who achieved holiness because of it. This was the counter-inspirer's hope for Ignatius. It will be the counter-inspirer's hope for you as well. The counter-inspirer understands what good you can accomplish for the Kingdom of Christ and will work to undermine it at all cost. Yet, the Divine Inspirer will always offer graces and insights to lead you home. Be Not Afraid! But be attentive.

CR

Additional Guidelines on Life Choices

Grace illuminates your mind and heart. What used to be in darkness is now being illuminated. You begin to awaken and to see more clearly: (1) the world as it is; (2) the world as a whole; and (3) your authentic human nature. Grace alone facilitates this journey from the spirit's dark night, and the darkened consciousness of counter-inspiration. You will discover in reaching this spiritual passage why narcissism and overweening pride are much more difficult to identify and eliminate than are the "sins of the flesh".

The pain of Original Sin, early life trauma, and lost innocence fuel your narcissism. The narcissistic ego closed to the Spirit rationalizes, self-empowers, and legitimizes whatever it needs to fill its painful void. The defenses that blind your conscience from seeing your narcissism match the intensity of the hidden pain and suffering at the center of your heart. You defend your use of these illegitimate vices and addictions because they protect you from feeling the pain in your heart. When you accept the Divine Physician's graces to break through your defenses, and heal the pain in your heart, your *Sacred Story* begins. This is the true path to mystical awakening. There are no shortcuts. There is no other way home.

The humility Ignatius discovered in surrendering control of his life—his pride and narcissism—is what opened his consciousness to new possibilities never before imagined. This new consciousness has its own graces and threats, as Ignatius well knew. Grace abounds no matter one's state of life and vocation. Grace brings illumination and clarity and a more cohesive portrait of yourself, the world, faith, God, your past and present commitments, and your choices—both well and ill conceived. This is where Ignatius found himself after his spiritual and psychological trials at Manresa.

The graces that transform a heart formerly divided and opposed to the values of the Gospel—as was Ignatius' heart—create possibilities and opportunities never before imagined or thought possible. Purifying graces rush in with new scenarios for your life and take the place of the void. Old thoughts, words, and deeds are replaced by the new. What else would you expect when your heart is touched directly by Divine grace and flush with the energy, enthusiasm, and the vitality of God? When this happens Ignatius has clear advice for you.

A person in this stage of integrated conversion and healing, who has received these graces of illumination, must consider them very attentively. She or he must cautiously distinguish the actual time of the consolation from the period that follows it. In the afterglow of these illuminations and insights, when the consolations themselves have ceased, your soul is still passionate and blessed with the graces and their aftereffects.

In the time of the afterglow, your heart and soul frequently form various resolutions and plans that are not directly inspired or granted by God. They may come from your own reasoning. They can emanate from ideas based on your own judgments, or they can be the direct inspiration of either the Divine-Inspirer or the counter-inspirer.

It is critical to distinguish between the illuminations themselves and the period of time after the illuminations and graces are given. Carefully, thoughtfully and cautiously examine your afterglow reflections and plans before approving them or acting on them.

Ignatius' advice is especially important if you are coming out of long established habits and lifestyles—thoughts, words, and deeds—rooted in inauthentic expressions of your human nature. These long-established patterns of sin and dysfunction create spiritual, mental and psychological grooves. The grooves are your default narratives for defining "normal" and "successful". These familiar yet false narratives are narcissism's anti-story. They feed on and draw strength from your broken heart and wounded innocence.

The pain of lost innocence has wounded our hearts. It is the spiritual and physical wreckage of the Original Fall combined with the evolution of sin in our families and social groups. The energy and effort pumped into your narcissistic anti-story shields you from the pain and shame that is too much to face. As you gradually receive the grace and illumination to let go of the anti-story, you experience a void. A powerful anxiety to fill that void is easily exploited by counter-inspirations. You will also have the desire to make up for lost time and to correct the mistakes of the past. These too can fill your heart with urgent and pressing agendas for change. No matter how honorable and right those inspirations might feel, especially in light of your past misdeeds and errors, they can, if acted upon, lead away from the truths, positive resolutions, and commitments recently illumined by Divine grace.

If you receive these inspirations, test any imagined future plans they represent. Do the inspirations of this afterglow period strike the heart gently, softly and with delightful peace, with no traces of electrical energy or urgency to act on them? Or do the inspirations and ideas of this second period instead strike the heart violently, noisily, and disturb the heart with electrical excitement, and a compelling urgency to immediately enact the good ideas or plans being pondered (like Ignatius' urgent desire to be done with his new life)? This later effect is a clear sign that the inspirations and ideas will lead you away from an evolution toward life and love—fruit that endures to eternity—no matter how enlightened and good they are, or appear to be in and of themselves. Be alert and forewarned! But be not afraid!

◯ঽ

10

Listening To Your History: Weeks One to Five

FIRST WEEK

Foundational Exercises

For those new to the practice of prayer and Ignatian spirituality, and even for those who are familiar, it is beneficial to begin the *Sacred Story* method with a month or two of foundational exercises. These foundational exercises will help you gain better personal knowledge and humility. They are designed to help you listen to your history, know yourself better, and begin your *Sacred Story* on a firm foundation, like Ignatius did.

The foundational exercises will make your spiritual journey towards eternity all the more fruitful. *Sacred Story* prayer is a life-long habit. There is no need to rush! These preparatory exercises have proven themselves of great benefit to hundreds of others. They will aid you in the practice of powerful prayer and your life in God.

CR

FIRST WEEK
First Exercise

Days One-Three: Listening to Sacred Story Narrative

Enter at your leisure into reading St. Ignatius' *Sacred Story* narrative. Take no more than fifteen minutes a day for this exercise. Read slowly and listen reflectively. Take note of your own life history as you listen to St. Ignatius' life story. Read the narrative with your heart. Notice what inspires hope, joy and peace. Notice what causes anxiety, stress, fear, and anger. You will have three days to slowly absorb this story. Break it into three parts and focus on one section each day. For day one, read up to, but not through the section titled "A Journey to the Heart." For day two, read up to, but not including "The Universal Call to Reconciliation" section. Finish the narrative on day three. Give yourself permission to re-read one or more sections of Ignatius' *Sacred Story* narrative.

If you feel there is more to absorb and reflect on in one or more of the sections, or if you prefer to read at a slower pace and can't comfortably finish a section in fifteen minutes, give yourself a second day and fifteen-minute period, or even a third day to re-read or finish a section. There is absolutely no rush to finish any of these exercises. You can't do it better by doing it faster!

Purchase a notebook for your *Sacred Story* reflections. In your notebook, write down two phrases or sentences for each day's reading exercise. Never skip a day. If you do skip, just pick up the writing exercise the next day. What you write at day's end ought to only take a minute or less. Write only two sets of thoughts: The first sentence or phrase should reflect what caused you the most fear or anxiety that day. The second sentence or phrase should reflect what inspired you and/or gave you hope. If your reading extends to more than one day for each of the three sections, still write two phrases or sentences for each day's reading/reflection exercise, no matter how many days it takes to finish the reading.

SACRED STORY
Part One: St. Ignatius and His Legacy

A Fallen Soldier

Until his thirtieth year Ignatius Loyola was unconscious of the sacredness of his life. Instead, he was sincerely devoted to life's pleasures and vanities. His life was not easy. Ignatius' mother died when he was an infant and his father died when he was sixteen. Perhaps that had some impact on his personality. He was a gambling addict, sexually self-indulgent, arrogant, hotheaded and insecure.

By our contemporary measures, Ignatius' family was dysfunctional. Was this person a possible candidate for sainthood? It did not look promising. But God does not judge by human standards. It is God's nature to pursue all who have fallen asleep through sin, addiction and selfishness. God judges the heart; with unbounded grace and patient mercy God reaches into the ruins that sin makes of our lives and transforms them into *Sacred Stories*.

Ignatius, with all his narcissism, psychological problems and sinful vices, was awakened by God's great love. A failed military campaign and a shattered leg forced him into a lengthy convalescence. Ignatius' time of recuperation provided an opportunity for Love to shine a light on much more serious and life-threatening wounds that were spiritual, emotional and psychological in nature.

These wounds were supported by the evolution of a destructive, sinful narcissism. For thirty years Ignatius' narcissism had rendered him unconscious to his true human nature and oblivious to his life as *Sacred Story*. The pleasures he indulged in and the power he wielded functioned like a narcotic to numb the pain of his hidden spiritual and psychological wounds. His sinful vices and self-indulgent pleasures blinded him to his authentic human nature and a fruitful life guided by a well-formed conscience.

God's grace reached into the reality of Ignatius' life and awakened in him a desire for innocence. His long-buried aspirations for living authentically suddenly became his prime motivation. He noticed it first while convalescing at Loyola. He became aware of new desires and a different energy while he daydreamed in reading stories of Christ and the saints. Pondering the saints' lives he imagined himself living a different, selfless life.

He compared these new daydreams to his usual vain, narcissistic daydreams. The old daydreams drew energy from a life of sin, addiction and vice while the daydreams of selfless generosity produced their own energy. Ignatius noticed a significant difference between the two sets of daydreams and the feelings they produced. The vain fantasies entertained him when he was thinking about them. But he noticed that when he set them aside, he felt empty and unsatisfied.

The new holy daydreams also entertained him when he was thinking about them. Yet when he set these aside, he remained content and felt an enduring calm and quiet joy. By paying close attention to the ultimate affective signatures of these two sets of daydreams and discerning their difference, Ignatius made a discovery that transformed his life and the history of Christian spirituality.

The Voice of Conscience

Ignatius discovered that the new, selfless aspirations were influenced by Divine inspirations. He further discovered that these inspirations reflected his true human nature and that the vain fantasies deadened his conscience. His narcissistic daydreams led him away from enduring peace because they masked his authentic human nature.

The old daydreams were powerful, ego affirming, and familiar. He knew in his heart that living their fantasy was the path to self-destruction. On the one hand he would be judged successful by the standards of the world, a world that measured success in terms of riches, honors, and pride. On the other hand, he would be judged a failure by the standards of the Gospel, standards that advocated a life of spiritual poverty, humility and consequential service—a *Sacred Story* that endures to eternal life.

Ignatius was awakened to the emotional wisdom and spiritual truth of his new daydreams. He became aware of the significant damage that his old lifestyle had done to both himself and others. What had been awakened in him was the divine gift of conscience, and with it, Ignatius experienced profound regret and sorrow for having wasted so much of his life on self-indulgent pleasures and fantasies, seductions that could never bring him lasting peace and satisfaction. He began to understand that living in pleasure and fantasy destroyed his authentic human nature and silenced his deepest desires.

As usually happens when people respond to the grace of conversion, Ignatius' new aspirations confused and disconcerted many of his closest family members and friends. Nonetheless he acted on these aspirations. Ignatius was now able to understand a path to God, a pattern of conversion that countless thousands would imitate.

A graced experience of God's love opened Ignatius to: ⇨ ⇩	**GIVE THANKS FOR FAVORS RECEIVED** ⇩
A dissatisfaction with vain fantasies which led to surrendering to holy daydreams, characterized by consolation, which in turn: ⇨ ⇩	**PRAY FOR GRACE TO SEE CLEARLY** ⇩
Caused him to review his life and actions leading to: ⇨ ⇩	**GIVE A DETAILED ACCOUNT OF CONSCIENCE: GENERAL AND PARTICULAR** ⇩
Grief with yearning for penance and repentance for his past sins, culminating in: ⇨ ⇩	**ASK PARDON FOR ONE'S FAULTS** ⇩
Ignatius' passion to amend his life and a desire to love God wholeheartedly. ⇨	**RESOLVE AND AMEND TO SERVE GOD**

A Menacing Fear Unmasked

After some months of living in the light of these new positive virtues, habits, and Divine inspirations, Ignatius was suddenly gripped by terror and panic. How could he manage to live the rest of his life without the pleasures of the past? It was easy to live virtuously for some months, but for the rest of his life? This was a real crisis because Ignatius began to wonder if this was an impossible goal.

Ignatius had two vital insights about this menacing fear. First, he realized it was a counter-inspiration prompted by the enemy of his true human nature. The panicky fear led him to think that it would be impossible to live virtuously for such a long time. Second, the counter-inspiration tempted him to return to his old narcissistic vices and habits. Seduced by their powerful influence, Ignatius would abandon all hope for a life of virtue. In essence, Ignatius was tempted to surrender living the authentic life that had finally brought him peace. He sensed an evil source inspiring this menacing fear and he challenged it head-on: "You pitiful thing! Can you even promise me one hour of life?"

A Decisive and Enduring Commitment to Remain Awake

Ignatius dismissed the counter-inspiration and its evil author by re-committing to this new wakefulness for the remainder of his life. This was Ignatius' second insight: NEVER trust the messages prompted by menacing fears. Counter them with a firm commitment to stay the course, to awaken and remain conscious.

This decisive, enduring commitment to persevere restored tranquility, and his fear abated. Ignatius had discovered, unmasked and confronted the deceiver. In this Ignatius learned another lesson about speaking truth to power that would guide his new life and help shape his first set of foundational discernment principles.

A enemy voice evokes Ignatius' fear of a lifelong struggle with his sinful habits. ⇨ ⇩	**CONSCIOUS FEAR AND ANXIETY OVER SURRENDERING SINFUL AND ADDICTIVE HABITS** ⇩
Ignatius rejects the "enemy of human nature" and confronts his false promises. ⇨ ⇩	**CONFRONTING THE THREATENING "VOICE" OF SIN AND ADDICTION WITH THE "TRUTH" THAT THEY BRING DEATH, NOT LIFE** ⇩
Peace is restored after truthfully naming sin and addiction as death dealing. ⇨	**PEACE RETURNS AND ANXIETY DISSOLVES**

Ignatius had to face these same fears many, many more times. Eventually he knew they were false fears, inspirations of the enemy of his human nature. Most importantly, he gradually learned how to diffuse them, and to defend against them.

Our Christian life is a labor of love. In order for God's love to heal us we must do our part to open ourselves to God's graces. This requires conscious and ongoing effort to abstain from sinful, addictive habits in thoughts, words and deeds. There is a need to pray for God's grace. First we must awaken to that grace. With that same grace, we have the strength to resist and abstain from sinful, addictive attitudes and behaviors, both spiritual and material. God's grace makes our spiritual disciplines fruitful, activating the on-going healing of our human nature. Grace helps us climb out of the spiritual, mental physical and emotional ruts of our bound self toward a future of increased hope, holiness and balance and freedom.

Part Two: A Journey to the Heart

Ignatius in Control

Ignatius' decisive and enduring commitment to his conversion launched him directly into the center of his heart's brokenness and the pride masking those wounds. After leaving home Ignatius traveled to Montserrat and spent three days reviewing his life. It was at this time that he made a general confession of all his past sins. This first life confession initiated an enduring habit of weekly confession and communion. In this written confession Ignatius consciously detailed his sinful attitudes, behaviors and passions: gambling addiction, sexual self-indulgence, arrogance, and violent outbursts of temper. It took three days to write the story of his past life.

Yet he discovered that simply detailing and confessing his sinful habits and addictions did not disarm them. That would require going deeper to their source in his heart and history. Only in these deepest recesses could he confront the pattern of spiritual and psychological dysfunction that was most responsible for eroding his freedom and distorting his authentic human nature.

It is this inward journey that fully awakened his conscience. It was only at this depth that he discovered his authentic human nature and regained the creativity of childlike innocence. We do well to understand the tipping point of Ignatius' life from his root vices and narcissism to his new life of wakefulness, light, peace and hope. This is how his story unfolded.

Ignatius' new, pious habit of regular confession evolved into a destructive obsessive and compulsive torture. He confessed and re-confessed past sins multiple times, never feeling he had gotten to the bottom of his immoral deeds. This excruciating spiritual and psychological torment lasted for months. He was so anguished by his obsessive guilt that numerous times he wanted to commit suicide by throwing himself off the cliff where he prayed.

Even awareness of the emotional damage caused by this obsessive confession habit did not help him surrender it. Instead he initiated new, harsher physical disciplines and spiritual regimens. His goal was to gain complete control and self-mastery over his immoral and dissolute past. He wanted to remember every detail of his past sins so he could be perfectly cleansed, but nothing worked.

Finally, exhausted and disgusted with his efforts, he realized he intensely despised the spiritual life he was living. Ignatius had an urgent and compelling desire to "stop it!" This thought alarmed Ignatius, and his spiritual radar went on high alert. Ignatius discerned the inspiration came from another source but what could it be? He discovered the inspiration's origin and author only by understanding where the inspiration was taking him. It occurred to him that the inspiration was leading him in the same direction as the menacing fear he had previously experienced. Inspired to abandon his newly awakened life, Ignatius was being tempted to abandon the peace, the service to others, and the virtuous life of his *Sacred Story*. But how did this counter-inspiration succeed in gaining control? Ignatius realized it was rooted in his damaging confession habit and so he ceased the habit then and there of re-confessing past sins.

Surrendering Control to Embrace Powerlessness & Innocence

Ignatius' description in his *Autobiography* to stop his damaging confession habit appears inconsequential. But the choice was the most significant spiritual decision in his entire life. It was also the most difficult, because that one choice meant fully surrendering his life to God. It meant admitting his powerlessness over his sins and in humility allowing God, not himself, to be the source of his holiness.

Reflecting on the temptation to walk away from his new Christian life, Ignatius received an insight that the burdensome, destructive habit of re-confessing past sins was rooted in a pride to try and save himself. This pride forced him to his knees. On seeing this he "awoke as if from a dream," and was given the grace to stop the habit.

Ignatius' first life confession at Montserrat documented the visible manifestations of this deep distortion in his human nature. The Divine Physician next led Ignatius to the source of those visible sins. It was his wounded human nature that fueled the controlling, narcissistic personality. The pattern of visible sins, vices and addictions was only the tip of the iceberg.

From that moment of surrender at Manresa, Ignatius acknowledged his powerlessness and surrendered control of his life to God. For his entire life God waited to transform Ignatius' deepest desires into a *Sacred Story* whose legacy would endure to eternity. This surrender defines Ignatius' second set of foundation discernment principles.

Ignatius' struggle with scruples hiding his vainglory ⇨ ⇩	The initial confrontation with one's root sin ⇩
Ignatius' constant re-confessing to seek salvation by willpower alone ⇨ ⇩	The effort to control one's root sin ONLY by personal effort or force of will ⇩
Ignatius' suicidal impulses, disgust and the desire to walk away from his new found faith ⇨ ⇩	Despair and desire to give up faith when human effort alone fails ⇩
Ignatius' tracing the spirit of disgust to a demonic source ⇨ ⇩	Insight that desire to reject the spiritual journey is a temptation ⇩
Ignatius abandoning his compulsive confessing of past sins ⇨ ⇩	Admitting powerlessness to save one-self and surrendering prideful actions ⇩
Ignatius being taught as a child and receiving graces according to God's design ⇨	Allowing God to shape one's *Sacred Story* according to His will and graces

An outpouring of mystical grace flooded Ignatius at this point. More importantly a humble and obedient spirit was beginning to emerge which enabled him to respond to the slightest movements of God's grace in his thoughts, words and deeds. In this humility and docility he discovered a life of service that changed the Church and the world. Later in life he reflected:

There are very few who realize what God would make of them if they abandoned themselves entirely to His hands, and let themselves be formed by His grace. A thick and shapeless tree trunk would never believe that it could become a statue, admired as a miracle of sculpture...and would never consent to submit itself to the chisel of the sculptor who, as St. Augustine says, sees by his genius what he can make of it. Many people who, we see, now scarcely live as Christians, do not understand that they could become saints, if they would let themselves be formed by the grace of God, if they did not ruin His plans by resisting the work which He wants to do.

The proud narcissist, the man who was master of his own universe, became a humble and obedient servant of the universe's true Master and Creator. To arrive at this point, Ignatius had to admit his powerlessness. He had to surrender control over his life and the distorted aspects of his human nature that had evolved over the years. He had to learn how to live out of his newly emerging authentic self, his true human nature previously hidden behind his wounded heart.

Ignatius also learned how to dismantle the narcissism that had evolved over the first thirty years of his life. The counter-inspirer, the enemy of his human nature, had cleverly concealed his true human nature and Ignatius had to begin life over again, this time allowing God to reveal his authentic self. This was why, after the resolution of this greatest of his life's crises, Ignatius experienced himself being taught by God. It was, he said, exactly like "a child is taught by a schoolmaster."

The Divine-Inspirer and the counter-inspirer

This harrowing crisis taught Ignatius a most vital lesson about counter-inspirations. The willpower and resolute commitment to live virtuously for the rest of his life could be manipulated and turned against him by means of subtle inspirations. What seemed like a holy, pious, and noble practice—a serious approach to confession—evolved into a damaging habit that made him loathe his spiritual life, and in frustration, inspired him to abandon it. He learned that the counter-inspirations of the enemy of his human nature could act like "an angel of light." These inspirations appear holy but when followed, they end in disaster, distancing one from God and from one's authentic self.

The counter-inspirer conceals our original wounds, counseling and guiding our steps to build a false identity, an anti-story, characteristically identified by a distorted ego and defended by narcissism. Our narcissistic pride rationalizes the habits, vices, addictions and lifestyles that form our anti-story. The counter-inspirer renders us unconscious to our *Sacred Story* and to our true Divinely shaped human nature.

God led Ignatius through this distorted evolution back to the lost innocence of his true human nature. The shattering of his powerful defenses and the unmasking of his prideful, narcissistic ego proved to be the tipping point of Ignatius' entire conversion process.

Ignatius, justifying himself, anxiously recoils and focuses on his sinfulness ⇨ ⇩	Panic over one's salvation due to weakness and sinfulness ⇨	**PURGATION** ⇩
Ignatius, no longer fearful, regrets not having responded sooner to God's graces ⇨ ⇩	Sadness at slowness of one's response to God's love and invitation to intimacy ⇨	**ILLUMINATION** ⇩
Ignatius' intense joy at the thought of dying and being with God ⇨	An ardent, all-embracing love of God and desire for complete union with the Trinity ⇨	**UNION**

Wakefulness, Holiness, and Heightened Consciousness

Ignatius' conversion from his anti-story and his full awakening to his *Sacred Story* was not a single event but rather a gradual process. His full evolution from a vain egomaniac to a saint took the rest of his life. His was a gradual, steady evolution from a sinful narcissist in control of his own life to an innocent, obedient servant of God. Growth in holiness requires desire, patience and daily effort to awaken to our authentic human nature. It takes time for grace to penetrate the influence of our anti-story so that our *Sacred Story* can more fully emerge. There are no short cuts to holiness, not even for saints.

A Life-Long Commitment to Christ in the Church

If you desire to surrender your anti-story and open to your *Sacred Story*, grace will awaken you, like Ignatius, to places in your heart's memories you might not wish to visit. The awakening will begin like Ignatius'. It starts with an honest identification of the visible manifestations of those spiritual and psychological distortions in the particulars of your human nature. These distortions disclose your lost innocence and a heart broken by the Original Fall and the cumulative sins of your family, clan and culture. Ignatius started this process with his life confession. He truthfully identified the habits, addictions, sins and compulsions characteristic of his lost innocence and broken heart.

Open yourself to the graces that will illumine the distinctive narcissistic elements fueling your sinful, compulsive behaviors. Ignatius needed much grace to overcome his defenses and unlock this hidden truth about his life. Everyone who embraces this path can confidently rely on the same grace to successfully navigate the journey to the center of one's heart. As confused as life is due to Original Sin, the Lord can and does penetrate our hearts and leads us to truth.

More tortuous than anything is the human heart, beyond remedy; who can understand it? I, the LORD, explore the mind and test the heart, Giving to all according to their ways, according to the fruit of their deeds (Jer 17: 9-10).

Part Three: The Call to Universal Reconciliation

Your Sacred Story

As with Ignatius, God extends an invitation to awaken to the pattern of spiritual, emotional and psychological dysfunction that has formed our anti-story. God invites us to awaken to our lives as *Sacred Story* and to produce fruit that endures to eternity. The awakening and growth will reveal where our freedom is compromised and how we close our hearts to our authentic human nature. Christ compassionately shows us how our selfishness and pride have corrupted our creativity, robbing us of the joy of innocence. God's invitation is gentle. God's awakening is merciful. Rest assured that God's passion is to pursue us, rescue us, heal us and bring us back to our original innocence. God's passion is Personal. God's passion is Love. God's passion is Christ Jesus. Be Not Afraid!

God's intention is to gradually heal and transform our thoughts, words and deeds. For every thought, word and deed influences my history in the direction of an anti-story or a *Sacred Story*. Every thought, word and deed, for good or ill, touches all people in my life, all the world and all of creation, shaping history's final chapter. The effects of sin and narcissism—as well as the effects of virtue and selflessness—have individual, social, physical, spiritual, and ecological ramifications that reach to the ends of creation. For everything and everyone is one in Love—one in Christ Jesus—through whom and for whom everything was made (Rom 11:36).

Every thought, word, or deed, no matter how discreet, has positive or negative significance in the interconnected web of life that God has fashioned through Christ. It is Christ's being—His *SACRED STORY*—that links each of our individual *Sacred Stories*. It is in Christ that the entire cosmos is joined together. God in Christ has made us responsible for and dependent upon each other and upon the earth that sustains us.

The Christ of the Cosmos—through whom and for whom everything was made—became man, and confronted, absorbed, and diffused all the destructive force of evil's evolutionary anti-history running through human nature and the created cosmos. Christ reconciles in Himself everything in the heavens and on the earth to bring peace to all by the blood of His cross. His *SACRED STORY* redeems and renews every chapter in our history, individual and collective.

Christ Jesus passionately awaits our participation to join His work of universal reconciliation. Our willingness to accept the path of conversion entails truthfully identifying our sins, dysfunction and addictions. It entails experiencing and admitting our powerlessness to save ourselves. It requires the patience of a lifetime while Christ writes our *Sacred Story*.

My participation in Christ's work of reconciliation is the only worthy vocation and the only labor that produces fruit enduring to eternity. My accepting the invitation unlocks the very mystery of life. When I accept the invitation, Christ promises to share His universal glory. Accepting the invitation to intentionally enter my *Sacred Story* has momentous consequences.

Now is the Time to Wake from Sleep

Our time on this earth is so very brief. Since the time of Christ's birth, life, death and resurrection, our story can only be measured and valued in light of His eternal mission of Reconciliation. Intentionally entering my *Sacred Story* will, over time, enable me to know God more intimately and serve God more generously. Like Ignatius, I am called to awaken from sleep—to awaken to wholeness and holiness. I was created and infused with the gift to awaken to a life that reverences the God, who in Christ and the Holy Spirit, is present in all things—all persons, and all creation.

Awakening to my *Sacred Story*, like Ignatius, calls for courage in the cleansing of the spirit and psyche that it initiates. The process requires discipline in the face of temptation and monotony. It requires consciously asking, even begging if necessary, for God's graces. It requires time and patience; deliberately choosing each day to be faithful to time and space for God. Awakening requires the patience of a lifetime. The journey is rich with blessings beyond our wildest expectations. Encountering Christ daily in *Sacred Story* forever changes life, relationships, the earth, and eternity.

What is needed for the journey will be provided each day. In my journey through the memories and experiences, past and present, I am promised the power and mercy of the LOVE that maintains and guides the entire cosmos. It is this LOVE that waits to transform your sins, addictions, angers, fears, grief, guilt and shame.

It is this LOVE that restores your broken heart into a vessel of forgiveness, light and peace. The more embedded and impenetrable the web of darkness, compulsion, sin, and addiction in your life, the more strategic and magnificent is God's grace in breaking its grip, for nothing is impossible with God (Lk 1:37).

Your Sacred History

There are no short cuts to the story's unfolding. Conversion is lifelong but measurable when I intentionally, daily, consistently, and faithfully enter my *Sacred Story*. Recall that Christ Jesus Himself has traveled the path. He will guarantee my journey's safe passage and carry my burdens, failures, shame, broken heart, and confusion.

I will hold in my heart the humble example of Jesus washing my feet. He endured humiliations, torture, and a disgraceful death, so that I can find hope and healing for everything in my life that needs healing, forgiveness, and redemption. From the beginning of time His *SACRED STORY* is mystically imprinted into the souls of His chosen people and the Church. Through the pattern of His *STORY*, I, the Church, and all people can have their history rewritten as *Sacred Story*.

I will intentionally enter my life narrative for 15-minute intervals once or twice each day. My story linked to Christ's *SACRED STORY* and to all people and to all creation, runs from my birth in all the thoughts, words and deeds to shape my destiny here, and in the hereafter. The prayer will help me attune to Creation, Presence, Memory, Mercy, and Eternity. When I encounter the fears, stresses, angers, temptations, failures, addictions and sins in my day, I can briefly attune to Creation, Presence, Memory, Mercy, and Eternity, and ask for the grace to see my whole story. By so doing, the Divine Physician can heal me and awaken my heart to its true human nature.

Christ extends the invitation and His Love, at the Heart of the Universe, awaits my response. I pray for the courage and generosity to enter with Christ into my *Sacred Story* on this ten-week journey. Be Not Afraid!

CR

FIRST WEEK[2]
Second Exercise

Spiritual Diagnostics: Cultivating God's Perspective on Your Life History

Introduction

The purpose of all the Spiritual Diagnostic exercises is to help you to see yourself and your whole history as God sees you. To gain this perspective, evaluating trends and patterns in your personality is essential: examine thoughts, words, and deeds that express any tendency away from love, forming your anti-story. In addition, examine all the same moving you towards love, forming your *Sacred Story*. The movement is always: toward or away from peace; toward or away from healing; toward or away from freedom; toward or away from God.

The individual acts (i.e. trends, habits, addictions, sins, vices) are what Ignatius confronted when recuperating from his injuries at Loyola. This was his first and foundational conversion. In identifying these painful parts of his life anti-story, Ignatius began a new journey toward his *Sacred Story*.

We want to imitate his honesty and courage as we begin our *Sacred Story* prayer. More importantly, we want to identify those individual threads of our life tapestry that distort the authentic character of our human nature. With God's grace, we want to unmask the events, trends, and habits that rob us of peace and hope. We want to examine anything keeping us from achieving a higher consciousness, an integrated life, and a peaceful, whole and holy heart.

Sacred Story prayer continues its first week with spiritual diagnostic exercises designed to help create a whole life narrative. To help in forming the foundation of your life narrative, complete these First Week spiritual diagnostic exercises for days four through seven. Remember, a day is relative to the dictates of each person's spiritual schedule. Moving faster through these exercises is not doing them better.

Again, the aim of the spiritual diagnostic exercises is to help identify themes, events, and persons linked to your life narrative that shape and have shaped your life as 'quest and tendency' away from God into your anti-story or toward God into your *Sacred Story.*

- ✠ **Day Four**—Listen to your history in light of Ignatius' story.

- ✠ **Day Five**—Identify the Commandments of the Decalogue where you regularly miss the mark of the ideals they express.

- ✠ **Day Six Morning**—Identify compulsions, addictions, that grip you.

- ✠ **Day Six Afternoon/Evening**—Identify the capital vices that regularly entrap you.

- ✠ **Day Seven**—Write out the names of ten people and/or events that trigger in you strong irritation, anger or grief. Write a single name and/or event. After each name or event, write a single word to define the emotion that best captures that person and/or event. Begin with your closest family members and friends and significant life events. Only list the ten persons and events that come most immediately to mind.

In doing these diagnostic exercises, simply watch and pray. Try to step outside of your experience—your life narrative—and notice what you have identified. Do this observation without condition, without judgment, and with compassionate curiosity. Just watch and pray. Don't form agendas around the people, commandments, capital sins, addictions, obsessions, etc., that you identify as part of your life narrative. As best as you can, simply watch and pray about what you have identified.

It will take time and grace for the mysteries of all the things you identify to be revealed. The Church has always described the history of iniquity—of sin, vice, evil, injustice, addiction—as the mystery of iniquity. The information you glean in looking at your life holistically through these diagnostic exercises are just facts. You need time, patience, and God's grace for the mystery and presence of these facts and patterns in your life to unfold—to see your life as God sees you.

If your goal in doing these exercises is to immediately reform your life you are way off the mark! Such a goal will only discourage you. You are merely engaging in diagnostic exercises and for some this can produce anxiety. Yet these diagnostic exercises will prove to be very valuable and informative if initiated with patient intention and discipline. Be curious and observe your life and actions compassionately, not with anxious fear. God watches you with great love and compassion. Imagine you are becoming conscious—waking up—so that Christ Jesus, the Divine Physician, can diagnose where to begin your life-long healing regimen. It will take the rest of your life, working with God's grace, to grow toward wholeness and healing. It will be accomplished in mercy on God's schedule, and not your own. Let God be God and learn to accept being God's beloved.

What is most important is consciously attending to your feelings and emotions linked to the facts of your life. Is that not what any doctor asks? Where do you hurt? What are you feeling? Jesus, as the Divine Physician, wants to know where you are hurting and what you are feeling.

So watch and pray while doing these exercises. Listen to the feelings and emotions that surface as the issues and people most significant in your life narrative take shape. Listen to these emotions and consider them dispassionately, without condition, and without judgment. If you want to cultivate an attitude of judgment, use Jesus' judgment. Be judged by the love and compassion of the Divine Physician who, without judgment and without condition, wants to bring you hope and healing (Jn. 3:16-17).

Note the significant issues and people in your life narrative with Christ Jesus as your companion. Jesus watches you compassionately, lovingly and without judgment. Observe the issues and persons that take shape like you would look at roses in a garden. Your dispassionate attention will, as time passes, unlock the mysteries in your heart about all these issues and persons. You will slowly understand how they are linked, and how, by grace, you can best cooperate with the Divine Physician in responding to each. What you are noticing is truly a matter and a mystery of the heart. Only the heart, by God's grace, can reveal the meaning of these facts of your history.

God has no interest in using the facts of your past as evidence against you. God is interested in how these experiences fractured your consciousness, eroded your freedom, or masked your true identity. Jesus wants to know what robbed you of peace. He wants to know what broke your heart and the hearts of others. God desires that you have knowledge about your life that is rooted in knowledge of the heart, because God is love and master of the heart. Watch, listen, and pray, without condition, without judgment. Ask for knowledge of the heart. Ask for knowledge of God's heart as you uncover these mysteries of your life narrative that will become chapters in your *Sacred Story*.

Watch and pray with these exercises as you did in your reading of Ignatius' life narrative. Watch and pray and ask for God's grace. Ask God that the facts of your life disclose to you their mysteries imprinted in the memory of your heart. For these too are only remembered by God in the heart of the Son. The heart is where God wants to make a home and where we will find our way home.

The heart is the place where all the important work of the *Sacred Story* prayer program will be accomplished. The mind reveals facts. The heart reveals the mind of God. Scripture uses the heart in all its most important descriptions of the human condition: to describe the state of corruption caused by sin (Gen. 6:5; Jer. 17:9-10; Mt. 15:9.); to articulate the process of conversion and forgiveness (Ez. 36:26; Mt. 18:35; Rom. 2:29). The heart is the place where self-condemnation and hope in God's power unite (1 Jn. 3:19-20). The heart is the place of purity that sees God (Mt. 5:8). The heart is the locus of compassion (Lk. 7:13), memory, and contemplation (Lk. 1:29; 2:19, 51), and the heart holds ultimate human significance and meaning (Mt. 6:21; Lk. 24:32; Ps. 85:9).

The heart is defined as the center of human consciousness and action and is where God helps us discern right from wrong. The heart is the center from which an individual will stand before God and render an ultimate account of their thoughts, words, and deeds (Heb. 4:12-13).

It is the heart that perceives love as the ultimate end, gift, and purpose of being (1 Cor. 13). The testimony of Christ in Scripture speaks to the heart's desire for innocence, based on the weariness of life and the burdens it carries resulting from corruption (Mt. 11:28-30) Christ also promises to respond to the heart searching for him. Christ gives us the conviction that he can be found by those who seek him (Lk. 11:9-11).

Seek knowledge of the heart and pray to be given the grace to access a pathway to your heart. Seek also knowledge of God's heart in Christ's sacred heart. Pray that your heart and the heart of Christ can become one.

CR

FIRST WEEK
Third Exercise

Days Four-Seven
Day Four Diagnostic: Attuning to your Life History

Recall your listening/writing exercise while reading St. Ignatius' *Sacred Story* narrative. Read what you wrote in your journal. Notice the issue(s) that caused you the most anxiety as you listened to Ignatius' story. Try to focus on why you were anxious. Also, recall the most significant issue(s) that inspired or gave you hope. Try to focus on why you were inspired or hopeful.

Now, looking over all your journal entries, write in your notebook the one issue or idea that caused you the most anxiety. Also write down why you felt the anxiety, if you can understand why. Not everyone will know why something causes anxiety so don't be anxious if you don't know. Also write the issue that caused you the most hope or inspiration and why, if you understand the reason for the hope or inspiration.

Be brief in all your writing exercises but also exacting and specific. Take no more than fifteen minutes for this entire listening and writing exercise.[3]

CR

FIRST WEEK
Fourth Exercise

Day Five: Spiritual Diagnostic — Ten Commandments or Decalogue

Set aside fifteen minutes today for the *Decalogue* or Ten Commandments exercise. You may choose to take one, two, or three days for this exercise. Remember, a day is relative to your schedule and the time you want to take to leisurely and reflectively engage each exercise. No matter how many days you take don't spend more than fifteen minutes each day in your prayer exercise. Each day as you read and reflect mark down all the stress points you find in your life, those areas where you miss the mark in living the Commandments. Think of the Commandments as reflecting "right relationships".

The Commandments were given to the Chosen People in a covenant that was sealed with a blood sacrifice. The Church reflects that the power of the animal sacrifice sealing the covenant receives its power from Christ's blood; an event which it also foreshadows. The Commandments, as a gift to humanity, are a foundation for God's work to repair our broken human nature, to forgive us, and reopen the way to eternity. It is no wonder then that laws enshrining their truths have transformed stories of violence and injustice to stories of civility and justice for tens of millions of people in the last three millennia.

We have taken the individual Commandments for this exercise and developed each one so our prayer enhances our understanding of their richness and wisdom. Our goal is to show how the responsibilities and boundaries stated in the Commandments help us manifest "right relationships" in our lives. In the *Sacred Story* program we call them "Decrees"—a synonym for Commandment—so that we hear them with new imagination. They are decrees—statements by God—to help a people who had forgotten to remember and know the truth about God, humanity, and oneself. They are a gift so we can all find our way home—so our thoughts, words, and deeds bring life, not death. They are our first code indicator of what signifies "right relationships."

Before completing your daily prayer period, jot down where in your life you miss the mark in living each Decree. Be exacting and specific in what you write. Be honest and courageous because you are the only one who has access to the information so strive for integrity and openness in your responses.

Try it this way: identify the Decree (and the sub-themes in the Decrees) as mild, moderate, or strong regarding the challenge they present to you. For example, you may jot down: "6th—moderate, especially regarding xoxoxo"; "4th—mild regarding tytyty"; "7th/10th—strong regarding bnbnbn". Use codes if you prefer so you can be free of worry should someone see your writing.

Note: You are simply to observe your challenges with the Decrees. With Christ by your side, watch with curiosity, detachment, and without self-blame. God sees beyond any patterns of sin and failure you have, or think you have. God knows you for who you are. God loves you. He is the Divine Physician who wants to help you diagnose your life so he can bring forgiveness, healing, freedom, and peace. The text of the Decalogue Examination follows.

THE TEN COMMANDMENTS
A DECALOGUE EXAMINATION OF CONSCIENCE[4]

First Decree: I am the Lord your God, you shall have no strange gods before me.

Is God the center of my life? Has God been displaced by career, work, concern for wealth and pleasure? Does the worship and honor of God take shape in my weekly religious practices? Do I pray often? Do I turn to God for forgiveness often? Have I resorted to relying on superstition, the occult, or astrology in place of asking for God's assistance?

Second Decree: You shall not take the name of the Lord your God in vain.

Do I casually take God's name in vain? Do I have a habit of swearing in jest or when angry? Do I use God's name to damn other people? Do I nurse hatred of God in my heart? Do I harbor anger towards God for things in my life or things in the world? Do I have reverence for God in my heart?

Third Decree: Remember to keep holy the Sabbath day.

Sunday is the continuous celebration of the Easter event as the sign and source of salvation. Do I make every effort to prepare myself for the Sunday Liturgy? Do I make every effort to attend the Sunday Liturgy? Do I allow social or sporting events to displace or limit my attendance at the Sunday Liturgy? Do I limit unnecessary servile work on Sunday? Is Sunday a true day of spiritual rest and refreshment?

Fourth Decree: Honor your Father and Mother.

Do I give due reverence to my mom and dad for the gift of life? Do I thank them? Do I spend time with them? Do I strive to forgive the shortcomings of my parents? Do I hold anger or grudges against them in my heart? Do I try to respond with love and charity? Do I attend to them in their weaknesses, infirmity, and old age?

Fifth Decree: You shall not kill.

Do I strive to overcome the prejudices I have against individuals or groups? Do I strive not to act on my prejudices so as not to harm others with my words or deeds? Do I act with meanness towards others? Do I risk my life or the lives of others by using illegal drugs? Do I risk my life or the lives of others by driving recklessly or while intoxicated? Do I strive in words and deeds to promote the value of life from conception to natural death? Have I ever helped someone terminate a pregnancy or end his or her life? Do I strive to do everything I can to uphold the value of all people? Do I harbor satisfaction in my heart at the death of those people whom I consider evil? Do I vote for people because of their positions to protect and promote abortion, euthanasia, capital punishment or pre-emptive war? Do I mourn the loss of all human lives no matter the cause of death?

Sixth Decree: You shall not commit adultery.

Ninth Decree: You shall not covet your neighbor's spouse

(The Sixth and the Ninth Decrees are usually linked because of the subjects they cover). Do I protect my covenant relationship and uphold its sacredness? Do I strive daily to support my spouse? Do I turn to other persons for emotional support to make my spouse envious? Do I denigrate my spouse by comparing her/him to others? Do I speak harshly about my spouse behind her/his back to gain the affections of others? Do I uphold the sacredness of my covenant commitment by never seeking the sexual attention of those to whom I may be attracted? Do I uphold my covenant by never engaging in any sexual activity with someone other than my spouse? Do I use pornography to arouse my sexual appetites, or to avoid intimacy with my spouse? Do I denigrate the spiritual integrity of persons by focusing on their physical beauty or appearance?

Do I protect my covenant relationship by not purposely fantasizing about sexual relations with others than my spouse? Do I hold sacred the gift of sexuality for marriage? Do I strive to cultivate purity of heart as a sign of God's own single-heartedness? Do I reverence sexual intercourse first and foremost as the gift most akin to God's original gift to us - the gift of love to create a human life destined for an eternity with God? Do I casually inhibit God's presence in this divine gift of my physical body with drugs or medical procedures when there is no legitimate reason?

Seventh Decree: You shall not steal.

Tenth Decree: You shall not covet your neighbor's goods.

(The Seventh and the Tenth Decrees are usually linked due to the subjects they cover). Do I cheat on papers and exams to steal a better grade? Do I take things of others that don't belong to me? Do I keep things I have borrowed? Am I honest in my investments, taxes, and in all of my financial dealings? Do I use legal loopholes in tax laws or business practices to harvest financial rewards that ultimately hurt the less fortunate? Am I honest and truthful in my business dealings even if it means I might lose profits or customers? Do I vandalize or otherwise harm property or goods that don't belong to me? Do I envy those who have more than I do? Do I let concern for wealth and comfort take center place in my life? Do I live lavishly just because I have the resources to do so? Do I spend money on luxury goods I don't really need? Do I live with envy of those who have more than I do? Do I respect the limited resources of the earth as a divine inheritance to benefit all people? Do I give to the poor a percentage of my earned income? Do I strive to live so as to minimize waste and protect the environment? Do I examine my investment patterns to discern if companies I own or in which I have stock are treating their employees justly and are protecting the environment in their practices? Do I ever put the drive for profits ahead of the welfare of other persons or the environment?

Eighth Decree: You shall not bear false witness against your neighbor.

Do I live to uphold the honor of other people's reputations? Do I avoid spreading gossip and avoid seeking gossip from others? Do I share information about people with third parties, even if it is true, when that information could damage that person's reputation? Do I constantly avoid spreading lies or rumors about other people? Do I challenge people who gossip and spread damaging information about others? Do I avoid and denounce TV, radio, magazines, and newspapers that employ the tactics of personality destruction and malicious gossip to sell news and generate profits? Am I more concerned with managing my own life than telling others what they ought to do with theirs?

CR

FIRST WEEK
FIFTH EXERCISE

Day Six-Morning: Addictions

For day six take fifteen minutes to listen to your addictions. Ignatius was addicted to gambling and licentious behavior. Your addictions might take entirely different forms. Read the short description of addiction types- substance or psychological dependence- below. Mark in your notebook all the addictions that you think are obstacles in your life and living with the freedom you desire. This is not a time to look deeply into clinical definitions or causes but simply to identify what you believe to be problematic behaviors and dependencies. Be brief in your writing but exacting and specific about what addictions you have or think you might have. Identify which ensnare you and list if you believe you are: **O**ccasionally ensnared, **F**requently ensnared, or **C**onstantly ensnared by the specific addiction. For example, you may write:

Television—O; Exercise—F; Gambling—C.

This exercise, like all the others, requires courage and honesty. Remember, you are only invited to watch these components of your life narrative, nothing more. You are not to pass judgment, plan corrective therapies to counteract addictions, or get lost in anxiety and fear. You are simply to watch your addictions and allow the Divine Physician help you understand and see their context in your life history. Watch with curiosity and with dispassion. Jesus the Divine Physician watches compassionately with you. God sees beyond any addictions you have or think you have. God knows you for who you are and loves you. Christ the Redeemer carries the burden for all your addictions and sufferings.

ADDICTION DEFINED[5]

The term "addiction" is used in many contexts to describe an obsession, compulsion, or excessive psychological dependence, such as: drug addiction

(e.g. alcoholism, nicotine addiction), problem gambling, compulsive defrauding or tax evasion, money addictions, work addiction, exercise addiction, compulsive overeating, compulsive shopping, sex addiction, computer addiction, e-mail addiction, video game addiction, pornography addiction, television addiction, etc.

Common usage of the term addiction has spread to include psychological dependence. In this context, the term is used beyond drug addiction and substance abuse problems, and also refers to behaviors that are not generally recognized by the medical community as problems of addiction, such as compulsive overeating. The term "addiction," as applied to compulsions that are not substance-related, such as problem gambling and computer addiction, is a common usage that describes a recurring compulsion one engages in despite the activity's harmful consequences to one's individual physical, mental, social, or spiritual health.

Gabor Maté sums up addiction's profile: "Addiction is any repeated behavior, substance-related or not, in which a person feels compelled to persist, regardless of its negative impact on his life and the lives of others. Addiction involves:

a. compulsive engagement with the behavior, a preoccupation with it;

b. impaired control over the behavior;

c. persistence or relapse despite evidence of harm; and

d. dissatisfaction, irritability, or intense craving when the object—be it a drug, activity, or other goal—is not immediately available.

Compulsion, impaired control, persistence, irritability, relapse, and craving these are all the hallmarks of addiction—any addiction."[6]

CR

FIRST WEEK
SIXTH EXERCISE

Day Six-Afternoon/Evening: Spiritual Diagnostic—Capital Sins or Vices

For day six take fifteen minutes in the afternoon or evening to read the list of vices or capital sins listed below. They are called "capital" sins (from *caput*, the Latin word for *head*) because they are root habits or vices that lead to many other problems. In your notebook, mark down all the capital vices that hook you. Be brief in your writing but as exacting and specific as possible. List which capital sins/vices ensnare you and to what level they ensnare you: mildly, moderately, or seriously.

You are simply to recognize your capital sins or vices. Allow Christ the Divine Physician to help you understand their source and context in your life history. Watch with curiosity and with detachment. God sees beyond any vices you have or think you have. God knows you for who you are and loves you. Jesus the Divine Physician watches compassionately and carries the burden for all your vices.

CR

THE SEVEN CAPITAL SINS OR VICES[7]

Pride

Pride is an unrestrained and improper appreciation of our own worth. This is listed first because it is widely considered the most serious of the seven sins. Pride was the foundation Adam and Eve's sin that made them fall for the serpent's temptation "to be like gods". Adam and Eve displaced God (Creator) as the arbiter of truth and goodness. They made themselves (creatures) final judges of truth and goodness. Their action led to the loss of paradise and the entry of sickness and death into the world. Pride often leads to the committing of other capital sins. Pride is manifest in vanity and narcissism about one's appearance, intelligence, status, wealth, connections, power, successes, and all other things one uses to stand apart.

"Keep me from the dead works of vanity and the thankless labor in which artists destroy themselves for pride and money and reputation, and saints are smothered under the avalanche of their own importunate zeal."[339]

Greed

Greed is also known as avarice or covetousness. It is the immoderate desire for earthly goods and power and is a sin of excess. The object a person is desires need not be evil. The problem lies in the way a person regards or desires an object making it a god and investing it with inappropriate value. Greed can inspire such sinful actions as the hoarding of materials or objects, theft, fraud, tax evasion, environmental waste, and unethical business practices.

"Staunch in me the rank wound of covetousness and the hungers that exhaust my nature with their bleeding."

Gluttony

Gluttony comes from the Latin word meaning to gulp down or swallow. It is a sin of over-indulgence and over-consumption of food and drink. Gluttony can be eating too soon, eating too expensively, and eating too much. St. Alphonsus Liguori explained that "it is not a fault to feel pleasure in eating. In most instances it is impossible to eat without experiencing the delight which food naturally produces. But it is a defect to eat through the sole motive of sensual gratification, and without any reasonable object".

"Keep me from the sins that eat a man's flesh with irresistible fire until he is devoured."

Lust

The sin of lust refers to corrupted desires of a sexual nature. Sexuality is a gift from God and pure in itself. However lust refers to the impure thoughts and actions that misuse that gift. Lust deviates from God's law and sexuality's purpose in allowing woman and man to participate in God's creative power. Indulging in the sin of lust can include (but is not limited to): fornication, adultery, bestiality, rape, masturbation, pornography, and incest.

"Keep me from the murder of lust that blinds and poisons my heart."

Sloth

Sloth is often described simply as the sin of laziness. However, while this is part of sloth's character, the central problem with sloth, as a capital sin or vice, is spiritual laziness. The sin of sloth means being lazy and lax about living the Faith and practicing virtue. Here is a paraphrase from *The Catholic Encyclopedia*: In general sloth means aversion to labor or exertion. As a capital or deadly vice, St. Thomas calls it sadness in the face of some spiritual good that one has to achieve. In other words, a person is bothered at the prospect of what he or she must do for God to bring about or keep intact one's friendship with God. In this sense sloth is directly opposed to charity.

"Untie my hands and deliver my hands from sloth. Set me free from the laziness that goes about disguised as activity when activity is not required of me, and from the cowardice that does what is not demanded, in order to escape sacrifice."

Envy

The sin of envy or jealousy is more than just someone wanting what others have. Sinful envy leads one to emotions or feelings of upset at another's luck or blessings. The law of love naturally leads one to rejoice in the good luck of one's neighbor. Envy opposes such love. Envy is named among the capital sins because of the other sins to which it leads.

"Stamp out the serpent envy that stings love with poison and kills all joy."

Anger

Anger or wrath may be described as excessive and powerful feelings of hatred and resentment. These feelings can manifest as a passionate denial of truths expressed by others. Anger can also manifest in the form of self-denial of truths about one's one life and impatience with the procedure of law. Anger can also manifest in the desire to seek revenge outside of the workings of the justice system. Anger, in essence, is wishing to do evil or harm to others. The transgressions borne of vengeance are among the most serious, including murder, assault, and in extreme cases, genocide and other crimes against humanity. Anger is the only sin not necessarily associated with selfishness or self-interest, yet one can be angry for selfish reasons, such as jealousy.

"Keep me from the death of deadly sin which puts hell in my soul."

೮

FIRST WEEK
Seventh exercise

Day Seven: Spiritual Diagnostic—Persons/Issues/Events That Initiate Fear, Anger or Grief and Gratitude, Hope, or Love

Each of us has persons, issues, and life events that consciously and unconsciously give shape to our life story and history. We seek grace to understand those most capable of shaping—negatively and positively—our daily thoughts, actions, feelings, and beliefs linked to God, the world and ourselves. These persons, life events, and issues are often linked to the spiritual plotlines in our life story, leading towards or away from God.

In this exercise we seek God's grace to awaken to our affective memories. That is, we want to remember the person, life event, or issue, and feel their emotional weight—the heart value—in our personal histories. We ask God's grace because these most significant history-shapers often move out of our consciousness. We use "I" to make these following statements my own.

I seek insight for those elements most personal to my life story: parents, family, friends, important events, and loved ones. For one life event, I might feel fear (something that has the power to generate the anxiety I know as fear). For another life event, my predominant feeling might be anger (something that hurt me or a loved one). For one person, I might feel mostly love (someone who has cared deeply for me). For another person, I might feel anger (someone who has hurt me in some way). For one issue, my predominant feeling might be grief (the loss of a loved one or an opportunity that grieves my heart). For another issue, my experience might be gratitude or hope (an issue that has positively transformed my life for the better).

Pray that God will enlighten your mind and heart to know each element (person, issue or life event) and the single, predominant feeling (fear, anger, or grief—gratitude, hope, or love) each inspires. Pray for the knowledge only God can give.

Complete this exercise on the day you begin it. It is less important to get things exactly right than it is to simply complete each question with the first answer that comes to mind.

Keep working until you complete a full list of ten people/events/issues, even if you take longer than fifteen minutes. Give yourself a longer time period if necessary in order to finish the exercise in one sitting. You can also take breaks and then come back to the exercise until it is completed that same day you began. You must write an associated word for each person/event/issue. The word should best express your emotional and affective response to the person or event. For the sake of focus and precision, limit your definitions of emotion used to describe these persons, issues or events to: "anger," "fear," or "grief," "gratitude," "hope," or "love."

Remember, you are simply to watch these persons, issues, and events as they are remembered. Watch with curiosity and with as much detachment and indifference as possible. God sees beyond persons, events, and issues that cause you fear, anger, or grief. God knows you for who you are, loves and cherishes you. Jesus the Divine Physician compassionately watches with you.

CR

TEN PEOPLE/ISSUES/EVENTS THAT INITIATE FEAR, ANGER OR GRIEF

Person/Issues/Events	Fear/Anger/Grief
1	1
2	2
3	3
4	4
5	5
6	6
7	7
8	8
9	9
10	10

TEN PEOPLE/ISSUES/EVENTS THAT INITIATE GRATITUDE, HOPE OR LOVE

Person/Issues/Events	Gratitude/Hope/Love
1	1
2	2
3	3
4	4
5	5
6	6
7	7
8	8
9	9
10	10

CR

SECOND TO FIFTH WEEKS
Second Week

Day One: Setting Your Time

When you start the regular practice of *Sacred Story,* select a fifteen-minute time to practice each day and the number of times a day you will pray. In continuing these preliminary exercises, test the time(s) of day and the number of times a day that work best for your schedule and life patterns. Take fifteen minutes today to decide the fifteen-minute period(s) during your day you will consciously enter these next exercises. Think of all the exercises that follow as a focused process of entering into your authentic life story. Be specific and be consistent in determining the time of day and the number of times of day you will pray.

You can choose to consciously enter your life narrative in these fifteen-minute spiritual exercises either once a day or twice a day. Those who choose twice a day often achieve insights and growth more readily. Yet those who choose consciously to enter their life narrative once daily also experience significant growth. You determine which path to walk. Remaining faithful to a practice once a day is better than sporadic practice twice a day. You can always change by increasing your prayer practice to two times a day or by decreasing your engagement to one period a day.

Similarly, you can change the time of days you pray until you find a workable method that fits your life and schedule.[8] Feel free to move at your own pace through these daily exercises. Whichever way you choose, be mindful that there is no hurry. Remember, *Sacred Story* lasts a lifetime. There is no rush to wrap it up. In fact, you can't wrap it up this side of eternity. So take your time! This is not intended to frustrate you. Moving through the exercises faster does not guarantee success, prove you are getting it, or make you a better person.

CR

SECOND WEEK
First exercise

Days Two-Seven: Watch and Pray for the Grace to see Links in your Sacred Story

Whether you engage in *Sacred Story* prayer once or twice a day for fifteen-minutes, for these next six days (or as many days as you choose to take) simply watch and pray with the notes from all of your previous exercises: Ignatius' Sacred Story narrative; the *Spiritual Diagnostic* and its component sections, i.e., the *Commandments/Decalogue* Examination of Conscience, Addictions, Capital Sin/Vices, and the People/Issues/Events that trigger anger, grief, or fear.

More than just watching and praying, consciously ask God (or Jesus, the Holy Spirit, Mary, St. Ignatius, or some other favorite and trusted holy person linked to your *Sacred Story*) for the grace to see your life more clearly, in light of all these different themes, people, events, emotions, habits, and patterns that you have identified as part of your life narrative. Specifically, ask for the grace to see any connections between the people, events, issues, vices, command-ments, addictions, and the emotions of fear, anger, or grief. Ask the Divine Physician for help to awaken to profound comprehension of your life history.

You have already begun this linking process in a previous exercise. This new diagnostic exercise simply builds on the previous one. It invites you to add the new component of Commandment challenges, capital vices, and addic-tions to the mix. You are free to use the data from your previous chart or to augment it with new persons/events/issues that may have surfaced as a result of further reflection in these past days/weeks. If you choose to augment your chart, you most likely will add elements/things/persons that appear integrated to your life narrative. Create a new template in your journal for this new diag-nostic exercise similar to this one shown below:

Person/Event/Issue	*Commandments/Addictions/Vices*	*Fear/Anger/Grief*
1	1	1
2	2	2
3	3	3

Let the Commandments, vices, addictions, issues, names, events and emotions of fear, anger or grief that you highlighted, and the links you discover, surface naturally in the course of the day as you go about your business. Don't force thoughts to surface. Simply take note of the ones that do surface. God can bring important things to your attention at the most unusual times. It often happens outside the set time of your *Sacred Story* prayer. That is why your whole life is a *Sacred Story*. You are becoming conscious of everything. You are awakening from sleep.

Expect ideas and links between the component parts of your anti-story and your *Sacred Story* to pop into your head at any time. After all, you have been consciously thinking about many things that you normally only keep in the back of your mind. Most importantly, you have been asking for God's grace to see, feel, and remember these parts of your life history. God answers your prayers at the best time and in the best way. Your prayers are always answered.

When you sit down for your fifteen-minute *Sacred Story* prayers, bring images and emotions from your day and the memories from your notes. Simply watch and pray with them for the duration of the prayer period. Note especially the things or persons that cause you upset, annoyance, anger, or fear. Make no judgments. Take no action. Simply watch and pray. Step outside your life narrative and watch as if above the fray. Notice what surfaces during these fifteen-minute periods.

When you finish consciously focusing on your life narrative, and at the end of each session, note what thoughts, persons, and/or feelings occupied your attention the most. Make a very brief notation in your journal. This will help you remember both the subject and the emotion attached to it. Pass no judgments upon yourself, or upon others. Seek heart knowledge. These notations will help you perceive your life more clearly. The Divine Physician, with great compassion, is helping you every step of the way.

CR

THIRD WEEK
First exercise

The Ignatian Confession Letter

Days One-Four (or more): Reflective Reading

Read reflectively this section of the Ignatian Confession Letter. Take fifteen minutes for this exercise. You may profitably extend this fifteen-minute exercise from one to two, three, four or more days. Trust your heart. Only move forward with the next exercise when you are convinced that you have gained all the insights possible. The peacefulness in your heart will guide you and let you know when to proceed.

CR

THE IGNATIAN CONFESSION LETTER

When he travelled to Montserrat, Ignatius made a general confession of his first thirty years. In preparation for this confession—his spiritual self-diagnostic—he was given by one of the monks detailed examinations of conscience that followed the Ten Commandments and the laws and precepts of the Church. It was common in his day for a pilgrim to be given many lists of sins based on the Ten Commandments. One would spend days writing down both the number and type of each sin.

That it took Ignatius three days to complete this exercise should give us hope that even saints are "people with a past." Late in his life Ignatius told his Jesuit companion Luís Gonçalves da Câmera that he believed God had never combined in one person someone who had sinned so much and yet been given so many graces. Yes indeed, there is hope for all of us! Wholeness and holiness are not linked to a perfect life. Instead, wholeness and holiness are linked to the perfect surrender of our lives to the compassion, mercy, and healing graces of the Divine Physician. Ignatius' journey into the very heart his anti-story, and from there into the wholeness and holiness of his *Sacred Story*, had a written life confession as a primary foundation. Ignatius' written confession was a real spiritual exercise. It demanded of him both honesty and courage. But the courage and honesty with which he engaged in the exercises laid the foundation for all his subsequent spiritual growth and enlightenment.

Review the notes from your journal entries, and your various Spiritual Diagnostic exercises. Pay attention to the Commandments where you miss the mark, the vices that ensnare you, and the addictions that grip you. Recall too the persons, issues, and events that upset you most with anger, fear, and grief. All of these issues, temptations, trials, people, and feelings can appear distinct and separate.

They intertwine in your heart and soul and are all part of your life narrative, from the past all the way up to the present day. In the Kingdom to come, we will be able to discern clearly all these interconnections in our lives, between our lives and the history of all creation, and in the whole of the human race (1 Cor. 13:11). Today, however, the path to awakened consciousness and integrated holiness invites you to see and begin to understand these connections in the-here-and-now. St. Paul said that now is the time to wake from sleep (Rom. 13:11). Writing a life-narrative, a life confession, is your first effort to begin seeing life-as-a-whole and waking from sleep.

With Ignatius as a model, this narrative is your story, your confession. You are bringing to consciousness those events (thoughts, words, and deeds) that express what Ignatius would call life's excessive affections (wounding addictions and sinful habits). All these things undermine your freedom, and shape aspects of your history as 'quest and tendency' away from God's love, mercy, and peace (your anti-story). Jesus comes into history not to condemn us (Jn. 3:17) but so that we may have life and have it abundantly (Jn. 10:10). Truthfully, for most this exercise will stir up considerable anxiety, and in some, withering fear or dread. Others thinking about this exercise will feel themselves slipping into unconsciousness and fall asleep from fatigue. (When you look back to the section on spiritual guidelines you will note that fear and dread are not the fruit of God's spirit but of the enemy of human nature.)

If you believe that it is not possible for you to change your habits you can experience anxiety. All that really needs to change is your habit of not letting the mercy and love of the Divine Physician touch you when and where you need hope and healing. Christ is the one who brings change, not you. Let God be God. You may simply need to allow the Divine Physician's mercy and love to touch those dimensions of your history where you really need help.

Jesus, as the Divine Physician, is the only one who can help. He does not demand instant change in your life. He urgently desires to be with you now and during the rest of your *Sacred Story,* when and where you need his care. This is why the life confession will take the form of a written narrative—a letter— addressed to Christ Jesus. He is the one to whom you can be fully honest. He is the only one who can hold in mercy all that you say. He is the only one who has waited and dedicated his entire life to receive your trials, sadness, grief, anger, fear, failures, sins, and pain. He can transform all of it into your *Sacred Story.*

Why does he do this? The best gift you can give Jesus Christ is to allow him to accept and forgive the darkness and sin from your past. He is the first born from the dead and the one who, in love, has freed you by his blood (Rev. 1:5). It is the only gift you can give to him that fully recognizes his suffering and death. He endured everything, lovingly and patiently, to bring you forgiveness, hope, and healing. Your failures, addictions, fears, wounds, anger, and grief all are gifts to Jesus. He died so that you might have life and have it abundantly. He is not ashamed of you. He is not angry with you. Christ, the Divine Physician, loves you and desires with all his heart to help you. Any fear you might feel contemplating this exercise comes not from God but from the enemy of your human nature. For God searches for the lost sheep and proclaims that there is more rejoicing in heaven over one repentant sinner than over ninety-nine righteous persons who have no need of forgiveness (Lk. 15:7).

God's only judgment against you was to die for you so you can regain your freedom, authenticity, and innocence. Any movement on your part to take advantage of his gifts of forgiveness, and compassion, will be supported by his infinite grace and mercy. This exercise requires humility because it can be humiliating to be so honest about your life. And the exercise requires patience because your memory holds many experiences that only by your close attention and God's grace are you able to surrender to the light of day.

Pray to remember and to see your life as God sees it. Jesus told his disciples in Gethsemane to "watch and pray". He wanted them to watch him, see his suffering, and learn from what they saw, with both their eyes and hearts. Jesus asks the same of you; that you watch your life history and pray, so you can see the sufferings of the past with your eyes, yes, but more with your heart. He suffered to take on the burdens of your life, and to give you hope, healing, and peace. We know the disciples could not stay awake in Gethsemane. They fell asleep. What they saw was too much for them to bear. It could be the same for you at times. But you will be given the grace to watch your history in a way that you can see, feel, and understand with your heart.

This exercise is not about forcing. It is about asking God to help you wake up to become conscious of the past so that you can find healing and peace. Let God lead you. Simply ask for God's help to awaken you to your life and your history. God watches over you as tenderly as a mother or a father watches over their child who is in distress. God passionately desires to hear your story, and for you to be able to tell it. Awakening to your story is the supreme gift that you can give to God because you are offering God the opportunity to reveal to you why you are loved.

The Son redeemed you. The Divine Physician will transform your anti-story—addictions, sins, vices, grief, fears and angers, brokenness and failures-into the gift, grace, and blessing of *Sacred Story*. In so doing, you will join his Great Work of Reconciliation. For where sin abounds, grace abounds all the more (Rom. 5:20). What you believe angers God, destroys your relationships, or forever makes you unclean and unforgivable, is precisely what draws Christ Jesus to you. He will use whatever has created alienation, fear, death, and loneliness and transform it into blessings. Christ will use these curses, turned into blessings, to connect you with him, others, and all creation. Eventually, they will become the source of your holiness—your *Sacred Story*. Do not be afraid!

☙

THIRD TO FOURTH WEEKS
Second exercise

Week Three, Day Two–Week Four, Day Seven: Writing a Confessional Narrative

For this exercise, write your Whole-Life Confession. What is a Whole-Life Confession? A whole-life confession is different from a confession of your whole life. It is not helpful, nor is it required to twice confess sins and weaknesses you have already confessed. Your opportunity in a whole-life confession is to look at connections and patterns of sin and weakness in your whole life—what we have been trying to work on these past weeks. I am inviting you to ask for God's help to see a comprehensive picture of your life— your story—with Christ as your Divine Physician and healer.

> It must be recalled that . . . this reconciliation with God leads, as it were, to other reconciliations, which repair the other breaches caused by sin. The forgiven penitent is reconciled with himself in his inmost being, where he regains his innermost truth. He is reconciled with his brethren whom he has in some way offended and wounded. He is reconciled with the Church. He is reconciled with all creation. *Catechism of the Catholic Church 1469--John Paul II, RP 31, 5.*

Think of this confession as your report to Christ—your spiritual diagnosis—after these weeks of the prayerful reflection on your life. You can confess current issues and past issues that have been overlooked. As you do this you are telling Christ the chronic patterns of sin and weaknesses and how they are linked to your life history. As you look at your life story with Christ, the Divine Physician, you are also addressing him directly. You are telling him why you need him as your Savior. This could be the very first time that you have reviewed your life, seen clearly why you can't save yourself, and directly asked Jesus to be your Savior. What a profound grace to know why you can't save yourself and to ask Christ for this tremendous gift!

Look at this from Christ's perspective, too. There is no greater gift you give to Christ than acknowledging your sinfulness and weaknesses as you ask for his healing love, mercy, and forgiveness. By so doing, you take seriously the gift of his life, passion, death, and resurrection. You are telling Jesus you need his cross to be healed. You are thanking Jesus for suffering and dying for you so you can be renewed in him. This is the real focus of Christian life! Jesus really hears you and wants to hear what you have to say to him. He waits with compassion and great longing to hear your story.

The Pharisees and their scribes complained to his disciples, saying, "Why do you eat and drink with tax collectors and sinners?" Jesus said to them in reply, "Those who are healthy do not need a physician, but the sick do. I have not come to call the righteous to repentance but sinners." Lk. 5: 30-32

With Jesus as your Divine Physician, a whole-life confession makes perfect sense. He understands you and everything about your life. He has an intense desire to hear your life story and wants to respond as your Savior. Here are my suggestions for preparing this simple, holy, and graced letter/statement/confession:

1. One picture is worth a thousand words—Your life is a picture, a story. You are to write a letter to Christ that is **no more** than a thousand words. If typed, it would be about three and a half pages double-spaced. But you don't have to write that much. I repeat: write **no more** than 1000 words.

2. Personal words that are heartfelt—I invite you to find the name for Christ that speaks to your heart. Christ Jesus, Lord and Savior, My Lord etc. You are speaking to the one who won your victory and who came into the world to save you. This week, we want to speak directly to Christ Jesus. Speak to Jesus in the first person: "Please forgive, I remember, I suffered, please heal me…" Write the confessional story—your history—directly from your heart to the heart of Jesus.

3. Strive for honesty—Strive earnestly for courage and honesty in your letter. The letter is for you and only you, unless you choose to share it in Sacramental Confession. You need not impress anyone. What is significant is your courage and honesty. Be honest too about the forgiveness you need to extend to others. Write from your heart. (Write by long hand, or type or on a computer, whichever is your preference).

4. You are not climbing Mount Everest—PLEASE, pray for the grace not to turn this simple, graced letter/confession opportunity into a huge, exhausting task. You are not climbing a mountain. You are having a conversation with Christ about your life. Hear him say to you:

Come to me, all you who labor and are burdened, and I will give you rest. Take my yoke upon you and learn from me, for I am meek and humble of heart; and you will find rest for your selves. For my yoke is easy, and my burden light. Mt. 11: 28-29

5. Pray for patience and compassion—Your awakening to your life story will take the rest of your life. It takes a lifetime for Christ's work of healing and forgiveness to embrace you heart and soul. There is no finish line or ultimate enlightenment you can reach on this earth. You will always need healing at deeper levels. You will constantly grow in love and enlightenment, selflessness and humility, until the day you pass from this earth. You will not be finished until the day the Divine Physician and Eternal King sits you down at his Eternal Banquet.

But as for the seed that fell on rich soil, they are the ones who, when they have heard the word, embrace it with a generous and good heart, and bear fruit through perseverance. Lk. 8:15

6. Set the scene in your heart's imagination—Here is how you might set your heart's imagination as you write: imagine you have been given the opportunity to be alone with Christ when he is walking from town to town. You will have fifteen minutes with him…alone. See the road and the other disciples walking up ahead of you and the Lord. No one else can hear you. Write your letter as if you are speaking to Christ in this setting. He knows why you want to speak with him and is ready to hear you. Before you begin talking about your life, he looks you in the eyes and says: "Soon, I will be lifted up on my cross. I am doing this for you so that you can find forgiveness, healing, and hope for the sin, weakness, and suffering you experience in your life. As I conquer all death and sin—as I breathe my last breath—I will hold you and your life story in my heart. You will find victory and eternal life in me, and one day be with me in paradise."

Then Jesus said, "Father, forgive them, they know not what they do." Then he said, "Jesus, remember me when you come into your kingdom." He replied to him, "Amen, I say to you, today you will be with me in Paradise." Lk. 23: 34, 42-3

Here is my suggestion for how you might structure your heart-felt conversation/letter/confession to Christ Jesus, the Divine Physician:

- "Dear Jesus, I am so grateful for all the gifts you have given to me." (Spend some time writing from your heart why you are grateful. Use Jesus' name often, as you write, and give very particular examples of why you are grateful).

- "Lord, I am profoundly aware of how some of my past experiences [life history, family, friends, work, school, and neighbors] are linked to areas of un-freedom in my life and have created embarrassing and/ or discouraging habits and rooted patterns of sinfulness." (Spend some time looking back over your life and offer particular examples that capture the links and patterns of sins, addictions, vices, and the Commandments that cause you to stumble. If you can't discern patterns yet, just speak about these areas individually. If there are central people in your life story who are linked to these destructive patterns, mention them to Christ. If you are confused about some of the things you do, tell Jesus what they are and then ask for his help to better understand why you do what you do. From your heart, ask Christ's grace to gain greater freedom from these habits and sins).

- "But Lord, there is one central pattern of sin that causes me the most embarrassment, shame confusion and discouragement than all the others." (Spend some time being very specific in your conversation with Jesus about this pattern in your life and why it is so difficult for you. If you are aware of this, tell Jesus when you most seem to fall under its spell, the circumstances that seem to surround your failures, and how you feel when you fail. If there are specific incidences of this pattern of failure that you have not confessed, tell them to the Lord and ask for his healing and forgiveness).

- "Lord Jesus, I have come to realize that I can't save myself and I ask for your compassion. I ask that you be my Savior, rescue me and be with me all the rest of my days." (Spend some time speaking with Jesus, in very particular words, about how you have come to realize you can't save yourself and why you need his grace—why you need him to be your Savior. Tell him in very clear words why you know that—because of x, y and z you can't save yourself. Tell him about any persons you can't forgive and what they did to you. Tell him why it is difficult for you to forgive them. Tell Jesus that with his grace, you can desire to forgive them, and in time, be able to forgive them. Ask for that grace. Ask the Lord to keep his attention on the core issues in your life [name them] that constantly trip you up. Pray that you never tire in seeking his forgiveness and that you never lose hope in yourself. Ask the Lord to please be your Savior.)

- "Lord Jesus, I thank you that you have given me the courage to face any fears I had and to trust you with my life in this healing sacrament of your redeeming love." (Close your letter/conversation/confession with personal words from your heart, thanking Jesus that he has heard your prayer and that he will always be your Savior. With heartfelt words, thank Jesus that he understands your life and will continue to walk with you, give you grace, and be with you until the end of your days. Ask Jesus for the grace to serve him more each day with everything you think, say, and do—ask for the grace to work for the fruit that will endure to eternity.)
- "Thank you Jesus for being my Savior." (Close your heartfelt letter by thanking Jesus for being your Savior and asking for his continued grace as he writes your *Sacred Story*).

CR

FIFTH WEEK
First Exercise

Days One-Seven: Sacramental Reconciliation and Prayerful Contemplation

Take fifteen minutes to read over your confessional narrative. Make a decision about whether you can grow in integrity, honesty, freedom, and peace by bringing your narrative to Sacramental Reconciliation. The most marked spiritual and psychological growth of those who have engaged in *Sacred Story's* daily prayer discipline is in those who bring their letters to Sacramental Reconciliation. This is not surprising. Ignatius encouraged those who do the *Examen* prayer to also participate in frequent reconciliation. In fact Ignatius wanted Jesuits to make a life confession twice a year in order to make a *new book* of their lives. One whole-life confession and then regular (monthly) reconciliation is sufficient for you.

If you decide to bring your letter to Sacramental Reconciliation, make a special appointment with your pastor and let him know you want to make a life confession. Tell him the process you have engaged in as preparation for it. This will ensure that he gives you some special attention and care. You may benefit most by simply reading the letter in the context of confession. You have already done the work, and what is in your letter, is spoken from your heart to the heart of Christ. The letter is addressed to Christ, and anything we confess in Reconciliation is addressed to Christ. Christ is the one who receives your confession. The priest, in Christ's name, and in the name of the Church, is empowered to offer you Christ Jesus' complete forgiveness, and all the graces that flow from that forgiveness.

If you decide to bring your confessional narrative to Sacramental Reconciliation, use your fifteen-minute *Sacred Story* prayer time in the days prior to Reconciliation to center your heart, and listen to your narrative. Take a full week after your Reconciliation to absorb the graces and insights of the experience. Use your daily fifteen-minute prayer sessions for this. Write in your journal as usual, itemizing one main point for each day of a grace or an insight coming from the experience of making your Whole-Life Confession. These are entries that your heart and mind register as important and note-worthy. Remember, Ignatius' life-confession propelled him more deeply into the root issues that robed him most of peace, joy, hope, peace, and freedom. Sometimes a life-confession fills us with peace, and sometimes it opens flood-gates of fear, anger, anxiety, and grief that have built up over the years.

Feeling peaceful after a life confession does not mean you did it right. Neither does the presence of fear, anger, and grief after a life confession mean you did it wrong. Whatever you experience will be the grace that will lead you to greater peace, joy, hope, and freedom. Have the freedom to simply experience what you experience. Trust that Jesus, the Divine Physician, knows exactly what will lead you to the deep, integrated healing and peace you desire. Be Not Afraid! Fear comes from the enemy of human nature, not from God, and therefore fear never speaks the truth.

If you decide not to formalize your narrative in Sacramental Reconciliation take your fifteen-minute sessions this week to reflect and ponder on the narra-tive you wrote. Seek understanding about your life story and ask for the grace to be open to seeing your life as God sees it. Listen to your life history with your heart, before the heart of God. Write in your journal each day, and itemize one element that specifically captures your imagination.

Starting this week, begin to listen to your whole-life narrative. Ask for graced awareness to see and understand the links between the anger, fear, anxiety, grief, temptations, failures, addictions, and sins that most hinder your spiritual and emotional maturity. Pray for insights into their source and origins in your life history. You may be helped in this holistic listening and consciousness exercise if you consider using the *Sacred Story* template below (adapted from Ignatius' own sacred story).

The template reveals both the spiritual and emotional character of sin's originating events: the persons/events/issues that cause, and continue to engender sin, addiction, anger, anxiety, grief, and fear. Slowly, over time, you will learn how to backtrack from manifest issues, through the root issues, back to originating events. Eventually, you will also be able to see how the originating events evolved and how they gradually took shape in root issues that gave birth to your most manifest sins, disorders, vices, and addictions.

SACRED STORY TEMPLATE

VISIBLE SINS

The Fruit or Ornamentation

(Ignatius' addictive gambling, reactive anger,

and sexual self-indulgence)

Manifest fear, anger, and grief, moral weaknesses, vices, addictions,

and sinful habits that are the most visible to you.

↓   ↑

CORE SINS

The Trunk or Superstructure

(Ignatius' arrogance, blinded conscience, and narcissism)

Disobedience and narcissism, along with its fear, anger, and grief, that forms

the trunk or superstructure of your daily life,

feeding on originating sins and events.

↓   ↑

ORIGINAL SINS

The Roots or Foundation

(Original Sin and concupiscence that wounded Ignatius' heart and soul;

distinctive family/clan sin and/or early life-events that wounded him

spiritually, psychologically, and physically)

Ancient, originating events that rooted the patterns of disobedience and

narcissism, along with fear, anger, and grief.

Most people have some consciousness of their manifest sins, vices, and addictions. However, most people have little or no conscious awareness of the root issues and/or their originating events, where they exist. Ask Christ the Divine Physician, your mentor and guide, to gradually awaken you to your life history so you can see and understand where you need to receive forgiveness, freedom, peace, and enlightenment. It is your gradual awakening and healing that allow you to live your life as a *Sacred Story*, and serve the great work of reconciliation. Your awakening will take the rest of your life as Christ's work of healing and forgiveness deepens in your heart and soul. There is no finish line or ultimate enlightenment you can reach on this earth. You will always need healing at deeper levels, growing in love and enlightenment, selflessness, and humility until the day you pass from this earth—until the day the Divine

Physician sits you down at his eternal banquet. Never lose patience with your growth, no matter how slow it might be. Jesus has infinite love and patience for you and delights in your every effort to grow in his love.

CR

FIFTH WEEK
Second Exercise

Days One-Seven: Ignatian Daydream/Fantasy Exercise

The Second Exercise of Week Five is linked thematically to the First Exercise of Week Five. Remember in the Ignatian spiritual universe "weeks" are not so much units of time but stages of spiritual development. Take this full week after your reconciliation exercise for this Ignatian daydream/fantasy exercise. It will help you to get deeper into your history so that you can better understand the movements in your heart towards or away from God; towards or away from your authentic human nature; towards or way from freedom, integrated healing, and peace. If you desire, you can take an extra week to do this exercise. Taking an extra week might actually be very beneficial. You decide what is best.

Whatever you decide, do this exercise in the context of your daily fifteen-minute prayer sessions but also let it permeate your thoughts during the day. Write in your journal as usual, itemizing two entries each day that seized your heart. In light of this exercise, focus on themes related to the two main daydreams/fantasies that you unconsciously or consciously entertain. The daydreams/fantasies you entertain may appear to cover dozens, even hundreds of different themes. Yet no matter how many different themes you detect, there are really two central themes they are all linked to:

- **Narcissistic Daydreams/Fantasies:** their story lines are lusts, appetites, resentments, addictions, and narcissistic dreams and fantasies linked to your broken heart and wounded human nature. These daydreams/fantasies generate electrical energy, excitement, and urges to things low and earthly. They inflate your ego and excite you while you are fantasizing or engaging them, but they leave you dry, empty, yearning, and dissatisfied—depressed even—after the fact.

- **Grateful Daydreams/Fantasies:** their story lines are the hopes and high ideals of self-less love, desires for healing and forgiveness, and the hope that you will make a difference and live a meaningful life. These story lines are linked to your divine human nature, and the deepest dreams of your heart. These daydreams/fantasies generate peace, tears, quiet hope, and aspirations to all things innocent, beautiful, and noble. They humble your heart and fill you with gratitude while you are fantasizing or engaging them, and they leave you fulfilled, content, and satisfied— joyful even—after the fact.

Ignatius, while recovering from battle, discovered that his daydreams and fantasies were pulling his heart in two different directions. One direction was toward vain, self-serving, self-indulgent exploits rooted in his wounded human nature. The other direction was toward holy aspirations representing his authentic human nature, and the deepest aspirations of his heart. These later daydreams had been out of view for most of his life. The black noise of temptation, and a false self-portrait painted by thoughts, words, and deeds inspired by the enemy of his human nature, both deafened and blinded his heart. Aided by grace, however, he awoke to his fantasies and daydreams, and by grace, discovered only one of the two story lines expressed his authentic human nature—the deepest dream of his heart.

You will discover that hundreds of daydreams and fantasies fight for room in the conscious and unconscious spaces in your heart. No matter their differences, or the fact that they might seem unrelated, they always fall into the two story lines representing the two trajectories of your heart. One set of daydreams/fantasies always trend toward infinite love, holy appetites, integration, humility, reconciliation, hope, peace, wakefulness, sobriety, and gratitude. The other set of daydreams/fantasies always trend toward finite things, low and earthly appetites, disintegration, narcissism, resentment, cynicism, anxiety, unconsciousness, drunkenness, and lack of gratitude.

Begin this week to wake up to your daydreams and fantasies. Let them see the light of day. You will find their traces everywhere: in things you purchase, or want to buy; in your favorite songs, movies and stories; in radio and TV programs that claim your passionate loyalty; in the lives of artists, athletes, actors, saints, politicians—the heroes you emulate and admire; in your programs of study and your job applications; in the friends you have, or wish you had; in the things that happened, or things you wish hadn't happened; in the places you want to visit or make your home, and the places you want to leave and never return to; in your online virtual life, or your offline daily life; in the worlds you visit in cyberspace, or the one you visit in your inner sacred space; what motivates you to exercise and discipline yourself or what influences you to fall out of shape; in the individuals and groups you love, and those whose love you reject; the people you offer forgiveness, or those you refuse to forgive; in the people you envy, wishing you had their looks, talents, connections, wealth, happiness, or relationships; in what causes you to practice your faith or causes you to forget and forgo its practice; in the persons and events that stir your sexual lusts, or persons and events that stir your innocence; in what opens your wallet to give to the needy, or closes it to their need; in the stories, images, and experiences that break your heart, or those that cause it to be joyful; in the things that make you cry, or that make you laugh; in the person or group you want to spend the rest of your life with, or the person or group you want to spend the rest of your life avoiding; in what moves your heart to thanklessness, or makes it swell with gratitude.

The traces of your two daydreams are everywhere. Pray for the courage to wake up to them and see how they each claim your allegiance. Pray for the grace to see, feel, and hear the story line that stirs your heart to gratitude, hope, peace, forgiveness, and all things of heaven. Pray for the grace to see, feel, and hear the story line that stirs your heart to thanklessness, despair, anxiety, resentment, and to things low and earthly. Pray for the grace to wake up to your daydreams and fantasies. Pray for the grace to begin to desire and choose life, love, and hope in all your thoughts, words, and deeds.

11

Learning the Daily Exercises: Weeks Six to Eleven

SIXTH WEEK
First Exercise

Awakening to the Sacred Story Method
Day One: Contemplative Reading

At your leisure, read the instructions for the *Sacred Story* daily practice: Prayer On Waking. Take fifteen minutes to understand this discipline. Note briefly in your journal what you consider significant. If you decide to spend more than one session or day on this exercise, or on the exercises that follow, trust your heart to move forward at the proper pace. When you incorporate this exercise into your day, you should spend no more than fifteen to thirty seconds on it.

Sacred Story Daily Practice:
Prayer On Waking (Fifteen to thirty seconds)

Before arising from your bed, consciously awaken to Creation, Presence, Memory, Mercy and Eternity. Note any significant movements in your heart and mind that come from your dreams. Note the state of your heart regarding any planned events for the day. Pay particular attention to things that stir peace or anxiety in you. Anticipate any challenges that might confront you today, especially those linked to your wounded human nature that might stir fear, anger, or grief within you. With gratitude, offer the thoughts, words, and deeds of your day to God.

SIXTH WEEK
Second Exercise

Day Two: Contemplative Reading

Read, at your leisure, the instructions for the daily practice: During the Day Awareness Exercise. Take fifteen minutes to understand this discipline. Note briefly in your journal what you consider significant.

During the Day Awareness Exercise: Awakening to Sin and Narcissism
Awakening to Your Sins, Addictions, and Compulsions

Prepare your heart to watch and listen to your day as it unfolds. Always be attentive to the events and circumstances that stir you to temptation and incite your attraction to things low and earthly. Watch what triggers your addictions or hooks into your vices and the fault lines in your mind and heart. You are, in short, seeking to "wake up" to what makes living out the Commandments difficult. Discipline yourself not to react to them outwardly. Remind yourself to always be curious about why you are tempted. Look for links between the events that spark your temptations, addictions and attractions to things low and earthly. Be conscious of both the theme and the fact of the temptation. Wake up, and watch.

When you are tempted or when you fail Jesus is both personal Divine Physician and your Redeemer. As Divine Physician he is not your judge. Instead he wants you to awaken to patterns, addictions, and chronic failures that rob you of freedom and peace so you can be healed, forgiven, and have hope and peace. Establish this ritual each time you are tempted and each time you fail by giving into your core wounds, addictions, and sins:

- **Declare** the specific sin, addiction, or destructive compulsion to be a false lover.

- **Describe** the specific sin, addiction, or destructive compulsion as coming from the enemy of your human nature.
- **Descend** with Christ into your memory, to see and feel your first experience of this specific sin, addiction, or compulsion, asking him to compassionately reveal the stress fractures, loneliness, and wounds in your heart it promised to satisfy.
- **Denounce** the sin, addiction, or destructive compulsion for its ruinous effect in your life.
- **Decide** for Christ to heal this wound, diffuse the stress, anxiety, and fear feeding it, and transform its damaging effects on your life into a *Sacred Story*.

Over time, this will become a spiritual exercise that comes naturally. It takes people varying amounts of time to make it a habit, but it will become a positive spiritual discipline that decreases your fear, reveals your truest self, and deepens your trust in Jesus as your protector, healer, and Lord.

CR

SIXTH WEEK
Third Exercise

During the Day Awareness Exercise: Awakening to Your Narcissism

We have already introduced one of the two principal *during the day* exercises: awakening to your addictions, sins, and compulsions. A corresponding exercise sits alongside it to help you source your root sin of narcissism. This complementary exercise asks you first to identify and then awaken to the specific type of chronic narcissistic dysfunction that accompanies your anger, fear, and grief. Ignatius of Loyola discovered a narcissistic pride at the root of all his manifest sin, addiction, spiritual dysfunction, and emotional imbalance. The principal sin of Adam and Eve in Genesis is pride, or how we might define it today, sinful narcissism. The serpent tempted both Adam and Eve with eating the fruit of the forbidden tree because, he said, your "eyes will be opened" and you will "be like gods" (Gen. 3:5).

Narcissism or pride, both words describe the same dark force, makes the individual—me—the center of the universe and the ultimate arbiter of truth. Narcissism displaces God so that "I" can be "like a god." From that first sin of narcissism flows: humankind's banishment from paradise; the advent of pain, sickness, and death: the emergence of evolutionary evil in family structures as evidenced by Cain's murder of Able; and the fracturing of the human community as symbolized in the greed, competition, and overweening pride underlying the parable of the Tower of Babel.

When man and woman consciously displace God as their center and source, and make themselves center and source, the balance, the harmony in all of creation, in all human relationships and networks, and in the whole of the natural order, is fractured. A terminal virus, the virus of self-centeredness, infects the core of all living things. One can see that the corruption caused by this virus has even altered life at the cellular, molecular, and biological level. Nothing in the created order has been left untouched or unharmed by the virus of this sin.

The loss of paradise, and the guilt and sorrow of what was destroyed by human choice, are memories burned deep in the heart of each and every woman and man who has lived, is living, or will ever walk this earth. It is the wound, guilt, and grief of paradise lost that sets each woman and man on a journey back home. But that journey is itself compromised by the tortuous divisions in the human heart (Jer. 17:9). As a divided heart strives to place God back as its source and center, each person must confront the virus of his or her narcissism that still desires to make the self, not God, source and center of all. Narcissism is different than self-respect, self-regard, or self-confidence. Self-respect and positive self-regard are necessary for healthy human functioning and flourishing.

The sin of narcissism is known in how we each strive to make everything revolve around "my needs," "my angers," "my concerns," "my wounds," "my vision," "my talents," "my suffering," "my injustices," "my projects," "my leadership," "my ideas," in general, all revolve around me. I am the center of the universe. This sin results from the pain of an inner void we possess that makes us, to greater or lesser degrees, feel unloved, unlovely, and broken. In our brokenness we get stuck in a narcissistic whirlpool of self-centeredness.

We passively or aggressively seek to find meaning, power, and a sense of self by pushing other's legitimate needs and concerns to the side while we claw our way to the center of attention. Pushing others aside is the work of both aggressors and victims.

The evolution of sin and evil in the world, because of narcissism, is everyone's responsibility to bear. The dark force promoting self-centeredness since time immemorial is an equal opportunity employer. Women and men, young and old, Jew and Greek, slave and free, Catholics and Protestants, priests, bishops and laity, Muslims and Hindus, Buddhists and Shintoists, agnostics, atheists, jihadists—all are entrapped by narcissism, and the act of self-agodizing—making oneself a god—making oneself the center of the universe. Narcissism, self-agodizing, is the core sin of the human race, and conversion, at the integrated level, targets this sin.

Narcissism takes two principal shapes, depending on one's wounds and life circumstances. Sometimes the burdens of evil, sins, addictions, dysfunction in life circumstances, and the grief, guilt and anger at paradise lost, make one feel powerless. Such people generally evolve toward being passive narcissists. The passive narcissist uses powerlessness to gain control of his or her life and to be the center of attention, the center of the universe. The passive narcissist often feels like a victim who never gets his due. He or she feels like they can never get ahead and that he or she will always fail. The passive narcissist secretly despises the powerful. Passive narcissists are oftentimes individuals who, lacking physical or mental strength, use emotional manipulation to wrest control of situations.

Sometimes the burdens of evil, sins, addictions, dysfunction in life circumstances, grief, guilt and anger at paradise lost, make one both feel and need to be powerful in order to cope with life's difficulties. These people generally become aggressive narcissists. The aggressive narcissist uses physical power or intellectual prowess to gain control of her life and to be the center of attention, the center of the universe. The aggressive narcissist feels the victor who will always get her due. She will get ahead and is bound to never fail. She deserves it. The aggressive narcissist despises the weak, is terrified of losing, and works overtime to be always the winner.

It is spiritually valuable to understand the dominant form of narcissism your life circumstances have shaped in you. Do this by noting your reactions to events. Eventually you will begin to understand your dominant type. I say dominant because you may react to different events with characteristics of one or the other type. But one type of narcissism will be dominant overall. In the long run, the spiritual goal is to note your reaction response to events. Then ask God to help you understand the origins of your reactions. Our reaction response, no matter whether it is aggressive or passive, helps awaken us to grief, anger, and fear. It is our grief, anger, and fear that points us to the wounds in our heart and soul that only the Divine Physician can heal. The following two exercises are geared towards helping you identify your dominant type narcissism. Awaken to your reaction response to your grief, anxiety, anger, and fear and then turn to the Divine Physician for his healing graces. The chart below can help you begin this process:

THE PASSIVE NARCISSIST	THE AGGRESSIVE NARCISSIST
Self-identifies as a *victim*.	Self-identifies as a *winner*.
Is determined to have others notice how special he/she is by *pointing to his/her unfair suffering.*	Is determined to have others notice how special he/she is by *defeating all opponents*.
Is cynical and excuses bad behavior by insisting it is justified because of how much he/she *has suffered.*	Is cynical and excuses bad behavior by insisting it is justified because he/she *has earned it.*
Wallows in self-pity when hurt, whether the hurt is real or imagined.	*Is vindictive* when hurt, whether the hurt is real or imagined.
Blames anyone who criticizes or opposes him/her.	*Threatens* anyone who criticizes or opposes him/her.

Protects him/herself from being hurt again by *keeping wounds as fresh as possible*. If anything is too difficult or painful, he/she will *retreat into those painful memories* and turn *inward*, away from others.	Protects him/herself from being hurt again by *eradicating vulnerabilities*. If anything is too difficult or painful, he/she will act in a *conqueror role* and *dominate* others.
Wins by *emotional manipulation*.	Wins by *direct confrontation*.
Is secretly attached to his/her own woundedness.	Is secretly attached to the *power of defeating others*.
Is terrified of *taking control and personal responsibility*, and has difficulty admitting it to him/herself.	Is terrified of *surrendering control and being vulnerable*, and has difficulty admitting it to him/herself.

SIXTH WEEK
Fourth Exercise

Day Three: Contemplative Reading—The Passive Narcissist

Read at your leisure the instructions for the daily practice: The Passive Narcissist. Take fifteen minutes to study the content of this analysis of human dysfunction and Original Sin. Note briefly in your journal what you consider significant that causes anxiety or hope. Are the passive narcissist's qualities ones that typify you?

Be attentive to your reactive impulses and how your temptations, addictions, failures, and sins might be linked to one of two types of narcissist: the passive or the aggressive narcissist.

The Passive Narcissist: This type of narcissism rehearses and revels in the anger, fear, anxiety, and grief of old wounds. The passive narcissist complains, is grasping, is cynical, and makes excuses for everything, except his or her own behavior. The passive narcissist draws attention to herself or himself in every thought, word, and deed and says she or he is the center of attention in these ways: "see how I have suffered;" "see how I have been victimized;" "see how unfairly I am treated;" "see why I behave the way I do;" "see why I am justified in the way I behave…" The passive narcissist works hard to blame others for his or her wounds. The passive narcissist labors mightily in every thought, word, and deed to make sure others know of their suffering. The passive narcissist takes pride and finds both power and comfort in her or his victim status, whether it's real or merely perceived. The passive narcissist works very hard to maintain her or his victim status, and remain powerless, refusing to take responsibility for changing her or his situation. Because changing the situation means confronting pain and offering forgiveness for those who helped you evolve this way. Changing also means losing your core identity of being a powerless victim. To lose this identity is to lose power and control. Why?

There are three main reasons. First, losing your victim status means losing power and control of your world and the other people and things in your world. Second, the passive narcissist is disconnected from his or her authentic self. Losing the status of being a victim initiates an acute and fearful identity crisis. As a victim, your meaning and success have been intimately linked with being a powerless victim. Third, in losing the power and control of the identity your anti-story sustains, you will encounter the spiritual, psychological, and emotional wounds hiding behind your passive narcissism.

Pay attention to sudden feelings of anger, anxiety, fear, or grief that creep up on you during the day. Pay particular attention to how they might be linked to your core narcissistic wounds and Original sins. For those events that seem to jump out at you capturing your attention, do this short exercise below.

Speak to Christ from your heart:

✠ Ask not to react but instead to be conscious of what you are reacting to.

✠ Ask to feel the heart's fear, anxiety, anger, and grief present in the reaction.

✠ Ask for knowledge—the graced insight—to begin dismantling this immature, destructive, aggressive-electrifying or passive-depressing and self-glorifying process.

✠ Ask who or what initiated this particular pattern of reaction—of overpowering or blaming others—and why?

✠ Ask for the courage to face your anti-story of always being the passive victim, because facing this can be terrifying when you are so used to being its slave.

GR

SIXTH WEEK
Fifth Exercise

Day Four Contemplative Reading—The Aggressive Narcissist

At your leisure, read the instructions for the daily practice: The Aggressive Narcissist. Take fifteen minutes to study the content of this analysis of human dysfunction and Original Sin. Note briefly in your journal what you consider significant causes of anxiety or hope. Are the aggressive narcissist's qualities ones that you might possess?

Be attentive to your reactive impulses and how your temptations, addictions, failures, and sins might be linked to one of two types of narcissist: the passive or aggressive narcissist.

The Aggressive Narcissist: This narcissist rehearses and revels in the anger, fear, anxiety, and grief of old wounds. The wounded, prideful aggressor gets even, is grasping, and determined to best others. The aggressive narcissist justifies and excuses his or her behavior in the process. The aggressive narcissist draws attention to herself or himself in every thought, word, and deed and says "I am the center of attention" in these ways: "see how special and gifted I am;" "see that you never get in my way;" "see, you will never overpower me;" "see, I deserve what I have, because I earned it;" "'see, no one will ever hurt me again." The aggressive narcissist works hard never to let anyone best him or her. The aggressive narcissist labors mightily in every thought, word, and deed to make sure others get the message of his or her superiority. The aggressive narcissist takes pride and finds tremendous energy in her or his triumphs over others, real or perceived. The aggressive narcissist works very hard to maintain her or his winner status, for her or his anti-story is now totally associated with being the winner. To lose winner status is to lose power and control. Why?

There are three main reasons. First losing winner status means losing the power and control of your world and the other people and things in that world. Second, because as an aggressive narcissist, you are disconnected from your *Sacred Story*. Losing the status of winner initiates an acute and fearful identity crisis. The crisis results because your meaning and success have been intimately linked with your anti-story of being the winner. Third, in losing the power and control of the identity your anti-story sustains, you will encounter the spiritual, psychological, and emotional wounds hiding behind your aggressive narcissism.

Pay attention to sudden feelings of anger, anxiety, fear, or grief that creep up on you during the day. Pay particular attention to how these might be emerging from your core narcissistic wounds and Original sins. For those events that seem to jump out at you capturing your attention, do this short exercise below.

Speaking to Christ from your heart:

- Ask not to react but instead to be conscious about what you are reacting to.
- Ask to feel the heart's fear, anxiety, anger, and grief present in the reaction.
- Ask for knowledge—the graced insight—to begin dismantling this immature, destructive, aggressive-electrifying or passive-depressing and self-glorifying process.
- Ask who or what initiated this particular pattern of reaction—of overpowering or blaming others—and why?
- Ask for courage to face the false identity of always being the aggressive winner, because facing this can be terrifying when you are so used to being its slave.

CR

SIXTH WEEK
Seventh Exercise

Day Five: Contemplative Reading

Read, at your leisure, the instructions on the following pages for the daily practice: Prayer at Mid-Day and at Night. Take fifteen minutes to understand the purpose of this discipline. Note briefly in your journal what you consider significant, and any challenges you expect in practicing it daily.

CR

Sacred Story Daily Practice: Prayer at Mid-Day and Evening
(Fifteen minutes, no more, no less)

Find a quiet place apart where you won't be disturbed. Bring with you the particular issues that surfaced in your day related to any particular annoyances or strong emotional events you experienced. Bring also your particular graces and inspirations.

During this time, you may kneel or sit, as is better suited to your prayer style, and more conducive to contemplative reflection, prayer, and devotion. Keep your eyes closed, or if opened, in a fixed position, not allowing them to roam.

Take a full fifteen minutes for this exercise, no more and no less. Bring to consciousness the five chapters in *Sacred Story*: Creation, Presence, Memory, Mercy, and Eternity. Spend some time on each chapter, but consciously enter into the whole of your life story from the day's events. You can consciously enter *Sacred Story* prayer for these fifteen-minute periods in one of two ways. Try both and determine which best suits your character and personality.

First Way: Say "Creation" and continue meditating upon this word, as long as you find meaning, connections, delight, and inspirations in considering it and some positive fruit in the graces you seek. The same method of reflection should be followed for each chapter in *Sacred Story* (Presence, Memory, Mercy, and Eternity).

Second Way: With each breath, say interiorly, "Creation," and from one breath to another, say this word while you ponder the graces and inspirations you seek. For this same space of time, direct your attention mainly to the meaning of the word and graces you seek, the person who is addressed, and why you need those graces. Follow this method with the other words (Presence, Memory, Mercy, and Eternity) until you reach the end and finish all the other chapters in *Sacred Story*.

No matter which way you choose, at the beginning and at the end of the prayer time, see with your imagination your whole life and say inwardly, while breathing slowly and deeply: "Creation, Presence, Memory, Mercy, and Eternity". For the body of the fifteen-minute prayer, after the opening mantra, and before the closing mantra, you can be flexible. On some days, you may spend equal amounts of time on each chapter. On other days, you may spend most of your time on one chapter. Let you heart lead you, based on the events of the day, and the images and emotions that emerge in your reflections.

Close the fifteen-minute *Sacred Story* daily exercise with one or other of these two prayers:

Our Father, who art in heaven, hallowed be Thy name.
Thy Kingdom come, Thy will be done, on earth, as it is in heaven.
Give us this day our daily bread, and forgive us our trespasses,
as we forgive those who trespass against us. Lead us not into temptation,

but deliver us from evil. Amen. (Ignatius favored the Our Father for this discipline)

(Suscipe) **Take Lord**, receive, my liberty, my memory, my understanding, my entire will. Whatsoever I have or hold, You have given to me. I surrender it all back to you to be governed by your will. Give me only your love and grace. This is enough for me, and I ask for nothing more. Amen.

(This prayer concludes St. Ignatius' *Spiritual Exercises*)

C3

SIXTH WEEK
Eighth Exercise

Day Six: Contemplative Reading

Read at your leisure the instructions for the daily practice: At Day's End. Take fifteen minutes to understand this discipline. Note briefly in your journal what you consider significant.

Sacred Story Daily Practice: Journals at Day's End—Sacred Story Journal

Write in your journal daily after you end your last *Sacred Story* session. It is not a diary but a journal—jottings, actually. What you write should be only single words or short phrases. The goal is to track the most significant events from your day. You are looking first and foremost for patterns and trends in your life: patterns of fear, anger, and grief, and patterns of sin, compulsion, and addiction. In both of these patterns you are also looking for links to persons/events/issues. On the positive side you are looking for gratitude, hope, and peace linked to your *Sacred Story* and the daydreams and fantasies coming from the Divine Inspirer.

The patterns and trends that are most relevant to the *Sacred Story* method in awakening to your life as a whole and growing in interior freedom are those that help you identify damaging, addictive, sinful habits at their roots. This is the principle goal of the *Particular Examen* of St. Ignatius. You are looking for patterns and trends that reveal the triggering mechanisms that make you easy

213

prey to these habits, sins, addictions, and vices. You are also looking for patterns and trends that help you 'source' the 'origins' and 'roots' of those habits from your early life, where they exist.

Every day, take one minute before retiring to inscribe your brief journal entry. If the noteworthy experience of the day appears to align with a chapter of your life narrative (Creation, Presence, Memory, Mercy, and Eternity), highlight that point for yourself. Always see the importance of memory in light of any significant events from your day's awakening exercises that open you to anger, fear, and grief, or temptations, failures and sins. Strive to see your life holistically as God does. God longs for your freedom, forgiveness, peace and healing.

People who completed these daily journal exercises gained much more from the entire *Sacred Story* method than those who did not write in their journal. Those who persevered in journal practice are the ones who learned to be brief and to do as instructed: write no more than a few words or a short phrase. You will not succeed in the journal practice if it takes you more than a minute or two a day to accomplish. Be brief, but specific.

Prayer Upon Retiring

Upon retiring, listen to your heart and mark you spiritual state (peaceful or anxious), and what person or event inspires one emotion or the other. Speak to God a few words appropriate to your heart's peace or anxiety, and invite God into your dreams.

CR

SIXTH WEEK
Ninth Exercise

Day Seven: Contemplative Reading

Read at your leisure the instructions for the daily practice: At Week's End and at Month's End. Take fifteen minutes to understand this discipline. Note briefly in your journal what you consider significant as you come to understand the purpose of this exercise.

At Week's End—*Sacred Story* Journal

In place of the day's end journal exercise review the words and phrases from the preceding week. Reflect on the words and phrases and ask to see the story of your whole life (Creation, Presence, Memory, Mercy and Eternity), and notice what particular insights or inspirations arise in you. Don't try to force insights. They will either be there or they won't. Most likely you will awaken gradually to patterns and trends. Read over your journal entries from the week, then write a brief entry that captures any insights you have gained about your life over the course of the week's prayer and reflection process. Always look for connections between persons, events, temptations, sins, fear, anger, grief, strong emotions, etc.

Pay particular attention to insights that can help you unravel the manifest and root spiritual and psychological stresses (sinful habits and psychological stresses or addictions and vices) that might be linked to significant events from your past history. Write these insights in a section of your notes that you might entitle "Insight and Integration." Date these reflections if you want to watch your progressive growth and awakening.

At month's End—*Sacred Story* Journal

In place of the week's end journal exercise, review your summary insights from these end-of-week exercises. Look for any patterns that are emerging in your life story, especially those linked to the matrix of spiritual and psychological stresses these insights highlight. Write in your Insights and Integration section, short comments ("I think…" "I believe…" "I discovered…" etc.) that reveal any changes you experience in your life as a result of graced insights and healing you receive.

It is highly recommended that you initiate a ritual of receiving the Sacrament of Reconciliation monthly. This discipline of grace and sacramental accountability will give you energy to engage daily in the *Sacred Story* practice, and provide a clear focus for your life narrative exercises. Those who engage in this discipline of monthly Reconciliation, accompanied with *Sacred Story* prayer, advance immeasurably more than those who forgo the graces of this great sacrament of insight and healing.

When you receive the sacrament do so as you did when you made your Ignatian Whole-Life Confession. Speak directly to Christ and talk about the events of your life and where you need healing and peace. Never tire of repeating the same problems and failures, and always ask for the grace to see more and more clearly the roots and origins of the challenges in your life. St. Ignatius even suggested that his followers make a life confession every six months! He said it would help them make a new book of their lives. However, monthly Reconciliation is sufficient for enlightenment and spiritual, psychological, and emotional growth that is measurable.

∞

SEVENTH WEEK
First Exercise
AWAKENING TO SACRED STORY'S CHAPTERS

CREATION

Days One-Seven: Creation

Every day consciously enter into *Sacred Story* prayer during your set time(s). For these first five weeks, say the entire mantra at the beginning and end of your fifteen-minute session (Creation, Presence, Memory, Mercy, Eternity), but for this week only focus on Creation for your fifteen-minute prayer session. This practice of praying/attuning at the beginning and end of your engagement session is foundational. It anchors your heart and your consciousness in this whole-life tableau--your entire *Sacred Story.* It will gradually transform how you listen to and engage in your life in the course of each day.

Spending an entire week on each of the five chapters will familiarize you with their substance. When you begin the combined practice, you won't need to refer to the written materials very often. You can even spend a complete month on each individual chapter before combining them into a single prayer.

For this week, your focus is Creation. For these next five weeks begin all the other disciplines associated with *Sacred Story* prayer as part of your daily practice: On Waking, During the Day Consciousness Exercise, Journal, and On Retiring Exercise. However do only the prayer on Creation for the fifteen-minute sessions as a way to familiarize yourself with it, so you can learn it by heart. It begins on the next page.

ଔ

CREATION

I believe God created everything in love and for love; I ask for heart-felt knowledge of God's love for me, for gratitude, and for the general and particular graces of this day.

Prelude: God created the universe—all persons and all things—in love and for love. Every thing, and every person in creation, is linked in Love, through Christ, in whom and for whom everything was made. We are made to reverence God and each other, and to delight in creation as both a divine gift and support for our lives. The God of all knows me personally and loves me, even before I was knit in my mother's womb. So fearfully and wonderfully made am I! (Ps. 139:13-14). My gratitude increases as my awakening to these truths is illuminated.

Illuminative Grace: Here I ask for what I desire—to know and feel God's tender and passionate love, and to know myself as beloved—a treasured creature in God's symphony of creation. I pray for the grace of gratitude to know in particular, for whom and why, I am loved, and that I am fearfully and wonderfully made.

ଔ

EIGHTH WEEK
First Exercise

PRESENCE

Days One-Seven: Presence

Every day consciously enter *Sacred Story* prayer during your set time(s). For these first five weeks, say the entire mantra at the beginning and end of your fifteen-minute session (Creation, Presence, Memory, Mercy, Eternity), but only focus on Presence during your fifteen-minute prayer session for this week. This practice of praying/attuning at the beginning and end of your engagement session is foundational. It anchors your heart and your consciousness in this whole-life tableau; your entire *Sacred Story*. It will gradually transform how you listen to and engage your life in the course of each day.

Spending an entire week on each of the five chapters will familiarize you with their substance. When you begin the combined practice, you won't need to refer to written materials very often. You can even spend a complete month on each individual chapter before combining them into a single prayer.

So, for this week, your focus is Presence. For these next four weeks begin all the other disciplines associated with *Sacred Story* prayer as part of your daily practice: the On Waking Exercise, During the Day Consciousness Exercise, Journal Exercise, and the On Retiring Exercise. However, do only the prayer on Presence for the fifteen-minute sessions, as a way to familiarize yourself with it, so you can learn it by heart. It begins on the next page.

$\propto$

PRESENCE

I believe God is present in each moment and event of my life, and I ask for the grace to awaken, to see, and to feel where and how God is present in each moment.

Prelude: The eternal God can only be experienced in the here and now. Everything in the universe is sustained by God's love in the present moment. When I worry about the past, or fret about the future, my consciousness of God, of creation, and of my deepest desires is blocked. My goal is to anchor both heart and mind firmly in the present: in each thought, word, and deed, as the story of my life evolves, in each moment, in God's presence.

Illuminative Grace: Here I ask for what I desire—to be present and awake to every feeling, thought, word, and deed—in the present moment. I beg for the grace to wake up to God's presence in every person, experience, event—good or ill—that I encounter in my day.

ⓒℛ

NINTH WEEK
First Exercise

MEMORY

Days One-Seven: Memory

Each day consciously enter *Sacred Story* prayer during your set time(s). For these first five weeks, say the entire mantra at the beginning and end of your fifteen-minute session (Creation, Presence, Memory, Mercy, Eternity), but for this week only focus on Memory during your fifteen-minute daily prayer session. This practice of praying/attuning at the beginning and end of your engagement session is foundational. It anchors your heart and your consciousness in this whole-life tableau; your entire *Sacred Story*. It will gradually transform how you listen to and engage your life in the course of each day.

Spending an entire week on each of the five chapters will familiarize you with their substance. When you begin the combined practice, you won't need to refer to written materials very often. You can even spend a complete month on each individual chapter before combining them into a single prayer.

So for this week, you focus is Memory. For these next three weeks do all the other disciplines associated with *Sacred Story* prayer as part of your daily practice: the On Waking Exercise, During the Day Consciousness Exercise, Journal Exercise, and On Retiring Exercise. However, do only the prayer on Memory for the fifteen-minute sessions as a way to familiarize yourself with it, so you can learn it by heart. It begins on the next page.

CR

MEMORY

I believe every violation of love committed by me and against me is in my memory, and I ask God to reveal them to me, especially those that have manifested themselves today, so I can be healed.

Prelude: I hold in my heart, by the power of God's grace, the memory of every action—of every thought, word, and deed—done to me and done by me, that has eroded my innocence. I affirm that these unloving thoughts, words, and deeds have spiritual, physical, and emotional consequences that wound God, me, others, and creation. I believe all these unloving actions have both generational and evolutionary consequences. At the root of my own narcissism are some events, that, more than others, have distorted my heart and mind, crippling my desire and my ability to love selflessly, and to freely forgive others.

Illuminative Grace: Here I ask for what I desire—to become conscious of my loss of innocence; the grace to see and the power to touch the original sins and wounds, especially the most vital ones, which shape an anti-story instead of a *Sacred Story*. I ask for the grace of an illumined consciousness to know intimately how these wounds and sins connect to everything I do that makes life burdensome; to know how and why they so often compel me to violate God's presence in myself, others, and creation. I ask God for the grace to wake up so I can see, feel, and name these thoughts, words, and deeds, and bring them to the light of day, to be healed by the Divine Physician.

CR

TENTH WEEK
First Exercise

MERCY

Days One-Seven: Mercy

Every day consciously enter *Sacred Story* prayer during your set time(s). For these first five weeks, say the entire mantra at the beginning and end of your fifteen-minute session (Creation, Presence, Memory, Mercy, Eternity), but for this week only focus on Mercy for your fifteen-minute daily prayer session. This practice of praying/attuning at the beginning and end of your engagement session is foundational. It anchors your heart and your consciousness in this whole-life tableau; your entire *Sacred Story*. It will gradually transform how you listen to and engage your life in the course of each day.

Spending an entire week on each of the five chapters will familiarize you with their substance. When you begin the combined practice, you won't need to refer to written materials very often. You can even spend a complete month on each individual chapter before combining them into a single prayer.

So for this week, your focus is Mercy. For these next two weeks do all the other disciplines associated with *Sacred Story* prayer as part of your daily practice: the On Waking Exercise, During the Day Consciousness Exercise, Journal Exercise, and On Retiring Exercise. However, do only the prayer on Mercy for the fifteen-minute sessions as a way to familiarize yourself with it, so you can learn it by heart. It begins on the next page.

☙

MERCY

I believe that forgiveness is the only path to
healing and illumination, and I beg for the grace of forgiveness,
and the grace to forgive, especially for the general and particular failures
of this day, and from my past.

Prelude: The path to Christian holiness and an illumined consciousness runs through the darkest memories and deeds of your life. These memories and deeds corrupt your innocence and blind your vision to the sacredness of all life. These memories and deeds can, by choice, act as a wall blocking the peace that leads to holiness and highest consciousness. Or they can act as a gate opening to holiness and highest consciousness. The gate is unlocked by forgiveness and compassion; both received from God, and then extended to all those entwined with the loss of innocence that broke your heart: those who hurt you, those whom you hurt, and the creation you abuse or misuse as a result. This miracle of peace and enlightenment is attainable through Christ, who, in love, bore the wounds of every sin and dark deed since time immemorial. Christ transformed them into grace for the salvation of the world.

Illuminative Grace: Here I ask for what I desire—for the grace to forgive any person who wounded my innocence, or who broke my heart. I pray to not only forgive them, but to have compassion and mercy on them. I ask for the grace of mercy and forgiveness for those whose hearts I have broken, and whose innocence I have wounded, and the creation I have misused. I beg to know personally the One who absorbed in his heart and body every wound and every sin of this dark evolution across the millennia. I beg for the dual knowledge of sin and mercy as it affects my life story. I beg for patience. I affirm that accepting and offering mercy and forgiveness, leading to holiness and highest consciousness, takes a lifetime.

ELEVENTH WEEK
First Exercise

ETERNITY

Days One-Seven: Eternity

Every day consciously enter *Sacred Story* prayer during your set time(s). For these first five weeks, say the entire mantra at the beginning and end of your fifteen-minute session (Creation, Presence, Memory, Mercy, Eternity), but for this week only focus on Eternity for your fifteen-minute daily prayer session. This practice of praying/attuning at the beginning and end of your engagement session is foundational. It anchors your heart and your consciousness in this whole-life tableau; your entire *Sacred Story*. It will gradually transform how you listen to and engage your life in the course of each day.

Spending an entire week on each of the five chapters will familiarize you with their substance. When you begin the combined practice, you won't need to refer to written materials very often. You can even spend a complete month on each individual chapter before combining them into a single prayer.

So for this week, your focus is Eternity. So for this week do all the other disciplines associated with *Sacred Story* prayer as part of your daily practice: the On Waking Exercise, During the Day Consciousness Exercise, Journal Exercise, and On Retiring Exercise. However, do only the prayer on Eternity for the fifteen-minute sessions as a way to familiarize yourself with it, so you can learn it by heart. It begins on the next page.

CR

ETERNITY

I believe the grace of forgiveness opens my heart, making my
every thought, word, and deed bear fruit that endures to eternity, and I
ask that everything in my life serve Christ's Great Work of Reconciliation.

Prelude: The *Sacred Story* book of all history, opened on the last day, will reveal that the loss of innocence and the broken hearts of humankind inaugurated the Great Work of Reconciliation. Because of Christ's mercy, each of us is now being invited to take our part in this work. The grace of mercy and forgiveness, both received and offered, is the reconciling work that brings true progress to the world. It is the only work that brings fulfillment and bears fruit that endures to eternity. A holy life and the highest consciousness attainable come in knowing personally the One who reconciles my life, and all creation. In this reconciling Love, I daily discern how to direct each thought, word, and deed to eternal glory—to the Divine Work of Reconciliation.

223

Illuminative Grace: Here I ask for what I desire—to be graced daily with a profound consciousness of Christ Jesus' healing love, personally experienced, that will so enlighten my heart and mind that each thought, word, and deed I do can serve His Great Work of Universal Reconciliation.

ᘉ

12

Living Your Sacred Story: Weeks Twelve to Eternity

Introduction

You have engaged in all of the spiritual disciplines of the *Sacred Story* program. Now is the time to combine the chapters into a single prayer and include the other daily disciplines you have practiced. Every instruction you need has already been detailed. On the next pages you can see all the spiritual disciplines and insights of the *Sacred Story* method in a single glance. If and when you have difficulty, temptation, stress, fear, or anxiety associated with the daily consciousness exercise or *Sacred Story* prayer (when, not if), read *Sacred Story Affirmations* and the *Guidelines for Health and Spiritual Growth*. Remember the anxieties Ignatius suffered as he began his journey. All emotional and spiritual crises soon pass. Christ Jesus will lead you home.

THE DAILY DISCIPLINES AT A GLANCE

✠ Prayer upon waking—*Attune to the day ahead and invite God's help*
✠ Exercises during the day—*Awakening to your life*
✠ *Sacred Story* prayer Mid-day—*Creation, Presence, Memory, Mercy, Eternity*
✠ Exercises during the day—*Awakening to your life*

✠ *Sacred Story* prayer Evening—*Creation, Presence, Memory, Mercy, Eternity*

✠ *Sacred Story* day journal—*Briefly note two significant event(s) of the day*

✠ Prayer upon retiring—*Attune to your heart, invite God into your dreams*

✠ Week's end journal—*Listen for trends, patterns, links*

✠ Month's end journal—*Listen for trends, patterns, links*

✠ Renew with monthly reconciliation—*You will be powerfully graced*

✠ Consult the Affirmations frequently—*Thumbnail discernment aids*

✠ Consult the guidelines—*For Healing and Spiritual Growth—You need them*

✠ Live your faith—*Engage its spiritual disciplines, serving God and neighbor*

Pray for Everyone on the Sacred Story Journey

ର

Invite Others to Walk It with You

ର

Entrust Your Heart and Sacred Story to Jesus, the Divine Physician

Sacred Story Affirmations

My Sacred Story takes a lifetime to write.

Be Not Afraid:
Fear comes from the enemy of my human nature.

The pathway to God's peace and healing runs through my heart's
brokenness, sin, fear, anger and grief.

God resolves all my problems with time and patience.

CR

I will have difficulties in this life.

There are just two ways to cope with my difficulties.
One leads to life, one to death. I will choose life.

CR

"Impossible" is not a word in God's vocabulary.

Sacred Story leads to my freedom and authenticity,
but does not always make me feel happy.

CR

My life's greatest tragedies can be transformed
into my life's major blessings.

Times of peace and hope always give way
to times of difficulty and stress.

Times of difficulty and stress always give way
to times of peace and hope.

CR

I will not tire of asking God for help
since God delights in my asking.

The urge to stop *Sacred Story* practice
always comes before my greatest breakthroughs.

CR

God gives me insights, not because I am better than others,
but because I am loved.

The insights and graces I need to move forward in life's journey
unfold at the right time.

CR

My personal engagement with *Sacred Story* accomplishes, through Christ, a
work of eternal significance.

Inspirations can have a divine or a demonic source. I pray for the grace to
remember how to discern one from the other.

CR

Christ, who has walked before me, shares my every burden.

Christ, who has walked before me, will help me resolve every crisis.

Christ, who has walked before me, knows my every hope.

Christ, who has walked before me, knows everything I suffer.

Christ, who walks before me, will always lead me home to safety.

༄

I will strive to curb temptations to react to people and events.

I will ask myself what causes my anger and irritation at people and events.

I will seek to identify the source of my anger and irritation.
I will give thanks for what angers and upsets me;
for identifying their source will help to set me free.

I will strive to listen, watch and pray; listen, watch and pray.
I will listen, watch and pray!

༄

Everyone has been mortally wounded spiritually, psychologically, and
physically by Original Sin and the loss of paradise.

Journeying with Christ to the roots of my sins and addictions
will help break their grip.

I will not waste time worrying about my sins and failures.
I will use my time wisely and ask God to help me
understand the source of my sins and failings .

I will trust that Christ came to heal all my wounds.

༄

I alone control Christ's ability to transform my life into a *Sacred Story*.
The process begins when I ask for the grace to
honestly name my sins and addictions.

The process continues when I invite Christ to illuminate my narcissism.

Only God's grace and mercy can write my *Sacred Story*.

☙

I will strive daily to pick up the cross, for it leads to my life.

The closer I get to holiness, the more I will see and feel sin's disorder in my
life.

The more I experience sin's disorder, the more tempted I will be
to disbelieve my life as *Sacred Story*.
The way through the temptation is to surrender my powerlessness to God.

☙

It is never too late to open my heart to Christ
and live my life as *Sacred Story*.

Christ, who is close to the broken-hearted, restores my lost innocence.

The path to my *Sacred Story* is
Creation, Presence, Memory, Mercy, and Eternity.

☙

TWO BENCHMARK GUIDELINES FOR
SPIRITUAL DISCERNMENT

To help your awakening and initiation into spiritual discernment, two benchmark guidelines are offered below that you will find helpful in many life situations. It is important to understand that divine inspiration (called consolation) does not always feel good. It is equally important to realize that an unholy inspiration (called spiritual desolation) does not always feel bad. We will explore this seeming paradox in a later lesson. For now, learn the two benchmark guidelines and realize both are intended to influence the direction of our life towards or away from God in every thoughts, word, and deed.

Benchmark One:

Authentic divine inspirations, called consolations, will always have specific features. They will:

1) Increase in your heart love for God and others.
2) Increase your heart's docility, humility, and selflessness.
3) Never oppose truths and teachings proposed by Scripture, the Tradition and the teaching Church, for the same Spirit guides both your life and the Church.

Consolation can be the consequence of the Divine Physician's Spirit working in you. This form of consolation helps strengthen your heart and soul, helping and encouraging you to turn to God. Consolation helps you to choose thoughts, words, and deeds that express your authentic human nature made in the Divine image. Consolation can also be the consequence of the body/spirit aspect of your divinely-shaped human nature. God created your human nature as a gift, in the divine image and likeness. Yet in spite of Original Sin's impact, cooperating with God's grace activates embedded life forces of your Divinely-shaped human nature. This helps heal biochemical, physiological, and emotional imbalances; energizing you, and increasing thoughts, words, and deeds that express your authentic human nature.

Benchmark Two:

Authentic counter-inspirations called desolations will always have specific features. They will:

1) Increase in your heart narcissism, displacing God and others.
2) Decrease your heart's docility and humility but increase your pride and self-satisfaction.
3) Stir in you hungers and desires that, although they feel good, will frequently contradict the truths and teachings proposed by Scripture, Tradition, and the teaching Church. This is because the spirit that brings counter-inspirations is opposed to Christ and will always lead you away from life and truth. You are led away from God and truth with counter-inspirations. The desires produced feel authentic because they are linked to fallen human nature's physical lusts and spiritual pride.

Desolation can be the consequence of the enemy of human nature working in you. This form of desolation helps weaken your heart and soul, discouraging you from turning to God. Desolation helps you choose thoughts, words, and deeds that are opposed to your Divinely-shaped human nature. Desolation can also be the consequence of your own fallen human nature. God created your human nature as a gift in the Divine image and likeness. Because of Original Sin' impact, not cooperating with God's grace erodes the embedded life forces of your divinely-shaped human nature. This helps diminish biochemical, physiological, and emotional balance; de-energizing you, and increasing thoughts, words, and deeds that are the opposite of your authentic human nature. When struggling with these issues, the *Guidelines for Integrated Healing and Spiritual Growth* will be of help.

GENERAL AWARENESS EXERCISES DURING THE DAY

When you experience your manifest sins and addictions, practice: Declare, Describe, Descend, Denounce, and Decide.

Speak in personal words to Christ in your heart to:

- **Declare** the specific sin, addiction, or destructive compulsion to be a false lover.
- **Describe** the specific sin, addiction, or destructive compulsion as coming from the enemy of your human nature.
- **Descend** with Christ into your memory, to see and feel your first experience of this specific sin, addiction or compulsion, asking him to compassionately reveal the stress fractures, loneliness and wounds in your heart that it promised to satisfy,
- **Denounce** the sin, addiction, or destructive compulsion for its ruinous effect in your life
- **Decide** for Christ to heal this wound, diffuse the stress, anxiety, and fear feeding it, and transform its damaging effects on your life into a *Sacred Story*.

When you are struggling with these issues, the *Guidelines for Foundational Healing and Spiritual Growth* will be very helpful.

Cষ

PARTICULAR AWARENESS EXERCISES DURING THE DAY

When You Find Yourself Conscious of Your Particular Sin of Narcissism and Reacting with Anger, Anxiety, Fear or Grief:

Determine if you are mostly an aggressive or a passive narcissist. Pay attention to sudden feelings of anger, anxiety, fear, or grief that creep up on you during the day. Pay particular attention to how they might be touching your narcissism and manifest sinfulness, and contributing to addictive tendencies. For those events that seem to jump out at you and capture your attention, do this short exercise below.

Speak to Christ from your heart:

- **Ask not to react** but instead ask to be conscious of what you are reacting to.

- **Ask to feel** the heart's fear, anxiety, anger, and grief in the present reaction.
- **Ask for knowledge**—for the graced insight—to begin dismantling this immature, destructive, aggressive-electrifying or passive-depressing and self-glorifying process.
- **Ask who or what** initiated this particular pattern of reaction—of overpowering or blaming others, and why—how far back does it go?
- **Ask for courage** to face your anti-story of always being the aggressive winner, or the passive victim, because facing this can be terrifying when you are so used to being its slave.

CR

ATTENDING TO MY REACTION RESPONSES: ANGER, FEAR AND GRIEF

THE PASSIVE NARCISSIST	THE AGGRESSIVE NARCISSIST
Self-identifies as a *victim*.	Self-identifies as a *winner*.
Is determined to have others notice how special he/she is by *pointing to his/her unfair suffering*.	Is determined to have others notice how special he/she is by *defeating all opponents*.
Is cynical and excuses bad behavior by insisting it is justified because of how much he/she *has suffered*.	Is cynical and excuses bad behavior by insisting it is justified because he/she *has earned it*.
Wallows in self-pity when hurt, whether the hurt is real or imagined.	*Is vindictive* when hurt, whether the hurt is real or imagined.
Blames anyone who criticizes or opposes him/her.	*Threatens* anyone who criticizes or opposes him/her.

THE PASSIVE NARCISSIST	THE AGGRESSIVE NARCISSIST
Protects him/herself from being hurt again by *keeping wounds as fresh as possible*. If anything is too difficult or painful, he/she will *retreat into those painful memories and turn inward*, away from others.	Protects him/herself from being hurt again by *eradicating vulnerabilities*. If anything is too difficult or painful, he/she will act in a *conqueror role* and *dominate* others.
Wins by *emotional manipulation*.	Wins by *direct confrontation*.
Is secretly attached to his/her own woundedness.	Is secretly attached to the *power of defeating others*.
Is terrified of *taking control and personal responsibility*, and has difficulty admitting it to him/herself.	Is terrified of *surrendering control and being vulnerable*, and has difficulty admitting it to him/herself.

SACRED STORY PRAYER CHAPTERS

Pray the whole fifteen-minute *Sacred Story* prayer once or twice daily and consciously repeat the mantra whenever you are in the grip of fear, anxiety, and grief, or sin, addiction, and destructive compulsion.

CREATION

I believe God created everything in love and for love; I ask for heart-felt knowledge of God's love for me, for gratitude, and for the general and particular graces of this day.

PRESENCE

I believe God is present in each moment and event of my life, and I ask for grace to awaken, to see and to feel where and how God is present in each moment.

MEMORY

I believe every violation of love committed by me and against me is in my memory, and I ask God to reveal them to me, especially those that have manifested themselves today, so I can be healed.

MERCY

I believe that forgiveness is the only path to healing and illumination, and I beg for the grace of forgiveness, and the grace to forgive, especially for the general and particular failures of this day, and from my past.

ETERNITY

I believe the grace of forgiveness opens my heart, making my every thought, word and deed bear fruit that endures to eternity, and I ask that everything in my life serve Christ's Great Work of Reconciliation.

☙

SACRED STORY INTEGRATION and AWARENESS TEMPLATE

The *Sacred Story* prayers and all its daily disciplines are helping God awaken you to patterns of sin and dysfunction, grace and healing. The Divine Physician is helping you unravel the diseases caused by Original Sin, so that you regain integrated healing and interior freedom to serve the *Great Work of Reconciliation.*

Be mindful that no thought, word, or deed is ever neutral. Everything one says, does, or thinks expresses a spontaneity of the Divine in human nature or of human nature's enemy. So as you listen to your life each day, keep the *Sacred Story* Template in mind. You are seeking a global vision of how the enemy of your human nature is working to keep you asleep, and a global vision of how the Divine Physician is working to awaken you. Watch your life with compassionate, patient, and merciful intelligence. That is the mind of the Divine Physician, who is working for your redemption and complete, integrated healing. As your memory awakens, and you become conscious of your life's issues, you will become sensitive and discerning of movements in both directions similar to the template below.

THE FOUR STAGES OF IGNATIUS' CONVERSION
THE AWAKENING

VISIBLE SINS

The Fruit or Ornamentation

(Ignatius' addictive gambling, reactive anger,
and sexual self-indulgence)

*Manifest fear, anger, and grief, moral weaknesses, vices, addictions, and
sinful habits that are the most visible to you.*

↓   ↑

CORE SINS

The Trunk or Superstructure

(Ignatius' arrogance, blinded conscience, and narcissism)

*Disobedience and narcissism, along with its fear, anger, and grief,
that forms the trunk or superstructure of your daily life,
feeding on originating sins and events.*

↓   ↑

ORIGINAL SINS

The Roots or Foundation

(Original Sin and concupiscence that wounded Ignatius' heart and soul;
distinctive family/clan sin and/or early life-events that wounded him
spiritually, psychologically, and physically)

*Ancient, originating events that rooted the patterns of disobedience and
narcissism, along with its fear, anger, and grief.*

SPEAKING TRUTH TO POWER

A graced experience of God's love opened Ignatius to: ⇨ ⇩	**GIVE THANKS FOR FAVORS RECEIVED** ⇩
A dissatisfaction with vain fantasies which led to surrendering to holy day-dreams, characterized by consolation, which in turn ⇨ ⇩	**PRAY FOR GRACE TO SEE CLEARLY** ⇩
Caused him to review his life and actions leading to: ⇨ ⇩	**GIVE A DETAILED ACCOUNT OF CONSCIENCE: GENERAL AND PARTICULAR** ⇩
Grief with yearning for penance and repentance for his past sins, culminating in: ⇨ ⇩	**ASK PARDON FOR ONE'S FAULTS** ⇩
Ignatius' passion to amend his life and a desire to love God wholeheartedly. ⇨	**RESOLVE AND AMEND TO SERVE GOD**
An enemy voice evokes Ignatius' fear of a lifelong struggle with his sinful habits. ⇨ ⇩	**CONSCIOUS FEAR AND ANXIETY OVER SURRENDERING SINFUL AND ADDICTIVE HABITS** ⇩

Ignatius rejects the "enemy of human nature" and confronts his false promises. ⇨ ⇩	**CONFRONTING THE THREATENING "VOICE" OF SIN AND ADDICTION WITH THE "TRUTH" THAT THEY BRING DEATH, NOT LIFE** ⇩
Peace is restored after truthfully naming sin and addiction as death dealing. ⇨	**PEACE RETURNS AND ANXIETY DISSOLVES**

SECOND CRISIS: SURRENDERING CONTROL & ADMITTING POWERLESS TO SAVE ONESELF

Ignatius' struggle with scruples hiding his vainglory ⇨ ⇩	The initial confrontation with one's root sin ⇩
Ignatius' constant re-confessing to seek salvation by willpower alone ⇨ ⇩	The effort to control one's root sin ONLY by personal effort or force of will ⇩
Ignatius' suicidal impulses, disgust and the desire to walk away from his new found faith ⇨ ⇩	Despair and desire to give up faith when human effort alone fails ⇩
Ignatius' tracing the spirit of disgust to a demonic source ⇨ ⇩	Insight that desire to reject the spiritual journey is a temptation ⇩
Ignatius abandoning his compulsive confessing of past sins ⇨ ⇩	Admitting powerlessness to save oneself and surrendering prideful actions ⇩
Ignatius being taught as a child and receiving graces according to God's design ⇨	Allowing God to shape one's *Sacred Story* according to His will and graces

LIFE-LONG PATIENCE
WHILE GOD WRITES OUR *SACRED STORY*

Ignatius, justifying himself, anxiously recoils and focuses on his sinfulness ⇨ ⇩	Panic over one's salvation due to weakness and sinfulness ⇨	**PURGATION** ⇩
Ignatius, no longer fearful, regrets not having responded sooner to God's graces ⇨ ⇩	Sadness at slowness of one's response to God's love and invitation to intimacy ⇨	**ILLUMINATION** ⇩
Ignatius' intense joy at the thought of dying and being with God ⇨	An ardent, all-embracing love of God and desire for complete union with the Trinity ⇨	**UNION**

Afterword

The Future of the Ignatian Examen

Gospel faith is necessarily linked to the needs of the poor and the powerless. Sin running through the center of human hearts disrupts not only our knowledge of God, but also our desire to care for others, especially the most disadvantaged. This spiritual blindness and sickness manifests in the glorification of the self, the desire for wealth, the seeking of worldly honors and the heart's unbending pride. Unattended, it constantly evolves in the horrors of war, insatiable greed, disrespect for life, ecological damage, injustice, and poverty.

Unless and until the spiritual superstructures of Original Sin, which are rooted in individual hearts and souls, are targeted and disarmed, no sustainable peace or justice in Church or human society is possible. This is true no matter how organized, expansive, and effective our social service networks become. The Second Vatican Council declared that human effort to achieve positive progress for the world is constantly "endangered by pride and inordinate self-love."[1] Both the language and the experience of the Council match Ignatius' life story and spiritual insights.

Awakening to spiritual and social realities—awakening to one's conscience and true human nature—are directly linked to the conversion process. Ignatius' foundational conversion after his wounding in battle led to his general examen and his night of the senses. The social awakening he experienced on his pilgrimage to Montserrat allowed Ignatius to see the beggar who became a recipient of his support and care. But it was at the deeper, integrated level of conversion at Manresa that Ignatius was led to his night of the spirit and his *Particular Examen*. This deeper conversion according to Nadal is where Ignatius' desire to help souls was "born."[2]

This begins Ignatius' *Sacred Story*. He finds soldiers of a different sort to help build a company whose purpose his *Constitutions* declare is to "aid souls to reach their ultimate and supernatural end". The tools of his ministry founded on his progressive conversion are the *Spiritual Exercises* and the daily *Examen*. Both are aimed at helping individuals conquer self by uprooting inordinate attachments. For these spiritual pursuits Ignatius says are "the interior gifts which make those exterior means effective toward the end which is sought."[3]

Spiritual writers and theologians too often focus on Ignatius' mystical gifts. Those seeking the keys to his spiritual genius should focus instead on when he received his mystical gifts. It is only after he surrenders his life to God his Savior. The surrender of his will enables him to see himself, the world and God. It is only then that he says "he felt as if he were another man with another mind."[4]

This is the tipping point of his history, transforming his life from an anti-story into a *Sacred Story*. He finally wakes up. No subsequent event or combination of events and graces will ever equal the rush of spiritual oxygen that renewed his mind and heart at this one moment in time. It was this moment when Ignatius saw himself, the world, and the kingdom of God, because he had been born from above (Jn. 3:3). That one-third of the *Autobiography* is dedicated to these critical first two years of his conversion journey should catch our attention.

Ignatius manifests three fundamental fruits of the classical path of purgation and illumination that each of us in our own way need to imitate: (1) he honestly named his sins and surrendered his life to God, admitting he could not save himself; (2) in so doing, he woke to see both his life and the world through the eyes of God—in this clarity of vision and depth of understanding, Polanco says, he wept even more bitterly over the sins of his past life and;[5] (3) understanding Christ as his Savior and Lord, he submitted his will, allowing God to lead him to the fullness of his authentic identity—his *Sacred Story*.

The late Cardinal Carlo Martini discussed the contemporary crisis of faith using the symbol of the barren tree. He recognized signs of renewal in many places, but to him, sterility appeared more evident: meetings, congresses, programs, renewals, encounters, many beautiful words, and gilt facades behind which there is almost nothing. Where is the fruit? Churches, seminaries, and novitiates are, in many cases, empty. Regarding the ratio of leaves and fruit in our individual Christian lives, he says:

> Each one has to wonder how the Lord looks at our leaves, i.e., the words, intentions, commitments, programs and little fruit, i.e., the ability to transmit the faith to others which, at its core, is the result, the

ability to convert others, and to communicate the love of God, to give them life. Our gift of self to God is manifested in the ability to give to the other the spark of love for the Lord that He has placed within us. Here surely we must ask not only about the fruits, that God in his goodness allows us to gather, but also about the relationship between leaves and fruits, between what we might do and the actual reality of our lives.[6]

Martini's vision encompassed Europe. His insights can be applied equally to the entire Christian West. He invited us to look closely at our lives and the apostolates to which we dedicate our time and treasure. Do our efforts at evangelization, our works for justice, our thousands of hospitals, grade schools, high schools, universities, and parishes produce fruit? Does the salt savor (Mt. 5:13)? In the Ignatian world, do we have many leaves and little fruit? Are we cultivating and sharing the fruits of the spiritual tree entrusted to us? Are Ignatius' spiritual methods, and the treasures of integrated conversion they facilitate, underutilized or their potency blunted?

Ignatius' pre-conversion life mirrors our contemporary faith and cultural crises. Out of his dysfunction, Christ gives the Church one of its greatest saints. A new dynamic spirituality that meets head-on the greatest social, intellectual, moral, religious, human, and psychological crises the Church has ever encountered is born. Paul VI understood the tremendous need of Ignatius' vibrant spirituality, especially in light of the crises facing the modern world:

> You have a spirituality strongly traced out, an unequivocal identity and a centuries-old confirmation which is based on the validity of methods, which, having passed through the crucible of history, still bear the imprint of the strong spirit of St. Ignatius...You are at the head of that interior renewal which the Church is facing in this secularized world, especially after the Second Vatican Council. Your Society, is we say, the test of the validity of the Church throughout the centuries; it is perhaps one of the most meaningful crucibles in which are encountered the difficulties, the temptations, the efforts, the perpetuity and the successes of the whole Church.[7]

Ignatius' life, conversion, and spiritual legacy are needed now more than ever. But the integrity of Ignatius' spiritual disciplines to promote integrated growth must be protected and their potency nurtured. There are temptations on all sides. Early on, the Inquisition prevented St. Ignatius from "helping souls" by prohibiting him from defining sin. We must be vigilant in our own day and not make their same mistake. Ignatian Spirituality, in its various methods including the *Examens,* must help souls properly identify sin. This is especially true at the foundational stage of conversion.

But evangelization must break the stalemate between arrogance and timidity. Evangelization that relies principally on the proclamation of laws and boundaries with little mercy is the Phariseeism condemned by Christ. Evangelization with no laws or boundaries except a bending, evolving definition of truth merely sanctions the individualist's desires and the narcissist's demands. Both methods are ultimately impotent and unsustainable. Success for the Church's evangelization is achievable along the narrow path of God's mercy and justice. Mercy is indispensable for humanity's sufferings, caused by the mortal damage to human nature in the Original Sin. And God's justice is that very same love in the form of boundaries protecting the created order and the distinctiveness of our human nature crafted in the image and likeness of God. When we evangelize with both mercy and justice, we help people find their way back to God and in freedom, serve the Kingdom—living life as a *Sacred Story.*

This interior freedom for service is the hallmark of Ignatian Spirituality and the goal of *Sacred Story.* Ignatius' practice of the daily *Examen,* and the interior freedom it brought him, changed the history of the Church and the world. Imagine what a handful of people in every religious community, parish, high school, and university around the earth could accomplish by living it daily.

છ

Notes

Author's Preface & Introduction

¹ [Valentin Tomberg], *Meditations on the Tarot: a Journey into Christian Heremeticism* (Shaftesbury Dorset, England: Element, 1991), 615. Cited hereafter as "Meditations."

² The Society of Jesus, *The Decrees of General Congregation 35.* (Washington, DC: Jesuit Conference, 2008), 15. Cited hereafter as "Decrees."

³ *Ibid.*, 73-75.

⁴ C.S. Lewis, was a medieval scholar and literary critic from Oxford University, and Josef Pieper, a philosopher from the University of Münster.

⁵ "For the present is the point at which time touches eternity. Of the present moment, and of it only, humans have an experience analogous to the experience which our Enemy has of reality as a whole; in it alone freedom and actuality are offered to them. He would therefore have them continually concerned either with eternity (which means being concerned with Him) or with the Present-either meditation on their eternal union with, or separation from, Himself, or obeying the present voice of conscience, bearing the present cross, receiving the present grace, giving thanks for the present pleasure. Our business is to get them away from the eternal and from the Present." C.S. Lewis, *The Screwtape Letters* (New York: Collier Books, 1982), 103), 68. Cited hereafter as: "Lewis."

⁶ "Or to put the matter more concretely: will it ever be possible to keep, or reclaim, some room for leisure from the forces of the total world of work? And this would mean not merely a little portion of rest on Sunday, but rather a whole 'preserve' of true, unconfined humanity: a space of freedom, of true learning, of attunement to the world-as-a-whole?" Josef Pieper, *Leisure, The Basis of Culture* (South Bend: St. Augustine Press, 1998), 37. Cited hereafter as: "Pieper."

⁷ Lewis, 103.

⁸ Pieper, 35.

⁹ Ps. 46:10; Lk 17: 21. (Unless otherwise noted, all Scriptural quotes are taken from the NAB).

¹⁰ "There is a pervasive form of contemporary violence, and that is activism and over-work. The rush and pressure of modern life are a form, perhaps the most common form, of this innate violence. To allow oneself to be carried away by a multitude of conflicting concerns, to surrender to too many demands, to commit oneself to too many projects, to want to help every-one and everything, is to succumb to violence. The frenzy of our activism neutralizes our work for peace. It destroys our own inner capacity for peace because it kills the root of inner wisdom which makes work fruitful." Thomas Merton: *Conjectures of a Guilty Bystander:* (New York, Doubleday, 1966), 73.

[11] George Aschenbrenner, SJ, "Consciousness Examen," *Review for Religious*, no. 31 (January 1972): 14. Cited hereafter as *Aschenbrenner.*

[12] Timothy M. Gallagher, OMV, *the Examen Prayer: Ignatian Wisdom for Our Lives Today* (New York: The Crossroad Publishing Company, 2006), 10.

[13] The *Sacred Story* method presented in this work forms the basis of a new evangelization project: The Sacred Story Institute (sacredstory.net). The Institute is developing multiple formats of the *Sacred Story Examen* method to introduce Third Millennium Catholics and Christians to this vital and dynamic Ignatian prayer. Our suggested book for adults is titled: *Forty Weeks – An Ignatian Path to Christ with Sacred Story Prayer.*

1. Fundamental Conversion and the General Examen

[1] See pages: 28-9; 80; 83-4, Abbot Garcias Cisneros: *A Book of Spiritual Exercises and a Directory for the Canonical Hours* (London: Burns and Oates, 1876).

[2] José Ignacio Tellechea Idígoras, *Ignatius of Loyola: The Pilgrim Saint*, trans. Cornelius Michael Buckley, SJ (Chicago: Loyola University Press, 1994), 538, 567. Cited hereafter as, "Idígoras."

[3] "If you cannot be continually recollected then at least be so at certain times, for example, in the morning and in the evening. In the morning make your resolution, and in the evening examine your performance, checking how you conducted yourself during the day. Scrutinize your speech, your actions, and your thoughts, because by these means you may have offended God and your neighbor." As cited in: Thomas à Kempis, *The Imitation of Christ*, trans. Joseph N. Tylenda, SJ (Wilmington: Michael Glazier, 1984), 55. See also: 86, 243-5.

[4] "...the Jesuits commended the Imitation enthusiastically and without reservation. This means that, as was true for other works that were not the objects of controversy among Catholics, they read it less with an analytical and critical eye than with the hope of utilizing what supported their spirituality...It encouraged frequent confession and Communion, though without defining what "frequent" meant. It encouraged daily examination of conscience." John W. O'Malley, *The First Jesuits* (Cambridge: Harvard University Press, 1993), 265. Cited hereafter as, "O'Malley."

[5] Joseph de Guibert on the level of esteem *The Practice of Perfection* is held in the Catholic tradition: "in the training of novices the name of Rodríguez has deservedly come to be linked with the names of St. Bernard and St. Bonaventure." Joseph de Guibert, SJ, *The Jesuits: Their Spiritual Doctrine and Practice* (St. Louis: The Institute of Jesuit Sources, 1994), 263. Cited hereafter as "de Guibert."

[6] Alphonsus Rodríguez, SJ, *Practice and Perfection of Christian Virtues*, vol. 1, trans. Joseph Rickaby (Chicago: Loyola University Press, 1929). 423. See also 421-442, 444-447. Cited hereafter as, "Rodríguez."

[7] George Ganss states in his *Spiritual Exercises* that Ignatius formulated two methods of examination that "were original" to him. George E. Ganss, SJ, *the Spiritual Exercises of Saint*

Ignatius: A Translation and Commentary (Chicago: Loyola University Press, 1992), 153. Cited hereafter as, "Ganss." Also, "Of the particular examination of conscience St. Ignatius is generally considered as the author or at least as the first who reduced it to a system and promoted its practice among the faithful." As cited in: "Examination of Conscience," Charles Coppens. The Catholic Encyclopedia, Robert Appleton Company, (New York 1909 Volume V), 675.

[8] "…y con esto no era menester demandalle nada, porque todo lo que importaba para hacer al hombre capaz, el Padre se acordaba de decillo." As cited in *Obras Completas de San Ignacio De Loyola*: Edicion Manual, ed. Iparraguirre, SJ, Ignacio (Madrid: Biblioteca De Autores Christianos, 1952), 27. Cited hereafter as "Obras."

[9] Idígoras, 50-51.

[10] "The Loyolas were among the ten great families called Parientes mayors; they had the vested right of invitation to the king's court on certain occasions. Hence, they felt that they really belonged to the court and the highest nobility, and therefore believed they were entitled from time to time to rebel against the king. It was owing to such self-willed rebellion that Inigo's grandfather was compelled to raze the tower that rose defiantly over Loyola castle and replace it by a less formidable structure." Hugo Rahner, *The Spirituality of St. Ignatius Loyola: An Account of its Historical Development.* (Westminster, 1953). Cited hereafter as: "Hugh Rahner."

[11] *Ibid.*

[12] William W. Meissner, SJ, MD, *Ignatius of Loyola: Psychology of a Saint.* (New Haven, 1992), 16. Cited hereafter as: "Meissner."

[13] Joseph de Guibert, SJ, *The Jesuits: Their Spiritual Doctrine and Practice* (St. Louis: The Institute of Jesuit Sources, 1994), 23.

[14] James Brodrick, SJ, *The Origin of the Jesuits*, (London: Longmans, Green, 1949), 45.

[15] de Guibert, 23-24.

[16] "The picture of the brash young courtier is permeated with signs of phallic narcissism. The narcissistic strain also carries with it certain lines of cleavage or vulnerabilities that portend future difficulties. The phallic narcissistic personality demonstrates a constellation of characteristics that include exhibitionism, pride in prowess, and often, counterphobic competitiveness and a willingness to take risks or court danger in the service of self-display. Such individuals are frequently quite self-centered but invariably have an intense need for approval and especially admiration from others. One often finds an arrogance or contempt for others that is basically defensive and masks underlying feelings of inadequacy or inferiority…At the same time, their strength of will, determination, and often ruthless drive to overcome all obstacles and conquer all dangers gives them the appearance of strength of character and resourcefulness…The history and traditions of the Loyolas, extending back to the earliest legends, to the 'band of brothers' and the battle of Beotibar, are a paean to phallic narcissism." Meissner, 26-27.

[17] Idígoras, 124.

[18] See Ignatius' account in: *St. Ignatius' Own Story*, trans. William J. Young, SJ. (Chicago: Loyola University Press, 1980), 7. Cited hereafter as "Loyola."

[19] *Ibid.,* 8. 20 *Ibid.*

[21] This Jesuit historian Michael Maher informed me the book Ignatius would have desired was Adamis of Gaul, the standard book on court life and chivalry.

[22] Idígoras, 124.

[23] Loyola, 9.

[24] Loyola. 10.

[25] Ignatius Loyola, *The Spiritual Exercises of St. Ignatius*, ed. Louis J. Puhl, SJ (Chicago: Loyola University Press, 1951), 60-63. Cited hereafter as, "Puhl." The standard of *riches, honor and pride* had defined his life-world, all his thoughts, words and deeds, up to this significant event. He will eventually characterize this standard as inspired by the enemy of human nature. The Jerusalem-bound daydreams characterize a radical departure—a new life—indeed a metanoia that is characterized by *poverty, humility and insults*. This standard is of Christ and influenced by his Spirit.

[26] Loyola, 10.

[27] *Ibid.* 10.

[28] *Ibid.* 11.

[29] Meissner discusses this particular event, and Ignatius' subsequent ascetic practices to control his libidinal impulses, as an introduction of a "repressive barrier, outlawing all sexual (incestuous) wishes." He concludes that Ignatius is *repressing* thoughts, words and deeds that contravene his new religious ego ideals (59). Meissner's theories on the origins narcissism are congruent with Freud. They do not adequately describe Ignatius' genuine spiritual transformation. Christian anthropology defines human nature as a conjoining of spirit and body. Recent studies on brain development, focusing on powerful transcendent experiences, indicate that intense religious events can alter brain function at a biochemical level, healing psychological wounds. These studies based on the latest research in neuroscience discuss how the spiritual character of human nature both shapes and supersedes primitive biological urges. The change in Ignatius' *horizon of desire* can signify a graced healing that restored his spiritual compass to its rightful place as guide and master of his integrated human nature: J.S. Young, D.S. Cashwell, and J Shcherbakova, "The Moderating Relationship of Spirituality on Negative Life Events and Psychological Adjustment," *Counseling & Values* 45, no. 1 (2000): 49-57. See also the study by Dartmouth Medical School, YMCA of the USA and Institute for American Values, "Hardwired to Connect: The New Scientific Case for Authoritative Communities," (2003), 29-32. Cited hereafter as: "Hardwired to Connect." See also Mario Beauregard & Denyse O'Leary, *The Spiritual Brain: A Neuroscientist's Case For The Existence of the Soul*, (New York: Harper One, 2007), 229 ff.

[30] Loyola, 11.

[31] Gilles Cusson, SJ, *Biblical Theology and the Spiritual Exercises*, trans. George Ganss, SJ, Mary Angela Roduit, RC (St. Louis: Institute of Jesuit Sources, 1988), 9-11. Cited hereafter as: "Cusson." Cusson suggests Ignatius' reading *The Imitation of Christ* and the lives of the saints in the *Flos Sanctorum* likely influenced his holy desires. He posits that Ignatius' reflections and reading materials are used by God to shape a fundamental new vision and mission for his future: an example of grace building on nature. "If we are familiar with the ideas of Ignatius and his conception of the Christian life, we can see (from his reading of the *Imitation*)...how faithful he remained to the way that was opened to him during his days at Loyola...and then developed them into a perspective that was much more clearly apostolic." 17.

[32] "God went on adorning his soul and filling it with tints of perfection the portrait of which at Manresa He had sketched on the outlines." Rodríguez, 464.

2. Integrated Conversion and the Particular Examen

[1] Loyola, 12.

[2] *Ibid.,* 13.

[3] *Ibid.,* 14.

[4] *Ibid.,* 15.

[5] *Ibid.,* 15-16.

[6] *Ibid.,* 17.

[7] *Ibid.,* 16.

[8] *Ibid.,* 14.

[9] "Answering that he had given the clothes (to the beggar), tears of compassion started from his eyes, compassion for the poor man to whom he had given his clothing, compassion for him because he had been suspected of stealing them." *Ibid.,* 16.

[10] *Ibid.,* 18.

[11] *Ibid.*

[12] *Ibid.*

[13] Ignatius understood human nature as good. Evil was without, not *by nature,* within. Ignatius' belief in human nature's goodness distanced him from Luther and specifically, Calvin.

[14] *SpEx* [315.2; 319.6; 320.7; 324.11; 325.12], Puhl, 142-45.

[15] The fact that Ignatius' custom was to read the passion during Mass is a fitting spiritual marker for this crisis. *Loyola* 18.

[16] "Up to his twenty-sixth year he was a man given over to the vanities of the world, and took a special delight in the exercise of arms, with a great and vain desire of winning glory." Loyola, 7.

[17] Meissner, 9.

[18] Idígoras, 42.

[19] Karen Horney, MD, *Self Analysis* (New York: W. W. Norton & Company, Inc., 1994), 38. Cited hereafter as: "Horney." Horney's theory differs from Meissner. His Freudian model posits external psychological forces and disturbances that frustrate instinctual drives.

[20] *Ibid.,* 42-43. A critical scholar of history may view the overlay of psychological theory on Ignatius' history as problematic. While ideas such as *deprivation* might be viewed as constructs or symptoms of Industrial society, the true human impact of such deprivation transcends historical epochs and intellectual constructs.

[21] Rudolf Allers, *Practical Psychology in Character Development* (New York: Sheed and Ward, 1934; repr., Fort Collins, CO: RC Books, 2002). For a discussion of childhood stresses that can damage the personality and lead to habitual and sinful complexes, see, 4-101 (page references are to the reprint edition) Cited hereafter as "Allers PPCD." [Allers broke early with Freud

and became a close collaborator of both Victor Frankel and Alfred Adler. Allers, a mentor to both the young Hans Urs von Balthasar and Edith Stein, was armed with doctoral degrees in medicine, psychiatry and philosophy. He published works in psychiatry, philosophy, theology, linguistics and physiology. He was uniquely attuned to the interplay between the spiritual, intellectual, and psychological components of the personality and developed a psychology sensitive to the best in the Christian tradition. His last teaching posts were at The Catholic University of America and Georgetown University. Most of Allers' works, and a large collection of his personal papers and conference notes, are available at Georgetown University's Lauinger Library].

[22] Such deprivation leads to stress and biochemical deficiencies that make forming intimate relationships difficult. All of which increase propensities to addictive substances and behaviors. Gabor Maté, *In the Realm of Hungry Ghosts: Close Encounters with Addiction* (Berkeley: North Atlantic Books, 2010), 197-210. Cited hereafter as: *Maté*.

[23] Maté, 390. See also these sections: "How the Addictive Brain Develops" and "The Addiction Process and the Addictive Personality (Maté's methods to deactivate maladaptive habits and addictions in order to establish emotional balance will be examined later, along with the awareness exercises of Michael Brown's *Presence Process*. Insights from both authors are used to highlight inherent aspects of Ignatius' methods in order to create a holistic updating of the vital *Examen* consciousness techniques and discernment principles).

[24] "(4). The neurotic need for power: Domination over others craved for its own sake; Devotion to a cause, duty, responsibility, though playing some part, not the driving force; Essential disrespect for others, their individuality, their dignity, their feelings, the only concern being their subordination; Great differences as to degree of destructive elements involved; Indiscriminate adoration of strength and contempt for weakness; Dread of uncontrollable situations; Dread of helplessness. (6). The neurotic need for social recognition or prestige: All things—inanimate objects, money, persons, one's own qualities, activities, and feelings— evaluated only according to their prestige value; Self-evaluation entirely dependent on nature of public acceptance; Differences as to use of traditional or rebellious ways of inciting envy or admiration; Dread of losing caste ("humiliation"), whether through external circumstances or through factors from within. (7). The neurotic need for personal admiration: Inflated image of self (narcissism); Need to be admired not for what one possesses or presents in public eye but for the imagined self; Self-evaluation dependent on living up to this image and on admiration of it by others; Dread of losing admiration ("humiliation"). (8). The neurotic ambition for personal achievement: Need to surpass others not through what one presents or is but through one's activities; Self-evaluation dependent on being the very best—lover, sportsman, writer, worker—particularly in one's own mind, recognition by others being vital too, however, and its absence resented; Admixture of destructive tendencies (toward the defeat of others) never lacking but varying in intensity; Relentless driving of self to greater achievements, though with pervasive anxiety; Dread of failure ("humiliation"). Trends 6, 7 and 8 have in common a more or less open competitive drive toward absolute superiority over others. But though these trends overlap and may be combined, they may lead a separate existence. The need for personal admiration, for instance, may go with a disregard of social prestige. (10). The neurotic need for perfection and unassailability: relentless driving for perfection; Ruminations and self-recriminations regarding possible flaws; Feelings of superiority over others because of being perfect; Dread of finding flaws within self or of making mistakes; Dread of criticism or reproaches." Horney, 53-56.

[25] Hugo Rahner, 5-7.

[26] Meissner, 16.

[27] Puhl, 61.

[28] Ignatius' sense of the *Magis* is at this point is purely ego-driven. His elder priestly brother had already brought "disgrace" upon the "princely line of Loyola" by fathering four children. Ignatius wanted much more, especially as his ambitions increased in his contacts with the royal court. Hugo Rahner, 7.

[29] Loyola, 15.

[30] A "harrow" is an agricultural tool with a sharp blade that digs up hardened soil. The word "harrowing" means a keenly painful, agonizing, excruciating, or torturous experience, if you will a painful digging up or slicing through the spirit and soul of a person. The word "harrowing" is chosen to capture this frightening episode in Ignatius' conversion—a point of extreme intensity in Ignatius' spiritual journey.

[31] Loyola, 19.

[32] "con asaz diligencia" Obras, 45.

[33] *(muy atribulado; mucho daño). Ibid.* [34] *Ibid.,* 19. 35 *Ibid.*

[36] (y así siempre quedaba con trabajo). Obras, 45.

[37] Ignatius Loyola, *A Pilgrim's Journey*, trans. Joseph N. Tylenda, SJ (Wilmington: Michael Glazier, Inc, 1985), 31. Cited hereafter as "Tylenda."

[38] *(Socórreme, Señor).* Obras, 46. [39] Loyola, 20. [40] Joseph W. Ciarrocchi, *the Doubting Disease: Help for Scrupulosity and Religious Obsessions* (Mahwah, NJ: Paulist, 1995), 22.

[41] "I insist especially that you think of God as loving you, as I have no doubt He does, and that you correspond with this love and pay no attention whatever to the evil thoughts, even if they are obscene or sensual (when they are not deliberate), nor to your cowardice or tepidity. For even St. Peter and St. Paul did not succeed in escaping all or some of these thoughts." As cited in: *Ignatius Loyola, Letters of St. Ignatius Loyola*, trans. William J. Young, SJ (Chicago: Loyola University Press, 1959), 430. Cited hereafter as, "Young." Also this: "It was especially with the tempted that the charity of Ignatius was given full scope." "Today" [January 29, 1555], Gonçalves tells us "the Father called a brother who was tempted, and remained two hours with him trying to get him to tell him why he wanted to leave. Suspecting that it was a matter of some sin committed in the world, the Father went over a part of his own life, even the evil he had done, to take away his shame; and thus, as a matter of fact, the brother admitted the cause of his temptation, which was next to nothing, to the Father, who was protesting that he would not go to dinner until he learned it.'" de Guibert, 99.

[42] *Ibid.,* 12.

[43] Loyola, 20

[44] *(con grande impetu).* Obras, 46.

[45] "The punitive demands and expected punishments that lie behind such scrupulous obsessions are possibly the result of a *superego regression* to more instinctual levels. It reflects

primitive destructive impulses deflected from the unconscious. The ego, of course, must defend itself from this punitive attack. For the pilgrim, the destructive and punitive inroads of the superego constituted a major battlefield…The psychological and spiritual crisis through which Iñigo de Loyola passed in Manresa was an extension of the conversion process begun on his sickbed at the castle of Loyola. The hypothesis we have been following here is that the strong, courageous, and fearless identity the young Iñigo had shaped, in the image of the chivalrous knight who feared no danger and sought glory and conquest on all sides, whether libidinal or aggressive, was formed around a phallic, narcissistic core that left him vulnerable to certain kinds of regressive stress. The core element in the pathological narcissist organization of his personality lies in the ego-ideal, in which the residues of archaic, narcissistic grandiosity and omnipotence were firmly embedded. The residues of earlier archaic narcissistic structures left him with a certain narcissistic vulnerability that carried with it the potentiality for regressive crisis." Meissner, 75, 77.

[46] (*tornaba a gritar*). Obras, 46.

[47] Loyola, 20.

[48] *Ibid.*

[49] (*le mandó que rompiese aqeulla abstinencia*), Obras, 46.

[50] (*pareciéndole que era obligado otra vez confesallos*). *Ibid.*

[51] (*con algunos ímpetus de dejalla*), *Ibid.*, 47.

[52] (*y con esto quiso el Señor que despertó come de sueño*), *Ibid.*

[53] (*con grande claridad*), *Ibid.*.

[54] Allers' insight linking pride and suffering is congruent with Augustine's. Rudolf Allers, *The New Psychologies* (New York: Sheed and Ward, 1938; repr., Fort Collins, CO: McCaffrey Publishing, 2000), 76 (page references are to the reprint edition).

[55] *Ibid.*, 77.

[56] Allers PPCD, 171.

[57] Young, 430.

[58] "And so, being in a stronghold which the French were attacking, and with everyone being of the opinion they should give themselves up and save their lives (for they saw clearly that they could not defend themselves), he gave so many arguments to the commandant that even then he persuaded him to make a defence, though against the opinion of all the knights." Loyola, 7.

[59] Loyola, 24.

[60] *Ibid.*, 27.

[61] Ignatius Loyola, *The Spiritual Journal of St. Ignatius Loyola*, trans. William J. Young, SJ (Woodstock, MD: Woodstock College Press, 1958), 6-7.

[62] Take, Lord, receive all my liberty, my memory, my understanding and my entire will. Whatsoever I have or hold, You have given to me. I give it all back to You, and surrender it to be wholly governed by your will. Give me only your love and your grace and I am rich enough, and I ask for nothing more.

[63] Loyola, 22.

[64] "The better to arrive at this degree of perfection which is so precious in the spiritual life, his chief and most earnest endeavor should be to seek in our Lord his greater abnegation and continual mortification in all things possible; and our endeavor should be to help him in those things to the extent that our Lord gives us his grace, for his greater service and glory." *Constitutions of the Society of Jesus and Their Complimentary Norms.* Edited by John W. Padberg, SJ. St. Louis: Institute of Jesuit Sources, 47. Cited hereafter as *Constitutions.*

[65] This is the Ignatian First Principle and Foundation from the forward of the *Spiritual Exercises* that concludes with; "our one desire and choice should be what is more conducive to the end for which we are created." Puhl, 12.

[66] "So it happens that the ideal and final objective Ignatius proposed to his followers, "finding God in all things," constituted his own inner attitude. Referring to this inner attitude, Nadal got to the essential idea when he summed it up this way: *ducentem Spiritum sequebature, non praeibat.* "He followed the Spirit who led him, he did not go before it." Rather than being a leader Ignatius was basically, as we have stated so often before, someone who was always being led. In the autumn of his life, a secret escaped his lips, a confidence that is typical of mystics: he said that his way was more *passive* than *active.* The proverbial man of action, therefore, was a man acted upon, more receptive than active, although without doubt he appeared to those who saw him to be more active than passive." Idígoras, 584.

[67] Gonçalves relates that his sharing with "the Father" about his own struggles with vainglory, brought this confession from Ignatius: "The Father related to me how he had struggled with this vice (vainglory) for two years, to the extent that when he took a ship in Barcelona bound for Jerusalem, he did not dare tell anybody that he was going to Jerusalem. He acted in this same way in other particulars, and, what is more, he added that he had enjoyed great peace of soul on this point ever afterwards." Loyola, 3.

[68] The conclusion of Ignatius' advice in, "Directions for the Amendment and Reformation of One's Way of Life in His State of Life," reads: "Let him desire and seek nothing except the greater praise and glory of God our Lord as the aim of all he does. For every one must keep in mind that in all that concerns the spiritual life his progress will be in proportion to his surrender of self-love and of his own will and interests." *SpEx* [189] Puhl, 78.

[69] For a modern narrative revealing the purification process Ignatius endured, I find Walter Ciszek's harrowing with his own pride a striking complement to Ignatius' struggles. Walter Ciszek, SJ, *He Leadeth Me* (Garden City, NY: Doubleday & Company, Inc. 1973), 83-5. (For the full account, read all of chapter seven: "Four Years of Purgatory: 78-88).

[70] In the Spanish transcription the phrase, *he was especially disturbed and sorry,* is stronger. It reads: *mas tenía grande confusión y dolor.* A different translation could read: *but he had great confusion and grief. Obras,* 50.

[71] Tylenda, 40-41.

[72] One thinks of Augustine's famous cry: "I have loved thee late, Beauty ever ancient, ever new." Saint Augustine, *Confessions,* trans. R. S. Pine-Coffin (London: Penguin, 1961), 244.

[73] Johnston, 193.

[74] Church tradition indicates that for the elect, most will undergo purification even after death. See *CCC,* 235: § 1030-32.

[75] "Gonçalves de Câmera has informed us that during all the last years of Ignatius' life he made this examen of his conscience as each hour of the day struck, and also of the night if he was awake. The examen was not a mere glance over the manner, more or less perfect, in which his actions had been performed, but also a humble search for faults that had escaped him. Ribadeneyra is once more the one who informs us of this in a note of 1554. Ignatius so feared the least shadow of sin that often he examined with the greatest care whether there had not been some fault in the actions where no trace of one seemed to be—a fugitive thought, a slight acquiescence of the will, and other minute details in which others would have found nothing even after a careful scrutiny." As cited in: de Guibert, 67.

[76] Michael J. Buckley, "The Structure of the Rules for Discernment of Spirits," *The Way Supplement*, no. 20 (Autumn): 28. Cited hereafter cited as "Rules."

[77] Puhl, 148.

[78] *Ibid.*, 4.

[79] Puhl, 11.

[80] The typical end of Ignatius' letters remains constant from early in his Roman years to late in his life. The refrain captures his hard-won docility and spiritual indifference while reflecting his desire to share its graces with others: "I close asking God our Lord by his infinite goodness to grant us his abundant grace, so that we may know his most holy will and entirely to fulfill it." *Letters*, 25, 669.

[81] Cusson sees a fundamental election by Ignatius during his spiritual awakening at Loyola denoting a major turning point in his life. Yet it is necessary to state that his willful ego at this juncture in his conversion is still in control. The man whose arrogance battled the French at Pamplona will remain in control up to the harrowing with his scrupulosity.

[82] Tylenda, 35-36.

[83] *Ibid.*, 7.

[84] *Letters*, 349, 468, 469, 635, 660, 694.

[85] Íñigo spent four years working on the spiritual crafting of Favre. He sent him to Dr. Castro to begin a schedule of weekly confession and Communion; he had him examine his conscience each day, and Favre ended up by choosing to follow the same form of life as his friend (Xavier). Idígoras, 311.

[86] Ignatius' linkage of the *Examen* to the First Week purgative process, and as a tool to help one follow Christ, adds further evidence that his methods are, indeed, unique to him. The foundational insights that produced these methods of examination of conscience likely resulted from his progressive conversion.

[87] "There is a new step taken by Ignatius with respect to the entire previous tradition of which the significance might be epitomized by saying: *the Ignatian name for union with God is 'election.'* Such union comes about in the act and art of choosing in each moment in terms of God's will, which declares itself in history for the transformation of the world…Thus the *Exercises*, beyond the formal frame of eight, fifteen or thirty days, constitute a way of living in God for the world and of living for God in the world. Such is Ignatius' contribution to the spiritual Tradition of the West…" Javier Melloni, SJ, *The Exercises of St Ignatius Loyola in the Western*

Tradition, trans. Michael Ivens, SJ, (Leominster, England: Gracewing, 2000), 50-54. Cited hereafter as, "Melloni."

[88] While Melloni speaks about a "mysticism of service," Ignatius does not mention the *Exercises* or the *Examens* as a means to mystical union. The closest one can come to understanding Ignatius' spirituality leading to such mystical union is the analysis of the near-death narratives discussed above, and the states of purgation, illumination and union they reveal. Ignatius' reluctance to speak about such lofty goals achieved by his methods might be explained by his frequent encounters with the Inquisition and their questions about his spiritual disciplines. Nadal, however, contextualizes the *Exercises* themselves as a means to perfection according the threefold path proposed by the mystical tradition: purgation, illumination and union. "The method and order of the *Exercises* is purgation, illumination, union; and the sequence followed is the proper one, beginning humbly and without undue curiosity from the bottom, with great faith and hope." Palmer, 36.

[89] Puhl, 1.

3. The Examen and its Use by the First Jesuits

[1] It is understood that the *GE* was to be a preparation for confession. In the context of the *Spiritual Exercises*, the *PE* was employed to deepen the conversion process. It is the *PE* that Ignatius employs as his principal means of daily spiritual growth and which he incorporates more fully into the structure of the *Exercises*. Puhl, 15-24.

[2] In Ignatius' day, "after dinner" would mean the mid-day meal and "after supper" the evening meal. The second examination might come after supper or before the end of the day as recommended by Rodríguez. Rodríguez, 446.

[3] The method of the *PE* as well as the chart to mark one's progress is original to Ignatius, as we concluded above: "He answered that the *Exercises* were not composed all at one time, but things that he had observed in his own soul and found useful and which he thought would be useful to others, he put into writing—the examination of conscience, for example, with the idea of lines of different length, and so on." Loyola, 69.

[4] Puhl, 22.

[5] *The Constitutions* of the Society of Jesus exhort Jesuits at all stages of formation to the following regarding the frequency of the *Examination of Conscience* for daily life: "Consequently, in addition to confession and Communion every eight days and daily Mass, they will have one hour, during which they will recite the Hours of Our Lady, examine their consciences twice each day, and add other prayers according to each one's devotion to fill out the rest of the aforesaid hours." *Constitutions*, 142.

[6] "(The) *GE* should be made always along with the particular; for immediately in the morning on rising we should offer to our Lord all that we are going to do that day...Afterwards, twice a day, at midday and at night, we must make the *GE* along with the particular. Such is the custom of the Society founded on our Constitutions and we find it expressed in the Common Rules." Rodríguez, 457.

[7] De Guibert confirms Rodríguez's instructions are consistent with both Ignatius' and the Jesuits' earliest practices. "Within the limits of the field which Rodríguez has marked out, he has the merit of being rigorously faithful to the lines of spiritual conduct indicated both by

St. Ignatius and by the Society's tradition which to no small extent is already time honored." de Guibert, 264.

[8] Rodríguez, 424.

[9] Puhl, 1.

[10] This attitude of docility and spiritual indifference is enshrined in three central statements and prayers of the *Exercises*: "The Fundamentum" (The First Principle and Foundation); "The Eternal Lord of All Things" (which concludes the First Week *Exercises*); and the "Suscipe" prayer that sums up the entire *Spiritual Exercises*: Puhl, 12, 45, 102.

[11] Another principal reason for enfolding the two modalities into a single structure is to incorporate elements of gratitude and God's love so essential to the Ignatian tradition when contemplating failure, addictions, sin and personal weakness.

[12] *SpEx* [5]: Puhl, 3. (The same generosity required of the *Exercises* is applicable to the *Examination of Conscience* when it is practiced as a daily discipline).

[13] "We should hold no occupation sufficient to justify our omitting this examen…Even sickness and indisposition, which is sufficient to excuse us from any long prayer, should not excuse us from making our examens. Thus it is right for all to hold as a first principle that the examens must never be omitted, neither the general nor the particular." Rodríguez, 424. See also, *Constitutions*: 261, 342, 344; da Câmara, 18, 68.

[14] "Regarding the faults of individuals, it is necessary that whoever knows himself should recognize the faults he has, for he will never be free of them in the state of our present misery until in the furnace of the everlasting love of God our Creator and Lord all our wickedness shall be entirely consumed, when our souls shall be completely penetrated and possessed by Him and our wills thus perfectly conformed to--or rather, transformed into--His will, which is essential rectitude and infinite goodness. But may He by His infinite mercy grant to all of us at least daily to regret and abhor all our faults and imperfections, and participate at last in the eternal light of which even the least of our defects will appear to be insupportable. By thus attacking them we will weaken and lessen them with the help of the same God our Lord." As cited in Ignatius Loyola, *Letters of St. Ignatius Loyola*, trans. William J. Young, SJ (Chicago: Loyola University Press, 1959), 153-4. Cited hereafter as *Letters*.

[15] Paul Doncoeur, SJ, *The Heart of Ignatius*, trans. Henry St. C. Lavin, SJ (Baltimore: Helicon, 1959), 34. Cited hereafter as "Doncoeur."

[16] "One reason is that it is easier to overcome an evil habit when one frequently turns his mind to the actions or omission he wants to be freed from, renews his resolution, and stiffens his will against the defect. Another reason is that by making this steady effort a person does what lies in his own power and merits from God the grace to be freed from the fault. For as a general rule God's grace is granted in proportion to our own efforts." Palmer, 127.

[17] "God's activity takes on many forms: He enlightens the understanding (2), He enters the soul, moves it, draws it toward loving Him (330), grants it abundance of fervor, overflowing love, and intensity of His favors (320), makes it attain intense affection, tears and other spiritual consolation (322), places in the soul that which the exercitant ought to do with regard to his choice of a state of life (180), and brings the soul's desires into order (16). God even communicates Himself to and embraces the exercitant (15)." As cited in William A. M. Peters, *The*

Spiritual Exercises of St. Ignatius: Exposition and Interpretation (Rome: Centrum Ignatianum Spiritualitatis, 1980), 1-2.

[18] "Every time one falls into the particular sin or fault, let him place his hand upon his breast, and be sorry for having fallen. He can do this even in the presence of many others without their perceiving what he is doing." Puhl, 16.

[19] This is from the Directory by Diego Miró: The one who remains in the world "should pray in the morning on the life and passion of Christ using the method of the *Exercises*; make an examination of conscience morning and evening; say the rosary; receive the sacraments using a definite spiritual method; cultivate devotion to the saints, his guardian angel, and his patron saint; read spiritual books; and help his neighbor according to his capacity." Palmer, 77. The Jesuit historian Michael Maher informed me of a "half rule" the early Marian Sodalities describe: two examines for Jesuits, one for lay people.

[20] There are three favors requested in the Third Exercise: "1. A deep knowledge of my sins and a feeling of abhorrence for them; 2. An understanding of the disorder of my actions, that filled with horror of them, I may amend my life and put it in order; 3. A knowledge of the world, that filled with horror, I may put away from me all that is worldly and vain." *SpEx* [63] Puhl, 31.

[21] Ignatius sought means of drawing persons to God based on the circumstances of their disposition and situation, *SpEx* [18]. However, he did not eschew using servile fear to motivate, especially as a means for drawing a person away from mortal sin, *SpEx* [370]. Perhaps the most noteworthy incident of his boldness is in a letter to Francis Jimenez De Miranda, the abbot of Salas. The abbot was living in sacrilegious wedlock and making illegal use of ecclesiastical funds: *"What you need is penance and much of it. This means that you must not only withdraw from your sin and be sorry for it, but that you must make satisfaction for past sins, and unburden your conscience of so much Church property that has been misappropriated... You do not know whether you will be summoned to the judgment this coming September, or this month, or this very evening. Many a man in better health than you enjoy, more conservative in his personal habits, has gone to bed without a care, and was not alive when morning came. Do not put your soul in such peril."* Young, 397-8.

[22] Doncoeur, 36.

[23] "Even during the purgation from sins in the First Week there is a kind of illumination, viz., through knowledge of sin, of oneself, and of God's justice. To some extent there is even a perfecting—through the increase or acquisition especially of those virtues opposed to the person's vices, as well as of contrition over sins for the sake of God and for love of him. Similarly, in the course of being enlightened with knowledge of Christ and God, which begins in the Second Week, attention is given to purging of sins: we are always looking out of the corner of our eye, so to speak, in order to remove any sins that may remain; this is why the examination of conscience is never given up. Here also there is a striving toward perfection by the augmenting of virtues and love of God. And finally, when at the conclusion perfection is being concentrated on—i.e., love of God and of the other virtues—one also reaches the highest degree of illumination in the knowledge of God and divine things; and there are always some residual sins, affections, or imperfections that need to be purged and rooted out. Nevertheless it is still true that in the first part the main and primary concern is purgation, i.e., the uprooting of sins; and this belongs by its very nature primarily to the First Week. After that the emphasis is on illumination, and in the third place, on perfection." Palmer, 104.

[24] "[T]he '*PE*' must be viewed as part of a positive growth-programme, characterized by the development of positive qualities, not just the eradication of negative ones."Michael Ivens, SJ, *Understanding the Spiritual Exercises* (Leominster, England: Gracewing, 1998), 34.

[25] "As a physician has effected not a little, but a great deal, when he has diagnosed the root of the illness, because then he will hit upon the right remedies, and the medicines will take effect; so we have achieved not a little, but a great deal, if we hit upon the root of our infirmities and ailments, because that will be to hit upon the cure of them by applying the remedy and medicine of the examen." Rodríguez, 427.

[26] "Next, he should have a great hope in God's goodness and generosity. God seeks out even those who go astray, and pursues those who flee from him; how much more will he receive and welcome those who come to him with a good will. The exercitant should therefore put his trust in that infinite clemency which has given him this good desire and so will give him also grace and strength to follow it through well and fruitfully. For 'his will is our sanctification' [I Thess. 4:3]." Palmer, 295.

[27] John English, SJ, *Spiritual Freedom* (Chicago: Loyola University Press, 1995), 56. Cited hereafter as "Spiritual Freedom."

[28] "He found great difficulty in staying in Salamanca because this prohibition on determining which are mortal and which are venial sins *closed the door* (italics supplied) on his helping souls." Tylenda, 82. In the Spanish transcription, the phrase *closed the door* is as definitive as most English translations: "*cerrada la puerta.*" Obras, 76.

[29] Idígoras, 567. Two accounts from the *Memoriale* offer similar testimony: "I must recall the way in which our Father deals with affairs: how he never uses emotions to persuade, but facts; how he does not adorn facts with words, but rather with the facts themselves, relating so many and so decisive circumstances that they convince, by their own force as it were." da Câmera,

59. Also, "It is very remarkable how the Father remembers what he has promised, and he fulfils his promises. The reason for this is, apart from his great constancy, that he never utters a word without having thought about it first and offered it to God." Ibid, 151.

[30] "We should speak only with necessity, and for the edification of ourselves and others, and avoid those things which offer no profit to the soul, such as the desire for news and worldly affairs...Let no one seek to be considered a wit, or to affect elegance or prudence or eloquence, but look upon Christ, who made nothing at all of these things and chose to be humbled and despised by men for our sake rather than be honored and respected...We should not dispute stubbornly with anyone. Rather we should patiently give our reasons with the purpose of declaring the truth lest our neighbor remain in error, and not that we should have the upper hand." Young, 440.

[31] Loyola, 12.

[32] "When one who is giving the Exercises perceives that the exercitant is not affected by any spiritual experiences, such as consolations and desolations, and that he is not troubled by different spirits, he ought to ply him with questions about the exercises. He should ask him whether he makes them at the appointed times, and how he makes them. He should question him about the Additional Directions, whether he is diligent in the observance of them. He will demand an account in detail of each of these points," *SpEx* [6]. Puhl, 3. (There is also this notation from

the *Official Directory of 1599* speaking about the importance of following the specific recommendations in the Annotations and rules for times of prayer: "This much however, should be said about them: the exercitant must devote the greatest diligence to observing these instructions, for the more fully he does so the sooner and more abundantly will he find the spiritual fruit which he seeks." Palmer, 296).

[33] Puhl, 16.

[34] And we read of our blessed Father that, not content with giving this method of the *PE* to anyone whom he wished to cure of any vice, he took means not to let him forget to put it into practice. He made him before dinner and before bedtime give an account to some confidential agent whom he assigned to him, and tell him if he had made the examen, how he made it, and whether he had made it in the manner appointed. Rodríguez, 423.

[35] The Directory index lists thirty-eight entries for the *PE* and only fourteen for the *GE*. *On Giving the Exercises: The Early Jesuit Manuscript Directories and the Official Directory of 1599*, trans. Martin E. Palmer, SJ (St. Louis: The Institute of Jesuit Sources, 1996), 361.

[36] *Ibid.*, 200.

[37] These men are: 1) Juan Alonso de Vitoria, who gave the *Exercises* in Rome under Ignatius' supervision. His notes find their way into the Official Directory (OD) of 1599 [Palmer, 16]; 2) Juan Alfonso de Polanco, Ignatius' secretary, whose Directory was prized as the finest of the group prior to the publication of the OD of 1599 [Palmer, 127]; 3) Diego Miró worked directly under Ignatius in giving the *Spiritual Exercises*, and borrows inspiration from Polanco, whom he considered somewhat lax in his application of Ignatius' disciplines [Palmer, 167]. Antonio Valentino, a novice director for 26 years in Italy, was likely in contact with the living tradition of the founder [Palmer, 86].

[38] "Finally, he should consider the causes, origins, and roots of his faults" (Palmer, 309) and; "Hence, in the first meeting after giving the Foundation, the director should give the Particular Examen. Here he should explain that every person usually has one or two principal faults or sins which are the source or root of others. And even if a person should have several main faults, it is still good to select one and focus all our efforts on uprooting it. Once it has been overcome, we then concentrate this special effort on a different one, and so on in succession. The Particular Examen will be of service here. Even though it is to be used throughout one's life after the Exercises, it should be begun now, both to…acquire skill in it and because it must be used on the exercises themselves and the Additions." Palmer, 313.

[39] Rodríguez, 426.

[40] "Thus the making of the PE against one vice is fighting against all vices, since this check and vigilance employed on one particular serves also for the rest." *Ibid.*, 426.

[41] *Ibid.*, 433-442.

[42] Joseph Rickaby in an early twentieth century commentary on the *Exercises*, echoes Rodriguez on the value of the PE's singular focus: "Nowhere in the Exercises does St. Ignatius enter into more minute detail than here…In the process of time, the file of the *PE*, steadily applied, will remove the rust of exterior defects, so far as they are removable, and not ingrained in the constitution. When the fault is brought down to an irreducible minimum, it is well to transfer the *PE* somewhere else, always however being ready to bring it back to the ancient defect should that show signs of growing again. Joseph Rickaby, SJ, *the Spiritual Exercises of St. Ignatius Loyola:*

Spanish and English with a Continuous Commentary (London: Burns Oates & Washbourne LTD, 1923), 55.

[43] "One of the reasons why some people make so little profit by their examen is very often this, that they do nothing but by fits and starts, making the Particular Examen on one thing for a week or a fortnight or for a month and then getting tired and passing on to another thing without having gained the first, and then make another new start, and then another...This is to tire yourself out without result, *always learning, and never arriving at knowledge of the truth* (II Tim

[iii] 7)." Rodríguez, 442.

[44] However as noted above, Ignatius tells Gonçalves that he struggled with vainglory for two years: Loyola, 3. The near-death narratives indicate a progressive purification that stretches over decades, indeed, the remainder of Ignatius' life.

[45] Rodríguez, 445.

[46] Rickaby echoes what has already been noted about the challenges presented by the *PE* in light of the second and third paradigms: "Still experience shows it is a practice extremely difficult to keep up. The difficulty arises, first, from want of heart and care in the matter; secondly from not finding a proper subject; thirdly from neglect to mark...But the chiefest difficulty is the subject. The most urgent subject is found in definite avoidable occasions of mortal sin. Such occasions should be avoided by the use of this examen." Rickaby, 55.

[47] William A. M. Peters, *The Spiritual Exercises of St. Ignatius: Exposition and Interpretation* (Rome: Centrum Ignatianum Spiritualitatis, 1980), 12.

[48] "Among the means that are of the great and interior assistance to people, Your Reverence is aware of one that is outstanding: the *Exercises*. I remind you, therefore, to make use of this weapon, so familiar to our Society—although it is the First Week that could be given to large numbers, together with some methods of prayer." Palmer, SJ, Martin E., and John W. Padberg, SJ, John L. McCarthy, SJ, *Ignatius of Loyola: Letters and Instructions* (St. Louis: The Institute of Jesuit Sources, 2006), 694. Similar advice can be found on pages; 468-9, 349, 635,

[660] Hereafter cited as "Palmer et all." (Androzzi is one of the first spiritual writers in the Society and a man who achieved great success in public ministries).

[49] The most prominent of Ignatius' apostles, Francis Xavier, developed a short version of Christian Doctrine for his missionary work that advises the practice of the five-point *GE* before retiring at night. The *Examen* itself, and instructions for praying it, were given to penitents after confession or posted on the doors of churches for the faithful to copy and take home. *The Letters and Instructions of Francis Xavier*, trans. M. Joseph Costelloe, SJ (St. Louis: The Institute of Jesuit Sources, 1992), 201-209. Cited hereafter as "Costelloe."

[50] Rodríguez, 423.

[51] "And we know also that he kept his first companions for a long time with no other support than that of the examination of conscience and frequentation of the sacraments, thinking that, if that was done, it would be quite enough to preserve them in virtue." *Ibid.*, 423.

[52] "Our Father has great skill in dealing with souls. He uses so many means that it seems almost impossible that anyone should fail to profit, if that person really wants to gain some advantage. The ordinary methods are: to recommend the making of examination [of conscience] and

the practice of prayer, to have syndics (a syndic is an admonitor or corrector) to urge the giving of an account to someone every day as to how much one is benefiting from these methods." da Câmera, 68.

[53] O'Malley, 87.

[54] "The daily examination of conscience that the Jesuits recommended so frequently in their works on piety did not necessarily look to confession. The examination was already a common place in the Christian tradition of asceticism. The contribution the Jesuits made was through their propagation of the so-called particular examination of conscience recommended in the *Exercises*. Along with a general review of the day went concern for a "particular sin or defect," which, because especially frequent or characteristic, grounded the others. The bookkeeping Ignatius recommended for this sin or defect is another manifestation of the moral foundation he and his disciples considered essential for the spiritual edifice. But such human calculation about moral performance was not meant to imply that God was an exacting bookkeeper. According to Nadal: 'Father Ignatius says that God deals with us differently than do worldly human beings. They look to find whatever is bad or imperfect in our actions, they take note of it and then hold it against us. God, however, looks to see what good we have done, and closes an eye to our imperfections.'" O'Malley, 151.

[55] Joseph F. Conwell, SJ, *Impelling Spirit: Revisiting a Founding Experience 1539 Ignatius of Loyola and his Companions.* (Chicago: Loyola Press, 1997). 157-8.

[56] O'Malley, 138-9.

[57] Francis Xavier made this connection in giving the *Examen* to those who came to confession. Indeed, it appears that one style of confession the Jesuits propounded was, like the *PE*, strategic. Pierre Favre, one of the first companions, composed in 1544 a work for confessors highlighting a *PE*-like focus on a root or core sin. "Although penitents should be encouraged to confess in any manner they wished, they should be guided by the confessor in locating their most characteristic sin that gives rise to others. The confessor should then indicate possible remedies and take care to instruct them in how to pray." *Ibid.*, 142.

[58] "Nevertheless what can be indicated is the fidelity of many Jesuits to the confessional where in practice the greater part of oral (spiritual) direction is given." "This fidelity was particularly noteworthy among the spiritual writers. The number of 23,000 confessions in one year has been given for Gabriel Hevenesi. More numerous still, at that time as today, were those who spent the greater part of their time, sometimes entire days, in hearing confessions. This is important to note about the penitents of these "perpetual confessors." As is still the case today, constantly the majority of these penitents did not consist of sinners to be converted. Rather they were simple and humble souls who found in those confessionals the path to a truly lofty piety and even, more often than one might be inclined to believe, to a genuine holiness completely unknown to all." de Guibert, 310-11.

[59] O'Malley, 83.

[60] Underlying the Jesuits' pastoral ideals and practice, therefore, were certain assumptions about God and about how the universe was governed. At least some of the more influential Jesuits shared an appreciation of the intimate immediacy and power of God's presence in the world and in the human soul, an appreciation undoubtedly related to what they learned from the "Contemplation to Obtain the Love of God." This appreciation led to conclusions about the efficacious power of that divine presence to conduct an individual in the way of salvation and peace.

The Jesuits by and large believed in a world in which God's grace was abundant. God willed all to be saved and had embraced the world with an even greater love because of the life, death, and resurrection of Jesus. *Ibid.*, 84.

[61] "Part of God's commitment to humanity is to remember also the sins and betrayals of his people. God remembers sin not to punish or avenge it, but to heal the brokenness that lies at the root of it. Unless human beings are enabled to remember, grieve for and repent of their sins they can never be made whole and free from guilt. What we forget we are condemned to repeat....For this reason Ignatius does all in his power to make the remembering safe." Lavinia Byrne, "Asking for the Grace," *The Way Supplement* 64 (Spring 1988): 33.

[62] It is hard to keep an appropriate balance between the spiritual and psychological. However it might be noted that a psychology that discounts the reality of evil, the fact of sin, and personal choice in collaboration with both, is as naïve as a spirituality that turns a blind eye to the psychological and emotional sources that can both generate, and fuel the capital vices in a personality already wounded by original sin, and weakened by concupiscence.

4. Five Challenges Point to the Examen's Future

[1] The Church continues to call on the Society to evangelize dynamically and faithfully. "All the same, while you try to recognize the signs of the presence and work of God in every part of the world, even beyond the confines of the visible Church, while you endeavour to build bridges of understanding and dialogue with those who do not belong to the Church or who have difficulty accepting its position and message, you must at the same time loyally fulfill the fundamental duty of the Church, of fully adhering to the word of God, and of the authority of the Magisterium to preserve the truth and the unity of the Catholic doctrine in its totality...As you well know because you have so often made the meditation "of the Two Standards" in the *Spiritual Exercises* under the guidance of St. Ignatius, our world is the stage of a battle between good and evil, with powerful negative forces at work...This is why I have asked you to renew your interest in the promotion and defense of the Catholic doctrine 'particularly in the neuralgic points strongly attacked today by secular culture,'...The issues, constantly discussed and questioned today, of the salvation of Christ of all human beings, of sexual morality, the marriage and the family, must be deepened and illumined in the context of contemporary reality, but keeping the harmony with the Magisterium, which avoids creating confusion and bewilderment among the People of God." Jesuit Life and Mission Today: The Decrees & Accompanying Documents of the 31st—35th General Congregations of the Society of Jesus (St. Louis: Institute of Jesuit Sources, 2008), 823-4. Cited hereafter as, "Decrees." The General Congregation responded positively to this invitation: "The 35th General Congregation expresses its full adherence to the faith and the teaching of the Church, as they are presented to us in the intimate relationship that unites Scripture, Tradition, and the Magisterium. The 35th General Congregation calls all Jesuits to live with the great spirit of generosity that is at the center of our vocation: "to serve as a soldier of God beneath the banner of the Cross...and to serve the Lord alone and the Church his spouse under the Roman Pontiff, the Vicar of Christ on earth." Ibid., 729-30.

[2] An analysis of the eight commentators and their writings can be found at <http:// sacredstory.net/resources/Examining The Examen/. The eight commentators and their writings are listed below:

George Aschenbrenner, SJ "Consciousness Examen," *Review for Religious*, no. 31 (January 1972). "Consciousness Examen: Becoming God's Heart for the World," *Review for Religious* 47, no. 6 (Nov/Dec 1988). Cited hereafter as *Aschenbrenner Heart*. "A Check on Our Availability: The Examen," *Review For Religious* 39, no. 3 (May 1980).

David Townsend, SJ, "The Examen and the Exercises: A Re-Appraisal," *The Way Supplement* 52 (Spring 1985): 54. "Finding God in a Busy Day," *Review for Religious* 50, no. 1 (January-February 1991). Cited hereafter as *Finding*.

Joseph Tetlow, SJ "The Examen of Particulars," *Review for Religious* 56, no. 3 (May-June 1997). Cited hereafter as *Particulars*. "Examen: Persons in Relationship," *Review for Religious* (March-April 2002). Cited hereafter as *Persons*. "The Most Postmodern Prayer: American Jesuit Identity and the Examen of Conscience, 1920-1990," *Studies in the Spirituality of Jesuits* 26, no. 1 (January 1994): 49-50.

John English, SJ, *Discernment and the Examen* (Guelph, Ontario: by Ignatius Jesuit Centre of Guelph, 1979). Cited hereafter as English. *Spiritual Freedom* (Chicago, Loyola University Press, 1995). Cited hereafter as *Spiritual Freedom*.

Joan L. Roccasalvo, CSJ, "The Daily Examen," *Review for Religious* (March-April 1986): 281. *Prayer for Finding God in All Things* (St. Louis: Institute of Jesuit Sources, 2005),

Peter G. van Breemen, SJ, "The Examination of Conscience," *Review for Religious* (July-August 1990): 601.

Sister Mary Hugh Campbell, "The Particular Examen—Touchstone of a Genuinely Apostolic Spirituality," *Review for Religious* (September 1971). Cited hereafter as Hugh Campbell.

Brendan Kneale, FSC, "Examining My Conscience: Do I Have an Attitude," *Review for Religious* (September-October 2001).

[3] Research for this project uncovered dozens of articles on the *Examen*. Not all could be classified as authentic to Ignatius and the *Ignatian Paradigm* I detailed in the first chapter. All components of this *Ignatian Paradigm* should be present for any *Examen* that wants to be identified as Ignatian. Other *Examen* modalities have inspirations that emanate from Ignatius' vision but are not necessarily consistent with a practice of the *Examen* and its formulation in the *Exercises*.

[4] Mary Hugh Campbell captures this full movement succinctly: "[T]he first point is a prayer of gratitude for the goodness and forgiveness which are man's twofold debt. Louis du Pont has probed the familiar method in order to discover its marrow: the optimism which prescribed gratitude first, thus guarding against sadness; the realism of seeing that the memory is so unfaithful, the mind so darkened, and the will so loveless that there is deep need of prayer for light. The examination itself, the third point, is a sincere acknowledgment of good, where this is recognized; and in the admission of sin or failure there is counsel to do this in a spirit of the untranslatable *douceur*—that that gentleness which refrains from turning bitter reproaches against itself, but rather grieves over the injury to One who has poured himself out, as fountain and light, in such generous giving. After the expression of perfect sorrow, one is urged in a fifth point to efficacious resolution—so practical as to foresee and so circumvent future failure." Hugh Campbell, 779-780.

[5] *Ibid.*, 780.

[6] "But. O Lord, you who alone rule without pride since you are the only true Lord and no other lord rules over you, there is a third kind of temptation which, I fear, has not passed from me. Can it ever pass from me in all this life? It is the desire to be feared or loved by other men, simply for the pleasure that it gives me, though in such pleasure there is no true joy. It means only a life of misery and despicable vainglory." As cited in: *Confessions*, 244.

[7] "No one who is in love with himself is capable of loving God. The man who loves God is the one who mortifies his self-love for the sake of the immeasurable blessings of divine love. If a person loves himself, he seeks his own glory...Once the love of God has released him from self-love, the flame of divine love never ceases to burn in his heart and he remains united to God by an irresistible longing. *The Liturgy of the Hours*, Divine Office Ordinary Time: Weeks 1-17, vol. 3 (New York: Catholic Book Publishing Co., 1975), 101-102.

[8] "But if a man goes on making his examen out of routine and for form's sake, without any true sorrow for his faults and any firm purposes of amendment, that is no examen, but a vain ceremony and a Christmas game. Hence it is the same evil propensities and the same bad habits and inclinations that a man brought from the world, he keeps after many years of religion. If he was proud, proud he is today...as self-willed, as greedy, as great lover of his own comforts." Rodríguez, 463. (The Jesuit historian, Michael Maher, suggests that a "Christmas game" likely refers to the very popular role-playing games commonplace in the Renaissance but especially during the Baroque period. These games included such parodies as a boy dressed up as a bishop. In this context, Maher suggests, Rodríguez's comment about the routine exercise of the *Examen* would be a game or a parody of the real event).

[9] "The awareness of the world as a dangerous and forbidding place, though it originates in a realistic awareness of the insecurity of contemporary social life, receives reinforcement from the narcissistic projection of aggressive impulses outward. The belief that society has no future, while it rests on a certain realism about the dangers ahead, also incorporates a narcissistic inability to identify with posterity or feel oneself part of a historical stream." As cited in: Christopher Lasch, *The Culture of Narcissism: American Life in an Age of Diminishing Expectations* (New York-London: W. W. Norton & Company, 1991), 51.

[10] "Diagnostic criteria for 301.81 Narcissistic Personality Disorder: A pervasive pattern of grandiosity (in fantasy or behavior), need for admiration, and lack of empathy, beginning by early adulthood and present in a variety of contexts, as indicated by five (or more) of the following: (1) has a grandiose sense of self-importance (e.g., exaggerates achievements and talents, expects to be recognized as superior without commensurate achievements); (2) is preoccupied with fantasies of unlimited success, power, brilliance, beauty, or ideal love; (3) believes that he or she is "special" and unique and can only be understood by, or should associate with, other special or high-status people (or institutions); (4) requires excessive admiration; (5) has a sense of entitlement, i.e., unreasonable expectations of especially favorable treatment or automatic compliance with his or her expectations; (6) is interpersonally exploitative, i.e., takes advantage of others to achieve his or her own ends; (7) lacks empathy: is unwilling to recognize or identify with the feelings and needs of others; (8) is often envious of others or believes that others are envious of him or her; (9) shows arrogant, haughty behaviors or attitudes." As cited in: The American Psychiatric Association, *Diagnostic and Statistical Manual of Mental Disorders: DSM-IV-RT* (Arlington, VA: American Psychiatric Association, 2007), 717.

[11] Those who work with high school or college students are aware of the discussions about the problem of entitlement and individualism. For some excellent research on the issues

see the books by Jean Twenge, PhD., Christian Smith, PhD., and David Kinnaman listed in the *Bibliography*.

[12] The Church's position on the sinfulness of these actions can be tempered by the degree to which any objectively sinful actions were committed with "full consent of the will." The APA is only concerned with narcissism in its most extreme manifestation where it becomes a debilitating psychological "pathology." The Church is concerned with narcissism in all its forms. As a spiritual disorder it is sinful for it blocks a person's openness to grace and conversion.

[13] Sin in English's paradigm is both Original and personal and both forms of sin have to be acknowledged and resisted by the examinee. Original sin for English has an evolutionary dimension, accruing power since the first sin of Adam. It is also traceable in the very structure of one's family. English affirms with theorists that the first five years of existence fix much of a person's responses to life. Each individual has the responsibility to sort through the *movements across one's being* and determine what is biological, psychological, and spiritual. Thus, English urges each individual to seek knowledge of her history, for in the spiritual realm of this history, she can discover where sin and love have made their home. In this regard, each individual is accountable for the presence of both sin and love as driving forces of the personality. John English, *Discernment and the Examen* (Guelph, Ontario: by Ignatius Jesuit Centre of Guelph, 1979), 48. Cited hereafter as, "English."

[14] The list of commandments in the *GE* encompasses all traditional moral categories. Also, Ignatius was direct in his denunciations of the kinds of immorality that he himself engaged in while a soldier (Loyola, 28, 31). He also publically challenged gambling, one of his former addictions, and lax sexuality like the practice of clergy taking concubines, of which his priest-brother in Azpeitia was guilty (Loyola 62).

[15] One assumes that Ignatius must have had a more integrated holistic focus to achieve such balanced and continuous spiritual growth. "Laynez said in 1547 that Ignatius had 'so much care of his conscience that each day he compared week with week, month with month, day with day, seeking daily to advance.' In the case of a person as faithful and fervent as he was, it is difficult to think that continuous increase in merit was the only development which took place in his interior life." de Guibert, 39-40.

[16] Charles Taylor's work, *A Secular Age*, will be referenced frequently in this section. It is a landmark study on the history and topic of secularization and helps in analyzing the religious fault-lines and the massive paradigm shifts affecting the contemporary world.

[17] "As we move from the Cambridge Platonists through Tillotson to Locke and the eighteenth century, apologetics, and indeed, much preaching, is less and less concerned with sin as a condition we need to be rescued from through some transformation of our being, and more and more with sin as wrong behavior which we can be persuaded, trained, or disciplined to turn our backs on. This concern with a morality of correct conduct has been observed by many historians of the period. Religion is narrowed to moralism." As cited in: Charles Taylor, *a Secular Age* (Cambridge, MA: The Bellknap Press of Harvard University Press, 2007), 225. Cited hereafter as "Taylor."

[18] "The disengaged, disciplined agent, capable of remaking the self, who has discovered and thus released in himself the awesome power of control, is obviously one of the crucial supports of modern exclusive humanism." *Ibid.*, 257.

[19] *Ibid.*, 264. Ignatius' correspondence typically closed with the phrase, "poor in goodness." Surely Ignatius did not see himself capable of benevolence unaided by God's saving love. One might see in his iconic expression an experience to both desire and emulate, i.e., the experience of a sinner rescued and humbled by God's mercy.

[20] "Hume distinguishes the genuine virtues (which are qualities useful to others and to oneself) from the 'monkish virtues' ('celibacy, fasting, penance, mortification, self-denial, humility, silence, solitude') which contribute nothing to, even detract from human welfare. These are rejected by 'men of sense', because they serve no purpose; neither advancing one's fortune, nor render one more valuable to society, neither entertain others nor bring self-enjoyment. 'The gloomy, hare-brained enthusiast, after his death, may have a place on the calendar; but will scarcely ever be admitted, when alive, into intimacy and society, except by those who are as delirious and dismal as himself." Taylor, 263.

[21] Friedrich Schleiermacher enshrined this class of detached intellectuals as religion's "cultured despisers."

[22] Taylor, 262.

[23] The *Examen* must not be a discipline that lacks mercy, nor can it be simply an exercise in mercy without discipline. The *Examen* needs both *discipline* and *mercy* to be effective.

[24] Taylor, 485.

[25] "Indeed, precisely the soft relativism that seems to accompany the ethic of authenticity: let each person do their own thing, and we shouldn't criticise each other's "values"; this is predicated on a firm ethical base, indeed, demanded by it. One shouldn't criticise others' values, because they have a right to live their own life as you do. The sin which is not tolerated is intolerance." *Ibid.*, 484.

[26] Hugh Campbell, 777.

[27] Aschenbrenner, 14; 19-20.

[28] "The fateful feature of roman-clericalism, which erects such a barrier between the Church and contemporary society, is not its animating spirituality; our world is if anything drowned in exalted images of sexual fulfillment and needs to hear about paths of renunciation. The deviation was to make this take on sexuality mandatory for everyone, through a moralistic code which made a certain kind of purity a base condition for relating to God through the sacraments. What Vatican rule-makers and secular ideologies unite in not being able to see, is that there are more ways of being a Catholic Christian than either have yet imagined...But as long as this monolithic image dominates the scene, the Christian message as vehicled by the Catholic Church will not be easy to hear in wide zones of the Age of Authenticity." Taylor 504.

[29] See, *The Boundaries of Ignatian Discernment,* page 78.

[30] Loyola, 17-18.

[31] "Consequently, when one who has received the sacrament turns to prayer and embarks on the way of purification, the person does not do so in order that sins may be forgiven (for they are already forgiven) but in order that he or she may be liberated from the shackles of concupiscence–that is to say, from the inclination towards evil, the inordinate affections, the uncontrollable appetites, the craving, the clinging, the attachments and all those debilitating tendencies that we

moderns call compulsive addictions, infantile fixations and ungovernable drives. In short, the path of purification is a path of liberation." William Johnston, *Mystical Theology: The Science of Love* (London: Harper Collins *Religious*, 1995), 194.

[32] The early history of the *Exercises* indicates that they were especially successful with those who were in some way dissatisfied with their lives. Ignatius himself indirectly, but successfully, healed certain types of affective instability, neuroses and psychological disturbances through the Exercises. We have already mentioned commentators who emphasize the psychotherapeutic usefulness of the *Exercises*." Egan, 159.

[33] For a discussion of childhood stresses that can damage the personality, leading to habitual sinful and psychological complexes, see: Allers PPCD, 4-101.

[34] English gives a strong nod to evolutionary, psychological stresses in shaping habits, but appears to define "sinful" behaviors requiring "examination and resisting" as those defined by the Commandments and Church tradition. Thus, he is using psychological and emotional history as a way to *explain* sinful habits, not explain them away. "Praying with graced history relies heavily on our faith memory (*anamnesis*)-a mystery in itself. Our memory retains all the events and responses to our life. These include those events that are immediately present to us and those that were unconscious or forgotten. Events are relegated to the unconscious for a number of reasons. Some are repressed. Releasing the secrets of repressed events usually requires psychological counseling. Often it is helpful for health reasons if as many life experiences as possible are externally expressed. '[E]verything exposed by the light becomes visible' (Eph. 5:13)." *Spiritual Freedom*, 263.

[35] *Particulars*, 241.

[36] "An honest repentant acknowledgment of sinfulness in the face of such love is neither obvious nor easy, because it cuts our consciousness in humiliation. The guilt and shame and embarrassment that come in the wake of such an acknowledgment sting and singe our consciousness. In the presence of such love, they make our spirits blush. The pain and hurt will, most often, and quite spontaneously, make us wary and seek to activate defense mechanisms such as the rationalizations of denial and the distractions, not of joy, but of pleasure. These are moments for careful discernment in the life of any believer. For the humiliating pain of acknowledging sin, as intended here, is not the result of some overly scrupulous conscience. Nor is it the unhealthy guilt of self-hatred. Rather it is the purifying consolation—not desolation, but consolation, however scouring—the consoling experience of God calling us to that greater love and life and faith. Despite the pain, therefore, this repentant blush of heart is a grace not to be rejected. It is essential to any mature faith, to any measured zeal for God's world, to any discipleship that hopes to brave the road's full distance." George Aschenbrenner, SJ, "Consciousness Examen: Becoming God's Heart for the World," *Review for Religious* 47, no. 6 (Nov/Dec 1988): 804-805.

[37] Brendan Kneale, FSC, "Examining My Conscience: Do I Have an Attitude," *Review for Religious* (September-October 2001): 475.

[38] George A. Maloney, SJ, *Alone with the Alone* (Notre Dame, ID: Ave Maria Press, 1982), 46.

[39] *SpEx* [345-351]. Read also how Ignatius dealt with Favre's scruples and sexual temptations: Idigoras, 310-11. There are many other accounts that reveal Ignatius' keen understanding of the complexities of the human personality. He was able to bring a person to integrated, spiritual

growth. Unaided by modern psychological disciplines, he was cognizant of the psychological dimension of human nature and the emotional stresses of the spiritual journey.

[40] All our commentators call for this integrated approach. They are aware that Ignatius' spirituality compels such integrated "sourcing" but none offer specific plans to achieve it.

[41] "It is important to remember that some people are deeply wounded because they have been sinned against. Ignatius does not consider this aspect of sin in the *Exercises*. Rather, he sets up exercises to help those who have truly sinned." *Spiritual Freedom*, 55.

[42] "Our memory retains all the events and responses to our life. These include those events that are immediately present to us and those that were unconscious or forgotten. Events are relegated to the unconscious for a number of reasons. Some are repressed....Other events, both positive and negative, are not repressed, but only forgotten. These events are significant for our life with God and other human beings. There are simple ways of remembering these experiences. For example, we can begin with our earliest recollection and move forward to the significant events in each year of our lives, or we can begin with the present and move back to our early years. Once we have done this we can reflect on these events and appreciate them. We are in a position to grasp their meaning in our lives, and then go forward with new energy and determination." *Ibid.*, 263.

[43] Ignatius grew up in a family culture immersed in "all other vices." Surely, then, he would not have second-guessed the *riches, honors and pride* that sourced them. Ignatius had to backtrack from those manifest sins to their roots before he could gain a complete picture of how the "enemy of human nature" helped him evolve, from infancy, to become the dissolute and vainglorious soldier of Pamplona. Thus, Ignatius' growth and illumination was progressive, from identifying and "controlling" his most manifest sins, to his graced discovery of the root pride underlying his disordered history.

[44] "The example which Christ our Lord gave of the first state of life, which is that of observing the Commandments, has already been considered in meditating on His obedience to His parents. The example of the second state, which is that of evangelical perfection, has also been considered, when He remained in the temple and left His foster father and His Mother to devote himself exclusively to the service of His eternal Father. While continuing to contemplate His life, let us begin to investigate and ask in what kind of life or what state His Divine Majesty wishes to make use of us. Therefore, as some introduction to this, in the next exercise, let us consider the intention of Christ, our Lord, and on the other hand that of the enemy of our human nature. Let us also see how we ought to prepare ourselves to arrive at perfection in whatever state or way of life God our Lord may grant us to choose." *SpEx* [135]; Puhl, 59.

[45] Tylenda, 37.

[46] Catholic doctrine declares: "the whole of human history is marked by the original fault freely committed by our first parents" (CCC 390). It is natural to view the transmission of sin, as a general evolutionary force, coming through those first parents. But we need to expand this view, and attune to the evolution of spiritual corruption, as a general force throughout time, but also *mutating* in specific ways because of the unique choices, personalities and histories of individual, cultures, nationalities, clans and families. Clearly Ignatius' *family* sins and traumas cast long shadows over his life.

[47] The beginning of this process should begin like Ignatius', i.e., a clear-eyed examination of those habits and vices—thoughts, words and deeds—contravening the Commandments and The Standard of Christ.

[48] Augustine speaks of sin as a wounding of the heart: "For in my wounded heart I saw your splendor and it dazzled me." *Confessions*, 249.

[49] Aschenbrenner had this insight. It is why he wrote his further reflection on the Examen as a verification of our availability. It is also the basis of Hugh Campbell's reflections on the PE as the touchstone of a genuine apostolic spirituality.

[50] *Particulars*, 238.

[51] "Do I have a God-centered, sacramental reverence for the earth? Do I see the cosmos as 'a body of God'? As a steward and co-creator of the planet, do I express gratitude for the beauty of God's creation and work responsibly with others to preserve it?" Joan L. Roccasalvo, CSJ, *Prayer for Finding God in All Things* (St. Louis: Institute of Jesuit Sources, 2005), 21.

[52] Teilhard de Chardin, *The Future of Man* (Glasgow: William Collins & Son Co. Ltd, 1959), 132-33.

[53] Joseph Ratzinger, *Introduction to Christianity* (New York: The Seabury Press, 1968), 178-179. Cited hereafter as: "Ratzinger."

[54] As an "I," man is indeed an end but the whole tendency of his being and of his own existence shows him also to be a creation belonging to a "super-I" that does not blot him out but encompasses him; only such an association can bring out the form of the future of man, in which humanity will achieve complete fulfillment of itself…From here onwards faith in Christ will see the beginning of a movement in which dismembered humanity is gathered together more and more into the being of one single Adam, one single body – the man to come. It will see in him the movement to that future of man in which he is completely "socialized," incorporated in one single being, but in such a way that the separate individual is not extinguished but brought completely to himself. *Ibid.*, 178-9.

[55] Paul's hymn forms the second Christmas preface pointing to this universal reconciliation of man and creation. *Today you fill our hearts with joy as we recognize in Christ the revelation of your love. No eye can see his glory as our God, yet now he is seen as one like us. Christ your son before all ages, yet now he is born in time. He has come to lift up all things to himself, to restore unity to creation, and to lead mankind from exile into your heavenly kingdom.* Rev. James Socias, ed., "Daily Roman Missal" (Chicago: Midwest Theological Forum Inc., 1998), 589. Cited hereafter as: *DRM*.

[56] For a comprehensive portrait of the exploitation of natural environments as a threat to humankind's survival see Jared Diamond, *Collapse: How Societies Choose to Fail or Succeed.* (New York, Viking-Penguin Group, 2005). For an overview of the Vatican's writings on environmental issues see *From Stockholm to Johannesburg: An Historical Overview of the Concern of the Holy See for the Environment.* Sister Marjorie Keenan RSHM, ed. (Vatican City: Vatican Press, 2002).

[57] "Destruction of the environment harms the good of creation given to man by God the Creator as something indispensable for his life and his development…We need to realize therefore

that there can be grave sin against the natural environment, one which weighs heavily on our consciences and which calls for grave responsibility toward God the Creator." Pope John Paul II, "Zamosc Homily," speech delivered to Polish Congregation, June 12, 1999, Zamosc, Poland.

[58] "In this global world marked by such profound changes, we now want to deepen our understanding of the call to serve faith and promote justice, and dialogue with culture and other religions in the light of the apostolic mandate to establish right relationships with God, with one another, and with creation...We are sent on mission by the Father, as were Ignatius and the first companions at La Storta, together with Christ, risen and glorified but still carrying the cross, as he labors in a world yet to experience the fullness of his reconciliation. In a world torn by violence, strife and division, we then are called with others to become instruments of God, who "in Christ reconciled the world to himself, not counting their trespasses." Decrees, 27.

[59] "Only the light of divine Revelation clarifies the reality of sin and particularly of sin committed at mankind's origin. Without the knowledge Revelation gives of God we cannot recognize sin clearly and are tempted to explain it as merely a developmental flaw, a psychological weakness, a mistake, or the necessary consequence of an inadequate social structure, etc." CCC, 87.

[60] *Finding*, 48-50.

[61] English, 13.

[62] *Persons*, 119.

[63] "We must never lose sight of the fact that we are pilgrims until we reach it (our heavenly country), and we must not let our affections tarry in the hostelries and the lands through which we pass, lest we forget our destination and lose our love of our last end. And the better to attain it, our eternal Father has given us the use and service of creatures....One can thus spend an entire lifetime seeking to pass these few days of our pilgrimage in the midst of honors, wealth, and self-satisfactions, without a thought of that which must be the cause of inestimable and unending riches, honor, prosperity, and satisfaction in our heavenly fatherland. Truly, that saying of the prophet applies to such men: "And they set at nought the desirable land." Or if they did have regard for it, they would do as much to live happily in it as they do to live contentedly in the pilgrimage in which God has placed us all on the way to that land. Letter to Anthony Enriquez: Rome; March 26, 1554 in: Young, 332-333. "I have a very great desire indeed, if I may say so, to see a true and intense love of God grow in you, my relatives and friends, so that you will bend all your efforts to the praise and service of God...It is none of my business to condemn a man who in this life lies awake with plans for adding to his buildings, his income, his estate in the hope of leaving behind him a great name and reputation. But neither can I praise him, for, according to St. Paul, we ought to use the things of this world as though we used them not, and own them as though we owned them not, because the fashion of this world passes and in a moment is gone (1 Cor. 7:29-31). God grant that it may be so." Letter of Ignatius to his brother, Martin Garcia De Onaz: Paris June 1532 in Young, 7-8. "For our profession requires that we be prepared and very much ready for whatever is enjoined upon us in our Lord and at whatsoever time, without asking for or expecting any reward in this present and transitory life, but hoping always for that life which lasts for eternity, through God's supreme mercy." *Constitutions*, 41.

[64] "Now the move to what I am calling "secularity" is obviously related to this radically purged time-consciousness. It comes when associations are placed firmly and wholly in homogeneous, profane time, whether or not the higher time is negated altogether, or other associations are

still admitted to exist in it. Such I want to argue is the case with the public sphere, and therein lies its new and (close to) unprecedented nature." Taylor, 196.

[65] "What is clear, however, is the present condition of belief and unbelief can't be described purely in terms of élite culture. One of the important events of the twentieth century is that the nova (of unbelief) has come to involve whole societies. It has become the "super-nova." Taylor, 412.

[66] An example of this is the prevalence in the Evangelical Christian world of preachers focusing on the Gospel of wealth and success. In my own work with Catholic executives, I have often been asked what *take home value* a particular retreat experience would give them. In both instances, the Christian message is understood in material and quantifiable categories. This sort of materialism (distinguished from "consumerist" and "materialistic") can also manifest in many Christian justice movements. The concept of *faith* is framed more or less exclusively as *action* for justice. Here, the challenge is an exclusive focus on the second of the two great Commandments. See Edward Vacek, SJ, "Religious Life and the Eclipse of Love for God" Review for Religious, 57 #2 (March-April 1998), 118-37.

[67] "Body, heart, emotion, history; all these make sense only in the context of (6) the belief that the highest being is a personal being, not just in the sense of possessing agency, but also in that of being capable of communion." Taylor, 278. And in relation to the "anthropomorphic shift": "Alongside this, I spoke of the lesser importance of grace in this scheme, the eclipse of mystery, and the foreshortening of the earlier views of the eventual human transformation at the hands of God, evoked by the patristic notion of 'theiosis.'" Taylor, 290.

[68] Jean-Pierre De Caussade, SJ, *The Sacrament of the Present Moment*, trans. Kitty Muggeridge (San Francisco: HarperCollins, 1982). See also De Caussade's: *A Treatise on Prayer from the Heart*, trans. Robert M. McKeon (St. Louis: Institute of Jesuit Sources, 1998), 103-124.

[69] Eckhart Tolle, *The Power of Now* (Vancouver: Namaste Publishing, 2004). See also: Andrew Ryder, "The Sacrament of Now," *The Way* 2 (April 2007); and Tolle's, *A New Earth*, (New York: Dutton, 2005).

[70] Brown's method accomplishes this much more systematically and effectively than Tolle, and does so in ways quite synchronous with Ignatius' *Examen*. Michael Brown, *The Presence Process: A Healing Journey into Present Moment Awareness* (Vancouver: Namaste Publishing, 2005). Cited hereafter as "Brown."

[71] Meditations, 615.

[72] *Ibid.*, 616.

[73] Joseph F. Conwell, SJ, *Contemplation in Action* (Spokane: Gonzaga University Press, 1957).

[74] Ignatius' spirituality embodies an "impressive prefiguring" of the characteristics the future Buddha-Avatar will possess: "He will bring human beings themselves to attain to the illuminating experience of revelation, of a kind that it will not be he who will win authority, but rather He who is "the true light that enlightens every man coming into the world" (John 1:9) – Jesus Christ, the Word made flesh, who is the way, the truth and the life. The mission of the Buddha-Avatar to come will therefore not be the foundation of a new religion, but rather that of bringing human beings to the first-hand experience of the source of all revelation ever received

from above by mankind, as also of all essential truth ever conceived of by mankind. It will not be novelty to which he will aspire, but rather the conscious certainty of eternal truth." Meditations, 614-15.

[75] *Ibid.*, 616.

[76] Chardin, too, recognized the malaise of modernity as an enervating boredom. Thomas King's reference to Teilhard de Chardin's last years is instructive: "Among the people whom Teilhard knew, there were many weary of life with little motive for living. He believed this number would increase as humanity became more reflective; people were losing the will to live." Thomas

M. King, S.J. "Teilhard de Chardin's Devotion to the Sacred Heart," *National Jesuit News*, May-June 2005, p. 8.

[77] Taylor, 308-10.

5. Contemporizing Ignatius' Discernment Principles

[1] "…an act and art of choosing which, the more profoundly they are exercised, the more they become in reality the act and art of 'allowing' oneself to be chosen. This ultimately is what discernment is all about; allowing oneself to be taken by God, allowing Him to act through oneself in every event of history. Thus for Ignatius union is always a quest and a tendency, never a definitive state." Melloni, 50.

[2] Michael Buckley's seminal essay on Ignatius' discernment *Rules* analyzes their origins can be sought in "his unfolding *Autobiography*" more than any place else. *Rules*, 26

[3] Egan, 21. Ignatius supports when he states in the Introductory Observations that Weeks One and Two of the *Rules* align with the purgative and illuminative stages of spiritual growth. *SpEx* [10]. Puhl, 4.

[4] Different commentators use the longer or shorter Latin abbreviation for "consolation without previous cause." Thus, CSC and CSCP are both accepted as an abbreviation for "consolation without previous cause." Likewise, "sin causa" and "sine cause" are Spanish and Latin forms of the same phrase.

[5] Toner, 291-313. It is valuable to identify aspects of CSC that are generally accepted and juxtapose them with Ignatius' progressive conversion detailed in the *Autobiography.*

[6] *Ibid.*, 99.

[7] Egan, 36-37.

[8] "One cannot find any adequate cause for it in sensible experience. Rather, it is an experience of being grasped or elevated by the love of the Trinity. The truth is in the experience. Simply, I know I am taken over by the Trinity's love when this happens. Paul speaks about this in Romans when he says: 'This hope is not deceptive for the love of God has been poured into our hearts by the Holy Spirit himself and our spirits bear witness that we are children of God' (Rom.

[8] 14-16). Such self-authenticated experiences of the unconditional love of God St. Ignatius calls "consolation without previous cause." John J. English, SJ, "The Mind and the Heart of Christ," *The Way* 23 (October 1983): 296.

[9] "Ignatius' transcendence is not without dogma, because the same Spirit who guides the exercitant's transcendence to Election also 'guides and governs our Holy Mother Church' (*Ex* 365). The CSCP, therefore, is intrinsically linked to established, historical, ecclesial norms which may be used to measure the CSCP's authenticity (*Ex* 170). For Ignatius, even a vocation discovered not to be from God cannot be changed, if that choice is deemed immutable by the hierarchical Church (*Ex.* 172)." Egan, 64.

[10] "It remains for me to speak of how we ought to understand what we think is from our Lord and, understanding it, how we ought to use it for our advantage. For it frequently happens that our Lord moves and urges the soul to this or that activity. He begins by enlightening the soul; that is to say, by speaking interiorly to it without the din of words, lifting it up wholly to His divine love and ourselves to His meaning without any possibility of resistance on our part, even should he wish to resist. This thought of His which we take is *of necessity* (italics supplied) in conformity with the commandments, the precepts of the Church, and obedience to our superiors." Padberg et al., 22. See also Toner, 217.

[11] Ignatius affirms that shedding tears for one's sins, in light of God's love and mercy, is spiritual consolation, *SpEx* [316.3].

[12] It has been disputed that CSC is a frequent and fundamental form of graced consolation that anchors all Ignatian discernment. The weight of evidence aligns with the argument toward the greater "frequency." Toner, 313. Rahner and Egan argue for the theory of greater frequency. See also: Lawrence Murphy, "Consolation," *The Way* 27 (Spring 1976) 38.

[13] Rahner states that Ignatius did not expect life in the Church to "be without pain or conflict." Nor can one simply "deduce" from doctrines how one is to make decisions. Otherwise he says: "Ignatius' Rules for an Election, which put the individual on his own before God, would make no sense and have no area where they could be applied." Neither is an election "anti-ecclesial for the "charismatic element" that informs election and conversion "belongs to the nature of the Church." Ibid., 293.

[14] Yet, it is possible to infer that Ignatius' explication of CSC in the Second Week Rules has less to do with the rarity of CSC as argued by Toner, than the *type* of temptation that is particularly destructive and deformative of its graces at this deeper and more integrated level of conversion; that conversion typified more by the purgation of the "spirit" than of the "senses." It is at this more critical stage of conversion and purgation that the enemy of human nature insinuates itself and "hides" behind the deeply entrenched vices of the intellect and spirit, like Ignatius' narcissism masked by his scruples. Here the "enemy" can mimic "an angel of light" and subtly lead one astray through "seemingly good" and even holy thoughts, just when one is on the cusp of a "fundamental" surrender of control of one's life to God in the purgative process, or during a vital "election" of a way of life. Hence, we have Ignatius' warning to be particularly wary during certain critical stages of spiritual development and election. See: Hugo Rahner, Hubert Becher, Hans Wolter, Josef Stierli, Adolf Haas, Heinrich Bacht, Lambert Classen and Karl Rahner, *Ignatius of Loyola: His Personality and Spiritual Heritage 116-1956*, ed. Friedrich Wulf (St. Louis: Institute of Jesuit Sources, 1977), 291.

[15] *Put to death, then, the parts of you that are earthly: immorality, impurity, passion, evil desire, and the greed that is idolatry. Because of these the wrath of God is coming (upon the disobedient). By these you too once conducted yourselves, when you lived in that way. But now you must put them all away: anger, fury, malice, slander, and obscene language out of your mouths. Stop lying to one another, since you have taken off the old self with its practices and have put on the new self, which is being renewed, for knowledge, in the image of its creator.* Col. 3: 5-10.

[16] *SpEx* [317.4]

[17] Catholic moralists can support culture's drift in this direction. They do this by positing an evolving view of human nature, the malleability of which is especially evident in the area of human self-experience and self-identity. Richard Gula is a good representative of this school of thought. See: Richard M. Gula, SS, *Reason Informed by Faith* (New York: Paulist Press, 1989), 228.

[18] *SpEx* [42]. As such, both St. Paul and Ignatius' benchmark of human nature appears to conform less with those who propose an evolving ethic of human nature and align instead with formulations of human nature and natural law like those put forth in more recent Church encyclicals. See: *Veritatis Splendor*, (Boston: Pauline Books and Media, 1993). [Especially: *VS*: §32, 34, 38, 42, 46, 48, 50, 53, 55, 64, and §84-94 on the role of faith in Christ in relation to freedom, truth, and the good].

[19] Ignatius is a strategist. He made his mark on Christian spirituality, and spiritual discernment, because of his attention to the *particular* details of his pre and post-conversion life. His introduction to the nuance of sin in its various guises came at Montserrat from the guides compiled by Abbot Garcia Cisneros. The *particular* details of sin and conversion are so critical to Ignatius that he walks away from his early ministry in Salamanca when the Inquisition forbids him from making distinctions between mortal and venial sin. *Obras,* 76.

[20] Blending spiritual and psychological insights into Ignatius' spiritual system is not new. Over a half century ago, Hugo Rahner identified aspects of Ignatius' prayer methods that are useful for their therapeutic benefits. Hugo Rahner, *Ignatius the Theologian*, trans. Michael Barry (New York: Herder and Herder, 1968), 181-213.

[21] "Men with their arms locked, singing bawdy songs on their way to the local whorehouse, are in desolation for Ignatius." Rules, 29.

[22] English, 13.

[23] "Decline has a still deeper level. Not only does it compromise and distort progress... But compromise and distortion discredit progress. Objectively absurd situations do not yield to treatment. Corrupt minds have a flair for picking the mistaken solution and insisting that it alone is intelligent, reasonable, good. Imperceptibly the corruption spreads from the harsh sphere of material advantage and power to the mass media, the stylish journals, the literary movements, the educational process, the reigning philosophies. A civilization in decline digs its own grave with a relentless consistency. It cannot be argued out of its self-destructive ways, for argument has a theoretical premise, theoretical premises are asked to conform to matters of fact and the facts in the situation produced by decline more and more are the absurdities that proceed from inattention, oversight, unreasonableness, and irresponsibility." Bernard Lonergan, *Method in Theology* (New York: The Seabury Press, 1971), 54-55.

[24] This is to deify what Rahner describes: "a finite reality, through the identification of my absolute worth that can only be related absolutely to God, with things that cannot be posited

absolutely." Karl Rahner, *Spiritual Exercises: Prayer and Practice* (London: Sheed and Ward, 1966), 40.

[25] John Horn's work on the Ignatian *Exercises* and the *Examen* as a source of mystical healing is based on the mending of broken hearts by the power of God's love and mercy. In particular, see the section on discernment and the *Examen*, (117-126) in: John Horn, *Mystical Healing: The psychological and Spiritual Power of the Ignatian Spiritual Exercises* (New York: Crossroads, 1996).

6. Discovering the Examen's Supernatural Powers

[1] "Both the reality and the mystery of sin seem to have become inaccessible to humanity, which now seems to be steeped in it. The hopeless "innocence" of modern man, who is so full of sin that he no longer experiences contrition and is consumed with guilt only for what is relatively inoffensive, is one of the most heartrending mysteries of our time. The very fact that even religious people have utterly confused the concept of sin, and the notion of guilt, goes far to prove that we have lost all sense of the reality of sin. For sin is an interior and spiritual reality: a real evil…the egg from which all other evils are hatched." Thomas Merton, *The Inner Experience: Notes on Contemplation* (New York, NY: Harper San Francisco, 2003). 118. And on the relation of sex to enlightenment: "According to most of the great religious traditions of the world, the restriction of all sex [is] to married life, and, within the married state, to certain ordinate norms. [Sex] is the most difficult of all natural appetites to control and one whose undisciplined gratification completely blinds the human spirit to all interior light." Thomas Merton, *New Seeds of Contemplation*. (Norfolk: New Directions Books. 1961). 87-8.

[2] Johnston and Merton also identify anger and lust respectively as the two capital sins most difficult to purge and control. For they too operate along this pleasure-pain axis that Buckley identifies with "triggers" that are virtually "instinctive" and "automatic."

[3] Maté, 397.

[4] Ibid, 397.

[5] "There are people who are not addicts in the strict sense, but only because their carefully constructed "personality" works well enough to keep them from the painful awareness of their emptiness. In such a case, they'll be addicted "only" to a false or incomplete self-image or to their position in the world or to some role into which they sink their energy or to certain ideas that give them a sense of meaning. The human being with a "personality" that is insufficient to paper over the inner void becomes an undisguised addict, compulsively pursuing behaviors whose negative impact is obvious to him or those around him. The difference is only in the degree of addiction or, perhaps, in the degree of honesty around the deficient self." Maté, 419.

[6] Maté, 374-384. "The Four Steps: Plus One"

[7] Ibid., 414.

[8] For those who need help awakening to their emotions, I recommend Brown's, "Presence Process." For those seeking a more holistic view of sin and addiction, I recommend

Gabor Maté's: "In The Realm of Hungry Ghosts." Two other books that detail the new studies in spirituality and brain science worth mentioning are: Mario Beauregard with Denyse O'Leary, *The Spiritual Brain: A Neuroscientist's Case for the Existence of the Soul.* (New York: HarperOne. 2008), and: Sharon Begley, *Train Your Mind Change Your Brain: How a New Science Reveals Our Extraordinary Potential to Transform Ourselves.* (New York: Ballantine Books. 2007).

[9] Brown, 10.

[10] *Ibid.*, 146.

[11] *Ibid.*, 215-17.

[12] *Ibid.*, 235.

[13] *Ibid.*, 320.

[14] *Ibid.*, 267, 323.

[15] Brown's conviction that anger forms the root of emotionally based blocked memory is harmonious with Johnston's mystical reflections on the soul's journey to holiness through the purification of anger. "At the beginning of the contemplative life the upper levels of the mind are swept clean, as one lets go of attachments, anxieties, reasoning, thinking and clinging of all kinds. When this happens, the unconscious begins to surface. Now the dark side of the personality (the part that has been thrown into the shade) rises up. One is faced with one's anger, just as one is faced with one's covetousness, lust, envy, pride and the rest. Now the good director tells the contemplative: 'Stay with your anger. Do not repress it. Go through it to the liberation.' But why give such advice? The reason is that at an even deeper level God is surfacing in the soul. The divine, uncreated energy is, so to speak, pushing into consciousness all the crud that has collected in the unconscious through the centuries. Needless to say, this causes great suffering. To be faced with one's darkness is painful. To be faced with the darkness of God is even more painful; for the meeting of the limited human with the unlimited divine is necessarily a terrible thing. Yet salvation comes in this way. As the human person is divinized by the inflow of the divine, so the human energies—the anger, the sexuality, the appetites—are divinized. The person whose anger has been transformed can face society with a divine anger that truly shakes heaven and earth." Johnston, 360.

[16] Brown's concept of a messenger triggering angers that can be mined for positive spiritual benefit is not without complement in Christian spirituality of East and West. The abbot St. Dorotheus of Gaza, whom the Church encounters yearly in the Office of the Readings in the ninth week of *Ordinary Time*, speaks of the same phenomenon in the context of false spiritual peace. Dorotheus, who lived between the years 505-565, is recognized as a saint in both the Eastern Orthodox and Catholic Church. "The man who thinks that he is quiet and peaceful has within him a passion that he does not see. A brother comes up, utters some unkind word and immediately all the venom and mire that lie hidden within him are spewed out. If he wishes mercy, he must do penance, purify himself and strive to become perfect. He will see that he should have returned thanks to his brother instead of returning the injury, because his brother has proven to be an occasion of profit to him. It will not be long before he will no longer be bothered by these temptations. The more perfect he grows, the less these temptations will affect him. For the more the soul advances, the stronger and more powerful it becomes in bearing the difficulties that it meets." *The Liturgy of the Hours: Book III* (New York: Catholic Book Publishing Co. 1975.) 299-300. See also, Discourses and Sayings, ed. and trans. Eric Wheeler, Cistercian Studies series 33 (Kalamazoo: Cistercian Publications, 1977).

[17] "A person who is in the grip of neurotic trends—or for that matter almost any person—is quite likely to feel offended or unfairly dealt with by a special individual, or by life in

general, and to take at face value his reaction of hurt or resentment. In such situations it takes a considerable degree of clarity to distinguish between a real and an imagined offense...It is much easier to feel a *right to be angry* (italics supplied) than to examine exactly what vulnerable spot in himself has been hit. But for his own interests this is the way he should proceed, even if there is no doubt that the other has been cruel, unfair, or inconsiderate." Horney, 257.

[18] *Ibid.*, 260-63.

[19] "My anxiety clothes itself in concerns about body image or financial security, doubts regarding lovability or the ability to love, self-disparagement and existential pessimism about life's meaning and purpose—or, on the other hand, it manifests itself as grandiosity, the need to be admired, to be seen as special." Maté, 355.

[20] "In Session Two, we were taught how to see the surfacing of our inner unintegrated memories as outer reflections in the world. This we call identifying 'the messenger.' In Session Three, we were taught how to access information from emotional content of these surfacing memories. This we called 'getting the message.' In Session Four, we were taught how to compassionately feel and thus attend to the pain and discomfort contained within these surfacing memories. We referred to this as 'feeling it to heal it.' In Session Five, we were taught how to re-establish our energetic connection with our child self   the causal point of these surfacing memories. The Emotional Cleansing Process is a procedure that entails combining these four individual steps into one complete perceptual tool." Brown, 196-98.

[21] It is important for two reasons. First, it modifies Brown's concepts of victim and victor in conjunction with the theme of narcissism advanced by Tetlow. It updates the Ignatian paradigm of pride with language easily understood by contemporary audiences. Second, the dual focus on the sins of power *and* powerlessness, (passive narcissists and aggressive narcissists) respond to feminist critiques that self-assertive male egoistic pride, like Ignatius', is uncharacteristic of women's sins. Dyckman, Garvin and Liebert in their feminist reading of the Ignatian Spiritual *Exercises* quote Judith Plaskow: "The 'sin' which the feminine role in modern society creates and encourages in women, is not illegitimate self-centeredness but failure to center the self, the failure to take responsibility for one's own life." The feminist view of victimization, powerlessness and lack of responsibility for self the authors propose as more characteristic of women's sin emerges as pride's passive face. Narcissistic pride—"illegitimate self-centeredness"—due either to gender or life differences, is an equal opportunity employer. See Catherine Dyckman, Mary Garvin, Elizabeth Liebert, *The Spiritual Exercises Reclaimed: Uncovering Liberating Possibilities for Women* (New York: Paulist Press, 2001), 160-166.

[22] Maté's advice is similar for those searching for the roots of addiction. He calls for compassionate curiosity, instead of self-hatred. The sinner open to his sins, and is treated with tender mercy by the Divine Physician (Lk. 18: 13-14).

[23] Brown, 106-114.

7. Ignatius' Life as Sacred Story

[1] "Ignatius' book, *Spiritual Exercises*, providentially absorbed the most important truths in God's plan of creating free human beings for his own glory and their beatitude. Furthermore it presented these truths in a chronological sequence which shows this divine design as evolving by

stages in the history of salvation. It teaches people how to lead their lives cooperatively with this divine plan and motivates them to do it. For them the *Exercises* are a practical application of this saving plan to their everyday living until they reach their rich self-fulfillment in the beatific vision. Life becomes an opportunity to fulfill the role offered by God during one's lifetime as the divine plan is evolving in history." Ganss, 201.

[2] The terms "higher consciousness" and "enlightenment" have been used along with the language of mysticism that forms the nexus of the final paradigmatic sequence of the conversion narrative. The intention is not to change the nature of the graces offered via purgation, but to use terms to describe those graces that have more resonance today.

[3] "All mystics are creative. Not all mystics are active, since some live and die in solitude; but all are creative. They give birth to a child who cooperates with Jesus in the salvation of the world. This child is the kingdom of God, the tiny mustard seed that becomes a great tree, and the beloved bride of Christ." Johnston, 231.

8. Sacred Story Practice and Structure

[1] Hugh Campbell, 776.

[2] "After retiring, just before falling asleep, for the space of a Hail Mary, I will think of the hour when I have to rise, and why I am rising, and briefly sum up the exercise I have to go through." Puhl, 35.

[3] This method was tested with hundreds of individuals and proved to help practitioners in two vital areas: 1) escape the narrow moralism that an exclusive focus on sinful failings can foster and, 2) to "see" their lives integrated by tracking spiritual, psychological and moral growth over days, weeks, and months.

[4] The Second and Third methods of prayer were used to frame *Sacred Story*. Puhl, 110-112.

9. Sacred Story Introduction

[1] Ignatius provides wise counsel for those tempted by evil thoughts and feelings and how to conduct oneself during such times. He writes this advice to Sister Theresa Rejadell: "I insist that you think of God as loving you, as I have no doubt He does, and that you correspond with this love and pay no attention whatever to the evil thoughts, even if they are obscene or sensual (when they are not deliberate), nor of your cowardice or tepidity. For even St. Peter and St. Paul did not succeed in escaping all or some of these thoughts. Even when we do not succeed fully, we gain much by paying no attention to them. I am not going to save myself by the good works of the good angels, and I am not going to be condemned because of the evil thoughts and weaknesses which bad angels, the flesh, and the world bring before my mind. God asks only one thing of me,

that my soul seek to be conformed with His Divine Majesty. And the soul so conformed makes the body conformed, whether it wish it or not, to the divine will. In this is our greatest battle, and here the good pleasure of the eternal and sovereign Goodness. May our Lord by His infinite kindness and grace hold us always in His hand." *Ignatius of Loyola: Letters and Instructions* (St. Louis: The Institute of Jesuit Sources, 2006), 25.

[2] Such panic attacks and terrors are similar to aspects of what psychologists call "catastrophic thinking" that obsesses anxiety sufferers. Catastrophic thinking's racing thoughts can even lead one to ideas of self-wounding or other types of bodily harm, similar to what Ignatius experienced at Manresa when, in the grip of severe scruples, he had an urge to throw himself off a cliff.

[3] Those suffering from bio-chemical addictions might need to seek professional guidance on extracting oneself from their grip. However, the "mind-body" can "feel" the same sense of menacing fear and dread both during the withdrawal of bio-chemical dependencies, and from habits and from sinful addictions that corrode the soul. It is obvious that eliminating these physical addictions will be a tremendous benefit to one's overall health. Therefore, it is obvious that the "mind-body" fear and menacing dread of withdrawing from sinful addictions that corrode the soul, is, like its physical counterpart, real but a lie. Withdrawal, from spiritual and physical addictions only leads to life.

[4] The counter-inspirations of spiritual desolation are real "inspirations" but just the opposite of those created by Divine inspiration: darkness and turmoil of a broken and wounded heart, soul, and spirit; magnetic attraction to sensual, base and animalistic appetites; restiveness, anger, cynicism, and temptations that erode love, hope and faith and makes all things geared towards faith, hope and love appear dull, absurd and destructive to one's heart. One has a lazy, lukewarm and sad spirit that feels separated from God. The counter-inspiration of desolation is everything that magnetizes a broken heart towards cynicism, isolation, despair and aloneness. The counter-inspiration of desolation is manifest in a pride that views eternal life, lasting love, and faith and hope in God as the illusions of the simple-minded and the product of those unwilling to risk seeing reality as it is.

10. Listening To Your History: Weeks One to Five

[1] Doncoeur, 34.

[2] The concept of a "day" and a "week" in these preliminary exercises should be flexible, as you may actually take six or nine days for *Sacred Story* Narrative or more than the suggested "days" or "weeks" for the other sections. Like the four "weeks" of Ignatius' *Spiritual Exercises*, many people who make the full *Exercises* will actually spend more than seven or less than seven days for completing an actual "week" of the *Exercises*. One should progress through any spiritual "exercise" as the Spirit prompts, and not according to a rigid schedule. The suggested time structure provided here is to simply aid your prayer and provide guidance.

[3] Ignatius is very specific that spiritual exercises should be kept to the *exact* time allotted for them. The *only* exception he makes is that an exercise *may* be extended by *a minute or so* if one is having difficulty or is experiencing some upset or turmoil. Ignatius believed that this extension

of an exercise in times of difficulty, however brief, works positively to help us confront and not be cowed by spirits of darkness or psychological and emotional anxieties.

[4] If you feel so called, you can reflect on the entire Decalogue as enumerated in the Catechism of the Catholic Church (CCC, 561-672). You can either purchase an inexpensive paperback or you can access the text on-line:

http://www.vatican.va/archive/ccc_css/archive/catechism/p3s2c1a1.htm

[5] Adapted from Wikipedia's definition of addiction.

[6] Maté, 136-7.

[7] The images used for the seven capital sins are the art of Jacques Callot (c 1592-1635), a Baroque printmaker and draftsman from the Duchy of Lorraine. The title of each vice is written in Latin. These images are in the public domain.

[8] All closing prayers on the capital vices are from Thomas Merton's *New Seeds of Contemplation*, 44.

[9] It is also possible to engage these foundational exercises as part of a focused week or two-week series of sessions with a group of people in a parish setting or even as a weekend retreat.

Afterword: The Future of the Ignatian Examen

[1] *Gaudium et Spes*, § 37.

[2] Cusson, 27.

[3] *Constitutions, Part X*: § [813]—2.

[4] Ganss, SJ, George E., and Parmananda R. Divarkar, SJ, Edward J. Malatesta, SJ, Martin E. Palmer, SJ, *Ignatius of Loyola: The Spiritual Exercises and Selected Works* (Mahwah: Paulist Press, 1991), 81.

[5] Cusson, 27.

[6] "Si miramos a nuestro alrededor, ciertamente esta situación nos impresiona. Pero si después la aplicamos a nosotros mismos, de seguro cada uno tiene que preguntarse hasta qué punto el Señor ve en nosotros hojas, es decir, palabras, propósitos, compromisos, programas y poco fruto, es decir, *capacidad de transmitir a otros la fe*, que, en el fondo, es el fruto, capacidad de convertir a otros de comunicar el amor de Dios, de hacer que vivan. Nuestra autodonación. A Dios se manifiesta el la capacidad de dar también a otros aqeulla chispa de amor al Señor que Él ha puesto en nosotros. Aquí ciertamente hemos de preguntarnos no solo acerca de los frutos que el Señor en su bondad nos permite recoger, sino también *acerca de la relación* entre hojas y frutos, entre lo que podríamos hacer y lo que en realidad somos durante toda la vida." Martini, Cardinal Carlo Maria. *Los Ejercicios De San Ignacio a la luz del Evangelio de Mateo*: 2a edición (Bilbao, Desclée de Brouwer, 2008), 55-56.

[7] GC 31-32, 527-8.

Select Bibliography

A New Introduction to the Spiritual Exercises of St. Ignatius. Collegeville, MD: Edited by Dister, John E. Michael Glazier, 1993.

Á Kempis, Thomas. *The Imitation of Christ*. Translated by Joseph N. Tylenda, SJ. Wilmington, DE: Michael Glazier, 1984.

Allers, Rudolf. *Practical Psychology in Character Development*. New York: Sheed and Ward, 1934. Reprint, Fort Collins, CO: RC Books, 2002.

. *The New Psychologies*. New York: Sheed and Ward, 1938. Reprint, Fort Collins, CO: McCaffrey Publishing, 2000.

The American Psychiatric Association. *Diagnostic and Statistical Manual of Mental Disorders: DSM-IV-RT*. Arlington, VA: American Psychiatric Association, 2007.

Aschenbrenner, George, SJ. "A Check on Our Availability: The Examen." *Review For Religious* 39, no. 3 (May 1980):321-324.

. "Consciousness Examen." *Review for Religious*, no. 31 (January 1972):14-21.

. "Consciousness Examen: God's Heart for the World." *Review for Religious* 47, no. 6 (Nov/Dec 1988):801-810.

Augustine, Saint. *Confessions*. Translated by R. S. Pine-Coffin. London, England: Penguin, 1961.

Beauregard, Ph.D., Mario and Denyse O'Leary. *The Spiritual Brain: A Neuroscientist's Case For The Existence Of The Soul*. New York, NY: Harper One, 2007.

. *Brain Wars: The Scientific Battle Over the Existence of the Mind and the Proof That Will Change the Way We Live Our Lives*. New York, NY: Harper One, 2012.

Brown, Michael. "One-on-One Session." *The Presence Portal*, 2008. / (accessed July 1, 2008).

. *The Presence Process: A Healing Journey into Present Moment Awareness*. Vancouver, BC: Namaste Publishing, 2005.

Buckley, Michael J., SJ. "The Contemplation to Attain Love." *The Way Supplement* 24, no. 2 (Spring 1973):3-9.

. "The Structure of the Rules for Discernment of Spirits." *The Way Supplement*, no. 20 (Autumn):19-37.

Campbell, Mary Hugh. "The Particular Examen—Touchstone of a Genuinely Apostolic Spirituality." *Review for Religious*, 30 (September 1971):775-781.

Carr, Nicholas. *The Shallows: What the Internet is Doing to Our Brains*. New York: Norton, 2010.

Ciarrocchi, Joseph W. *The Doubting Disease: Help for Scrupulosity and Religious Obsessions*. Mahwah, NJ: Paulist, 1995.

Cisneros, Garcia, Abbot. *A Book of Spiritual Exercises and a Directory for the Canonical Hours*. London, England: Burns and Oates, 1885.

Ciszek, Walter, SJ. *He Leadeth Me*. Garden City, NY: Doubleday & Company, Inc. 1973.

Congregation for the Clergy, *Directory on the Ministry and Life of Priests*. London: CTS Publications, 1994.

Constitutions of the Society of Jesus and Their Complimentary Norms. Edited by John W. Padberg, SJ. St. Louis, MO: Institute of Jesuit Sources, 1995.

Conwell, Joseph F., S.J. *Contemplation in Action*. Spokane, WA: Gonzaga University Press, 1957.

Cusson, Gilles, SJ. *Biblical Theology and the Spiritual Exercises*. Translated by RC; George Ganss, SJ Mary Angela Roduit, RC. St. Louis, MO: Institute of Jesuit Sources, 1988.

Daily Roman Missal. Edited by Rev. James Socias. Chicago, IL: Midwest Theological Forum Inc. 1998.

da Câmera, Luís Gonçalves. *Remembering Iñigo*. Translated by Alexander Eaglestone and Joseph A. Munitz, SJ. St. Louis, MO: The Institute of Jesuit Sources, 2004.

De Caussade, Jean-Pierre. *the Sacrament of the Present Moment*. Translated by Kitty Muggeridge. San Francisco, CA: HarperCollins, 1982.

. *A Treatise on Prayer from the Heart*. Translated by Robert M. McKeon. St. Louis, MO: Institute of Jesuit Sources, 1998.

de Guibert, Joseph, SJ. *The Jesuits: Their Spiritual Doctrine and Practice*. St. Louis, MO: The Institute of Jesuit Sources, 1994.

Doncoeur, Paul, SJ. *The Heart of Ignatius*. Translated by Henry St. C. Lavin, SJ. Baltimore, MD: Helicon, 1959.

Dyckman, Catherine, Mary Garvin, Elizabeth Liebert. *The Spiritual Exercises Reclaimed: Uncovering Liberating Possibilities for Women*. New York, NY: Paulist Press, 2001.

Egan, Harvey D., SJ. *The Spiritual Exercises and the Ignatian Mystical Horizon*. St Louis, MO: The Institute of Jesuit Sources, 1976.

English, John, SJ. *Discernment and the Examen*. Guelph, Ontario: 1979.

. "The Mind and the Heart of Christ." *The Way* 27 (October 1976):292-301.

. "Mysterious Joy of the Poor and the Complex Causes of Consolation." *Review of Ignatian Spirituality [CIS]*, no. 85 (1997).

. *Spiritual Freedom*. Chicago, IL: Loyola University Press, 1995.

Gallagher, Timothy M., OMV. *The Examen Prayer: Ignatian Wisdom for Our Lives Today*. New York, NY: The Crossroad Publishing Company, 2006.

Ganss, George E., SJ. *The Spiritual Exercises of Saint Ignatius: A Translation and Commentary*. Chicago, IL: Loyola University Press, 1992.

Gula, Richard M., SS. *Reason Informed by Faith*. New York, NY: Paulist Press, 1989.

Holy See. *Catechism of the Catholic Church*. Dublin, Ireland: Veritas, 1994.

Horn, S.J., John. *Mystical Healing: the Psychological and Spiritual Power of the Ignatian Spiritual Exercises*. New York, NY: Crossroads, 1996.

Horney, Karen, MD. *Self Analysis*. New York, NY: W. W. Norton & Company, Inc, 1994.

Idígoras, José Ignacio Tellechea. *Ignatius of Loyola: The Pilgrim Saint*. Translated by Cornelius Michael Buckley, SJ. Chicago, IL: Loyola University Press, 1994.

Ignatius of Loyola: Spiritual Exercises and Selected Works. Edited by George

E. Ganss, SJ. New York, NY: Paulist Press, 1991.

Ignatius of Loyola: Letters and Instructions. Translated and Edited by Martin

E. Palmer, SJ, John W. Padberg, SJ, and John L. McCarthy, SJ. St. Louis, MO: The Institute of Jesuit Sources, 2006.

Ivens, Michael, SJ. *Understanding the Spiritual Exercises*. Trowbridge, England: Cromwell Press, 1998.

Johnston, William. *Mystical Theology: The Science of Love*. London: HarperCollinsReligious, 1995.

Kneale, Brendan, FSC. "Examining My Conscience: Do I Have an Attitude?" *Review for Religious* (September-October 2001):474-478.

Kinnaman, David. *You Lost Me: Why Young Christians Are Leaving Church and Rethinking Faith*. Grand Rapids, MI: Baker Books, 2011.

Lallemant, Louis. *The Spiritual Doctrine of Father Louis Lallemant*. Edited by Alan G. McDougall. Westminster, MD: The Newman Book Shop, 1946.

The Letters and Instructions of Francis Xavier. Translated by Joseph M. Costelloe, SJ. St. Louis, MO: The Institute of Jesuit Sources, 1992.

Lewis, C.S. *The Screwtape Letters*. New York, NY: Collier Books, 1982.

Liturgy of the Hours. Divine Office Ordinary Time: Weeks 1-17, vol. 3. New York, NY: Catholic Book Publishing Co., 1975.

Lonergan, Bernard. *Method in Theology*. New York, NY: The Seabury Press, 1971.

Lonsdale, David, SJ. *Eyes to See, Ears to Hear: An Introduction to Ignatian Spirituality*. Chicago, IL: Loyola University Press, 1990.

Loyola, Ignatius. *St. Ignatius' Own Story*. Translated by William J. Young, SJ, Chicago, IL: Loyola University Press, 1980.

. *Letters of St. Ignatius Loyola*. Translated by William J. Young, SJ. Chicago, IL: Loyola University Press, 1959.

. Ignatius. *A Pilgrim's Journey*. Translated by Joseph N. Tylenda, S.J. Wilmington, DE: Michael Glazier, Inc, 1985.

. *The Spiritual Journal of St. Ignatius Loyola*. Translated by William

J. Young, SJ. Woodstock, MD: Woodstock College Press, 1958.

Maloney, George A., SJ. *Alone with the Alone*. Notre Dame, IN: Ave Maria Press, 1982.

Martini, Cardinal Carlo Maria. *Los Ejercicios De San Ignacio a la luz del Evangelio de Mateo: 2a edición*. Bilbao, Spain: Desclée de Brouwer, 2008.

Maté, Gabor. *In the Realm of Hungry Ghosts: Close Encounters with Addiction*. Berkeley, CA: North Atlantic Books, 2010.

Melloni, Javier, SJ. *The Exercises of St Ignatius Loyola in the Western Tradition*. Translated by Michael Ivens. Leominster, England: Gracewing, 2000.

Merton, Thomas. *Conjectures of a Guilt Bystander*. New York, NY: Doubleday, 1966.

. *New Seeds of Contemplation*. New York, NY: New Directions Books, 1961.

. *The Inner Experience: Notes on Contemplation*. New York, NY: Harper San Francisco, 2003.

O'Malley, John W. *The First Jesuits*. Cambridge: Harvard University Press, 1993.

On Giving the Exercises: The Early Manuscript Directories and the Official Directory of 1599. Translated by Martin E. Palmer, SJ. St. Louis, MO: The Institute of Jesuit Sources, 1996.

Peters, William A. M. *The Spiritual Exercises of St. Ignatius: Exposition and Interpretation*. Rome: Centrum Ignatianum Spiritualitatis, 1980.

Pieper, Josef. *Leisure, the Basis of Culture*. South Bend, IN: St. Augustine Press, 1998.

Rahner, Hugo, Hubert Becher, Hans Wolter, Josef Stierli, Adolf Haas, Heinrich Bacht, Lambert Classen and Karl Rahner. *Ignatius of Loyola: His Personality and Spiritual Heritage 116-1956*. Edited by Friedrich Wulf. St. Louis, MO: Institute of Jesuit Sources, 1977.

. *Ignatius the Theologian*. Translated by Michael Barry. New York, NY: Herder and Herder, 1968.

. *The Spirituality of St. Ignatius Loyola: An Account of Its Historical Development*. Translated by Francis John Smith, S.J. Westminster: The Newman Press, 1953.

Rahner, Karl. *Spiritual Exercises: Prayer and Practice*. London: Sheed and Ward, 1966.

Ratzinger, Joseph. *Introduction to Christianity*. New York, NY: The Seabury Press, 1968.

Rickaby, Joseph, SJ. *The Spiritual Exercises of St. Ignatius Loyola: Spanish and English with a Continuous Commentary*. London, England: Burns Oates & Washbourne LTD, 1923.

Roccasalvo, Joan P., CSJ. "The Daily Examen." *Review for Religious* (March-April 1986):278-282.

. *Prayer for Finding God in All Things*. St. Louis: Institute of Jesuit Sources, 2005.

Rodriguez, Alphonsus. *Practice and Perfection of Christian Virtues: Volume*

I. Translated by Joseph Rickaby, SJ. Chicago, IL: Loyola University Press, 1929.

Ryder, Andrew. "The Sacrament of Now." *The Way* 2 (April 2007):7-18.

Smith, Christian. *Lost in Transition: The Dark Side of Emerging Adulthood*. Oxford, Oxford University Press, 2011.

Society of Jesus. *The Decrees of General Congregation 35*. St. Louis, MO: Institute of Jesuit Sources, 2008.

Society of Jesus. *Thirty First & Thirty Second General Congregations*. St. Louis: Institute of Jesuit Sources, 1977.

Taylor, Charles. *A Secular Age*. Cambridge, MA: The Belknap Press of Harvard University Press, 2007.

Tetlow, Joseph, SJ. "Examen: Persons in Relationship." *Review for Religious* (March-April 2002):118-128.

. "The Examen of Particulars." *Review for Religious* 56, no. 3 (May-June 1997):231-250.

. "The Most Postmodern Prayer: American Jesuit Identity and the Examen of Conscience, 1920-1990." *Studies in the Spirituality of Jesuits* 26, no. 1 (January 1994):2-67.

Teilhard de Chardin, Pierre. *The Divine Milieu*. New York, NY: HarperCollins Perennial, 2001.

. *The Future of Man*. Glasgow, Scotland: William Collins & Son Co. Ltd, 1959.

Tolle, Eckhart. *The Power of Now*. Vancouver, BC: Namaste Publishing, 2004.

[Tomberg, Valentin]. *Meditations on the Tarot: A Journey into Christian Heremeticism*. Shaftesbury Dorset, England: Element, 1991.

Toner, Jules J., SJ. *A Commentary on Saint Ignatius' Rules for the Discernment of Spirits*. St. Louis, MO: Institute of Jesuit Sources, 1982.

Townsend, David, SJ. "The Examen and the Exercises: A Re-Appraisal." *The Way* 52 (Spring 1985):53-63.

. "Finding God in a Busy Day." *Review for Religious* 50, no. 1 (January-February 1991): 43-63.

Twenge, Jean M., Keith Campbell. *The Narcissism Epidemic: Living in the Age of Entitlement*. New York: Free Press, 2010.

van Breemen, Peter G., SJ. "The Examination of Conscience." *Review for Religious* (July-August 1990): 600-609.

Walker, Andrew. "Daydreaming Revisited: A Psychology for the Examen Explored." *The Way Supplement* 42, no. 3 (July 2003):95-105.

. *The Future of Man*. Glasgow, Scotland: William Collins & Son Co. Ltd, 1959.

Tolle, Eckhart. *The Power of Now*. Vancouver, BC: Namaste Publishing, 2004.

[Tomberg, Valentin]. *Meditations on the Tarot: A Journey into Christian Heremeticism*. Shaftesbury Dorset, England: Element, 1991.

Toner, Jules J., SJ. *A Commentary on Saint Ignatius' Rules for the Discernment of Spirits*. St. Louis, MO: Institute of Jesuit Sources, 1982.

Townsend, David, SJ. "The Examen and the Exercises: A Re-Appraisal." *The Way* 52 (Spring 1985):53-63.

. "Finding God in a Busy Day." *Review for Religious* 50, no. 1 (January-February 1991): 43-63.

Twenge, Jean M., Keith Campbell. *The Narcissism Epidemic: Living in the Age of Entitlement*. New York: Free Press, 2010.

van Breemen, Peter G., SJ. "The Examination of Conscience." *Review for Religious* (July-August 1990): 600-609.

Walker, Andrew. "Daydreaming Revisited: A Psychology for the Examen Explored." *The Way Supplement* 42, no. 3 (July 2003):95-105.